About Island Press

Since 1984, the nonprofit Island Press has been stimulating, shaping, and communicating the ideas that are essential for solving environmental problems worldwide. With more than 800 titles in print and some 40 new releases each year, we are the nation's leading publisher on environmental issues. We identify innovative thinkers and emerging trends in the environmental field. We work with world-renowned experts and authors to develop cross-disciplinary solutions to environmental challenges.

Island Press designs and implements coordinated book publication campaigns in order to communicate our critical messages in print, in person, and online using the latest technologies, programs, and the media. Our goal: to reach targeted audiences—scientists, policymakers, environmental advocates, the media, and concerned citizens—who can and will take action to protect the plants and animals that enrich our world, the ecosystems we need to survive, the water we drink, and the air we breathe.

Island Press gratefully acknowledges the support of its work by the Agua Fund, Inc., Annenberg Foundation, The Christensen Fund, The Nathan Cummings Foundation, The Geraldine R. Dodge Foundation, Doris Duke Charitable Foundation, The Educational Foundation of America, Betsy and Jesse Fink Foundation, The William and Flora Hewlett Foundation, The Kendeda Fund, The Andrew W. Mellon Foundation, The Curtis and Edith Munson Foundation, Oak Foundation, The Overbrook Foundation, the David and Lucile Packard Foundation, The Summit Fund of Washington, Trust for Architectural Easements, Wallace Global Fund, The Winslow Foundation, and other generous donors.

The opinions expressed in this book are those of the author(s) and do not necessarily reflect the views of our donors.

THE GLOBAL FARMS RACE

The Global Farms Race

Land Grabs, Agricultural Investment,
and the Scramble for Food Security

Edited by

Michael Kugelman
Susan L. Levenstein

Washington | Covelo | London

Library of Congress Cataloging-in-Publication Data

The global farms race : land grabs, agricultural investment, and the scramble for food security / edited by Michael Kugelman, Susan L. Levenstein; with contributions from Carl Atkin . . . [et al.].
   p.   cm.
   Includes bibliographical references and index.
   ISBN 978-1-61091-186-3 (cloth : acid-free paper)—ISBN 1-61091-186-5 (cloth : acid-free paper)—ISBN 978-1-61091-187-0 (paper : acid-free paper)—ISBN 1-61091-187-3 (paper : acid-free paper)   1. Farms—Foreign ownership.   2. Farms—Developing countries—Foreign ownership.   3. Agricultural industries—Foreign ownership. 4. Agricultural industries—Developing countries—Foreign ownership.   5. Investments, Foreign—Developing countries.   6. Agriculture—Capital investments.   7. Food security—Political aspects.   8. Food security—Environmental aspects.   9. Food security—Social aspects.   I. Kugelman, Michael.   II. Levenstein, Susan L., 1975–
III. Atkin, Carl.
   HD9000.6.G52 2013
   338.1—dc23
                              2012011492

Printed on recycled, acid-free paper ♻

Manufactured in the United States of America
10 9 8 7 6 5 4 3 2 1

Keywords: farmland acquisitions, food crisis, agricultural investment, food imports and exports, economic development, crop shortages, grain costs, land-poor countries, Daewoo

CONTENTS

ACKNOWLEDGMENTS

This book would not have been possible without the assistance and support of a number of key places and people. First, we thank Island Press for taking this project on, and especially Emily Davis for guiding us through the publication process from start to finish. Emily is one of those rare people who have a workable solution for every possible problem, and we are grateful for all her assistance. Also of great help for their ideas and suggestions were Elisio Contini of the Brazilian Agricultural Research Corporation; Oliver Coomes of McGill University; Derek Hall of Wilfrid Laurier University in Canada; Chris Huggins of the Land Conflict Research firm in Canada; Jackie Klopp of Columbia University; and Peter Messerli of the University of Bern. Finally, we thank Laura Jervis for her editorial assistance.

This book traces its origins to a conference hosted by the Woodrow Wilson International Center for Scholars in May 2009 entitled "Land Grab: The Race for the World's Farmland." A post-conference Wilson Center report, comprising early versions of some of the contributions in this volume, followed later that year. For this reason, we are indebted to a number of past and present Wilson Center staff members. They include, above all, Robert M. Hathaway of the Center's Asia Program. His support and counsel cannot be overstated. We also recognize Mame-Khady Diouf and Justine Lindemann of the Center's Africa Program; Geoff Dabelko and Kayly Ober of the Environmental Change and Security Program; Lauren Herzer of the Comparative Urban Studies Project; Paulo Sotero of the Brazil Institute; José Raúl Perales of the Latin American Program; and Jacqueline Nader of the Program on America and the Global Economy.

Back in 2008, when this project was in its very early conceptual stages, foreign land investments were not receiving nearly the amount of attention or coverage that they are now. The editors are deeply grateful to a number of experts who not only helped explain the topic and suggested angles to pursue, but also strongly encouraged that the May 2009 conference and report be undertaken. These people include Javier Blas of the *Financial Times*; Alex Evans of New York University; Zoe Goodman, formerly of the 3D organization; Gawain Kripke of Oxfam America; author Paul Roberts; and Carin Smaller of the International Institute for Sustainable Development.

Others deserving mention include Suraya Afiff of the KARSA Institute in Indonesia; Jun Borras of Saint Mary's University in Canada; John Lamb of the World Bank; Carola Lentz of Harvard; Peter Lewis of Johns Hopkins/SAIS; Henry Machina of the Zambia Land Alliance; Zachary Makanya of the Participatory Ecological Land Use Management (PELUM) organization in Kenya; Will Masters of Purdue; Kidane Mengisteab of Penn State; Bill Moseley of Macalester College; Roz Naylor and Walter Falcon of Stanford; Jesse Ribot of the University of Illinois; Jonathan Rigg of Durham University in the United Kingdom; Beatriz del Rosario of the International Federation of Agricultural Producers; Ibrahim Saif and Farah Shoucair of the Carnegie Middle East Center; Jean-Francois Seznec of Georgetown; Michael Taylor of the International Land Coalition; and Peter Vandergeest of York College in Canada.

The editors must also express their tremendous appreciation to this volume's 15 chapter contributors, some of whom have been with us since they served as speakers at the 2009 conference. They are all busy people, yet they generously took the time to contribute to this collection. We thank them for their time, efforts, and good cheer—even when deluged with our questions and requests.

Finally, we thank our patient and supportive families for tolerating our frequent disappearing acts during the most intense periods of the editing and production process. This book is dedicated to two very special members of our respective families, Adam Kugelman and Henry Levenstein. If large-scale farmland acquisitions are still occurring many decades from now, these two little boys will be in a better position than we will to take stock of the effects, whether benign or malign.

Michael Kugelman and Susan L. Levenstein
Washington, DC
March 2012

Chapter 1

Introduction

MICHAEL KUGELMAN

The world is experiencing a land rush. Wealthy, food-importing countries and private investors are flocking to farmland overseas.

These transactions are highly opaque, and relatively few details have been made public. What is known, however, is quite striking—and particularly the scale of these activities. Back in 2009, the International Food Policy Research Institute (IFPRI) estimated that 15 to 20 million hectares of farmland had been subject to negotiations or transactions over the preceding few years. In 2011, the International Land Coalition (ILC) presented data indicating that nearly 80 million hectares had been subject to negotiation with foreigners since 2001—an amount exceeding the area of farmland in Britain, France, Germany, and Italy combined. Also in 2011, the World Bank projected that about 60 million hectares' worth of deals were announced in 2009 alone.[1]

By early 2012, the ILC's estimates had soared to a whopping 203 million hectares' worth of land deals "approved or under negotiation" between 2000 and 2010. Some projections have gone even further; a September 2011 Oxfam study contends that nearly 230 million hectares—an area equivalent to the size of Western Europe—have been sold or leased since 2001, with most of this land acquired since 2008.[2]

One of the largest and most notorious deals ultimately collapsed: an arrangement that would have given the South Korean firm Daewoo a 99-year lease to grow corn and other crops on 1.3 million hectares of farmland in Madagascar—half of that country's total arable land. Popular opposition on the African island nation not only squelched the deal but also contributed to the demise of the government that had championed it. (Another mammoth bid, put forth by China to acquire up to a million hectares of land in the Philippines, was also unsuccessful.) However, other megadeals are reportedly in the works (see Table 1-1). Indonesia has opened up more than 1 million hectares of farmland to investors, while Mozambique has offered Brazil a staggering 6 million hectares to grow several different crops.[3] To get a sense of the magnitude of such deals, consider that most small farmers in the developing world own plots of less than two hectares (see Table 1-2).

Early characterizations of this trend portrayed capital-rich Arab Gulf states and the prosperous countries of East Asia preying on the world's farmland. In 2009, one specialist estimated that by the end of 2008, China, South Korea, the United Arab Emirates, Japan, and Saudi Arabia were controlling over 7.6 million cultivable hectares overseas—more than five times the usable agricultural surface of Belgium.[4]

However, such assessments do not capture the whole picture—one that has more fully emerged only since 2011, when organizations such as the World Bank, Oxfam, and the ILC began releasing in-depth research. It is not simply the richest countries targeting the developing world; North African countries are investing in sub-Saharan Africa, Brazilian and South African investors are angling for deals worldwide, and Southeast Asian countries are eying one another's soil. Meanwhile, keen interest in Australian and New Zealand farmland explodes the myth that these land acquisitions represent an assault solely on the soils of the developing world.

Additionally, the role of the United States often goes unreported. According to researchers and media reports, the US firm Goldman Sachs has purchased poultry and pig farms in China; American farmers have bought plots in Brazil; and North American investors hold 3.3 million hectares in Africa. In 2011, the Oakland Institute alleged that American universities—including Harvard and Vanderbilt—were investing heavily in African farmland through European hedge funds and financial speculators.[5]

The New Farms Race: Roots and Reasons

Why are we now witnessing this race for the world's farmland, and what propels its participants? A chief reason is food security.

In 2008, world food prices reached their highest levels since the 1970s. The skyrocketing costs of staple grains and edible oils triggered riots across

TABLE 1-1   The 100,000-Hectares-and-Above Club: Ten of the Largest Land Deals

Investor	Host Country	Scale (in hectares)	Crop	Status
Brazil	Mozambique	6 million	Soy and corn	Concession offered by Mozambique, 2011
Daewoo (South Korean)	Madagascar	1.3 million	Corn and others	Collapsed due to public opposition, 2009
Binladen Group (Saudi Arabian)	Indonesia	1.2 million	Various	Project launched but investments on hold, 2011
China	Philippines	1.2 million	Rice, corn, others	Suspended, 2007
Hong Kong and Philippine firms	Philippines	1 million	Rice, corn, others	MOU signed, 2008
South Korea	Sudan	690,000	Wheat	Deal signed, 2009
Nile Trading and Development (American) and local Sudanese investors	South Sudan	600,000	Jatropha and others	Lease signed, 2008
Karuturi (Indian)	Ethiopia	300,000	Various	Lease agreement in place, 2011
Heilongjiang Beidahuang Nongken Group (Chinese)	Argentina	300,000	Soybeans, wheat, others	Agreement in place, 2010
Libya	Mali	100,000	Rice	Agreement in place, 2009

This information is largely derived from media reports. Its accuracy cannot be confirmed, and the status of these deals may have changed by the time of publication.

TABLE 1-2   Farm Sizes Worldwide

Region	Mean Size (in hectares)	Farms of <2 Hectares (%)
Central America	10.7	63
East Asia	1	79
Europe	32.3	30
South America	111.7	36
South Asia	1.4	78
Southeast Asia	1.8	57
Sub-Saharan Africa	2.4	69
United States	178.4	4
West Asia and North Africa	4.9	65

Source: World Bank, Rising Global Interest in Farmland, 2011

the globe—particularly in the impoverished cities of the developing world, where many people spend up to 75 percent of their incomes on food. Some top food-exporting nations, in efforts to prevent food price spikes and public unrest at home, imposed bans on food exports. Such bans, by taking large amounts of grain supplies off the global market, exacerbated the food insecurity of food-importing nations dependent on such staples.

Prices have now stabilized and the world food crisis has receded from the media spotlight. However, food costs are still high and commodities markets remain unpredictable. Additionally, other factors—such as eroding topsoil, farmland-displacing urbanization, water shortages, and the spread of wheat-destroying disease—demonstrate the challenges nations and their populations continue to face in meeting their food needs. Indeed, food security remains an urgent global concern—and particularly for agriculturally deficient, water-short nations that depend on food imports to meet rapidly growing domestic demand.

Some of these nations have decided to take matters into their own hands. In an effort to avoid the high costs, supply shortages, and general volatility plaguing global food imports, these countries are bypassing world food markets and instead seeking land overseas to use for agriculture. Crops are harvested on this land and then sent back home for consumption.[6]

Energy security is another prime impetus. In an effort to avoid environmentally damaging and geopolitically risky hydrocarbons, many nations are searching feverishly for land overseas to use for biofuels production. In fact, according to the ILC, 40 percent—about 37 million hectares—of the world's land involved in agricultural deals is set aside for this purpose (keep in mind, however, that some biofuels crops, such as oil palm, soybeans, and sugarcane, can produce food as well as fuel).

Meanwhile, private-sector financiers recognize land as a safe investment in an otherwise shaky economic climate, and they hope to capitalize financially on the mushrooming food- and energy-security-driven demand for agricultural land. Estimates from early 2012 judged that $14 billion in private capital was committed to investment in farmland—a figure projected to double by 2015. Nearly 200 private equity firms are projected to be involved in farming, with just 63 of them seeking to generate $13 billion in agricultural investments.[7]

Far from being coerced into these land deals, many developing-country governments welcome them—and even lobby aggressively for them. Pakistan, for example, has staged "farmland road shows" across the Arab Gulf to attract investor interest, offering lavish tax incentives and even a 100,000-person-strong security force to protect investors.[8] Host governments hope that heavy injections of foreign capital will enhance agricultural technology, boost local employment, revitalize sagging agricultural sectors, and ultimately improve agricultural yields. They are also drawn to the new roads, bridges, and ports that some land investors promise to build. With such tantalizing incentives, many host-nation governments have no compunction about holding farmland fire sales.

Why This Book?

The global run on agriculture has sparked high levels of passion and polarization. Some regard it as the spark for a new green revolution—while others perceive it as a "new colonialism" or a "land grab," whereby powerful forces seize land long held (or used) by the more vulnerable. Indeed, supporters believe these capital-intensive, technology-heavy deals, by boosting agricultural productivity, can help bring down global grain costs and reduce the threat of future food crises. Critics, conversely, worry about pernicious impacts on small farmers, their land, their livelihoods, and the environment. Some argue that the deals' purported benefits could become moot if they result in mass displacements, land degradation, and natural resource shortages.

A more accurate picture can likely be found somewhere in between these two positions, and serious work on the topic must engage this middle ground. While such literature has begun to emerge, thanks to the output of organizations such as IFPRI, the International Institute for Environment and Development (IIED), the World Bank, and the ILC, the knowledge vacuum remains considerable, particularly in the United States.[9] This book's contribution to this new yet growing debate is to present a range of views on an equally broad array of issues flowing from the world's pursuit of farmland.[10] *The Global Farms Race* features contributions from agricultural investment consultants, farmers' groups, international organizations, and academics based in nine different countries across the developed and developing worlds. Its topical scope encompasses historical dimensions, environmental implications, and social effects. It provides regional perspectives covering all the major areas of investment: Africa, Asia, Latin America, and the former Soviet Union/Eastern and Central Europe.

The book's underlying argument is a simple one: Whether we support them or not, large-scale land acquisitions are a reality. We should accept this reality and seek to learn more about these deals with a spirit of inquiry that steers clear of undue alarmism and Pollyannaism alike. This is why even the chapters most critical of the deals do not issue shrill calls for their elimination, and why the most supportive chapters openly acknowledge that farmland investments are fraught with risks and challenges. The book deals with a topic that begs for more public debate, and for such debate to be healthy, it must not be contaminated with the poison of polarization.

With this in mind, the objective of *The Global Farms Race* is to equip readers with the proper grounding to understand the scramble for the world's soils—a trend with considerable implications for major twenty-first-century challenges such as food security, natural resource management, and climate change.

History Reinventing Itself

While often referred to as a new trend, today's land lust is simply the reappearance—in a new form—of a phenomenon that has occurred for centuries. In the nineteenth century, European colonialism gobbled up global farmland. In the early twentieth century, foreign fruit companies appropriated farmland in Central America and Southeast Asia. Later in the same century, Britain attempted (unsuccessfully) to convert present-day southern Tanzania into a giant peanut plantation. Indeed, the nightmare scenario invoked by critics of today's foreign land acquisitions—a wealthy nation whisking its newly grown crops out of a famine-scarred country—has a historical precedent: During the Irish potato famine of the nineteenth century, the British government was exporting fresh Ireland-grown crops back home to England.

Derek Byerlee's opening chapter surveys large-scale land acquisitions since the second half of the nineteenth century (the first era of globalization), with a focus on the six commodities that have dominated these deals over the last 150 years—sugarcane, tea, rubber, bananas, palm oil, and (more recently) food staples. Many of his examples involve the United States: American sugar companies acquiring Cuban forest and pasture land in the early 1900s, transforming the newly independent nation into the world's leading sugar exporter; powerful US landholding sugar firms in Hawaii contributing to the annexation of the territory in 1898; and the United Fruit Company controlling nearly 1.5 million hectares of banana plantations in Central America in 1935, "making it the largest farmland holder in the world at that time." He also describes how, in colonial-era Kenya, 3 million hectares of "prime" land were converted into European tea estates, displacing locals and helping spark the 1950s Mau Mau uprising; how a precursor company to Unilever obtained a 140,000-hectare concession to produce palm oil in early twentieth-century Belgian Congo; and how Nikita Khrushchev's Virgin Lands program of the 1950s plowed up 55 million hectares of the Central Asian steppe.

Byerlee, an independent adviser who coauthored the World Bank's 2011 *Rising Global Interest in Farmland* report, argues that despite this proliferation of large-scale deals, smallholders still managed to thrive. Even with colonial policies favoring estate production, he notes, smallholders produced half of Asia's rubber in 1940. Meanwhile, the tea sector experienced "a remarkable transition from foreign-owned plantations to a robust smallholder sector," a shift attributable to supportive government policies, smallholder innovation, and "forward-looking" companies. "The historical experience has shown the importance of providing a level playing field for smallholders," Byerlee concludes, asserting that once support services are put into place, smallholders can "dominate" their respective industries.

Byerlee emphasizes that today's overseas land investments do differ from their predecessors in significant ways—particularly in that the "high social costs" of past deals were more frequently tied to labor issues (such as poor working conditions) than to the land-related issues (such as displacement) witnessed today. He attributes this relative infrequency of land tensions to the fact that in the past, most land was acquired in sparsely populated areas. One can identify other differences as well: today the scale of the acquired land is much larger; the investments emphasize staples instead of cash crops; the deals are concluded on the basis of agreements instead of through the barrel of a gun; and they are spearheaded by more government-led investment than in the past.

David Hallam's contribution provides a broad overview of international agricultural investments, focusing on trends, motivations, impacts, and policy implications. Hallam, of the UN Food and Agriculture Organization (FAO), first provides a reality check. The number of implemented investments, he notes, "appears to be less" than what the media are reporting, and land controlled by foreigners "remains a relatively small proportion" of total land in host countries. Additionally, while government funds are fueling the deals to a significant extent, investors are "primarily" from the private sector. Finally, foreign farmland investment represents only one strategy for satisfying food-security needs. Others include regional food reserves and better international food-market information systems, both of which are "under active discussion."

The "key question" concerning land investments, Hallam writes, is the extent to which host-country benefits—capital inflows, technology transfers, more employment—"spill over" into host-country agriculture and create a "synergistic relationship" with existing smallholder systems. He asserts that these benefits will not materialize in local settings if land deals result in an "enclave" of "advanced agriculture" operating in isolation from indigenous, traditional smallholder agriculture. Contract farming (whereby small farmers produce crops for a larger entity, such as an agribusiness firm) can bring together smallholders and advanced agriculture; Hallam advocates this arrangement as an alternative to outright purchases and leasings of land. He acknowledges, however, that investors may favor land acquisitions or long-term leases when economies of scale prevail, or when major infrastructural expenditures (such as roads and ports) are required.

Farmland Acquisitions: Foolish or Fortuitous?

Be that as it may, Hallam underscores that large-scale foreign investments in agriculture "raise complex and controversial issues." Alexandra Spieldoch, a gender and food-systems consultant, and Sophia Murphy, of the Institute for Agriculture and Trade Policy, take a closer look at the troubling social and economic implications of these acquisitions. One issue is the presence of "lopsided" power relationships in "virtually every one" of the deals being proposed. Foreign investors are typically large, wealthy transnational firms or rich governments, while host governments are poor, are at war, or are embroiled in political conflict. Few of the host governments can boast of strong and independent democratic institutions—a concern not just for investors, but also for local affected communities who may find that their governments have no authority to speak on their behalf. Women, arguably those most impacted by the deals, are particularly vulnerable in this context, as they "have less access to information and less of a political voice than men." Spieldoch and Murphy reference a land scheme in central Ghana, where jatropha-seeking companies have taken over land long used by local communities for yam cultivation. Women, they report, have been "the hardest hit." They have lost access to the forested land that provided them with medicine, fuel, and the food crops that accounted for their modest incomes.

Another reason for concern is the ambiguous definition of *land use*. Government officials often claim that the land they plan to sell or lease is unused. However, "what the government may categorize as wasteland might very well be meeting an important share of rural people's household needs," Spieldoch and Murphy explain. Rural denizens often use uncultivated land as a source of wild foods, medicinal plants, and water. Indigenous use of fallow land to satisfy resource demand is particularly critical given the world's paucity of healthy land and natural resources. The writers point out that two-thirds of the world's agricultural land is currently degraded, and that by 2025 nearly 2 billion people could live in water-scarce regions. And the authors argue that the large-scale, industrialized agricultural production envisioned by foreign investors will only exacerbate this environmental blight. Fresh water will disappear, soil nutrients will be depleted "at unsustainable rates," and fossil fuels will be heavily expended to support fertilizers, pesticides, and farm machinery. Given that some of the prime investment targets—Central Africa, South America, and Southeast Asia—are home to the majority of the world's dwindling rain forests, such prognostications are particularly troubling.[11]

These environmental risks constitute the focus of the chapter by Laura A. German, Wouter M. J. Achten, and Manuel R. Guariguata. The writers (from, respectively, the University of Georgia, the University of Leuven, and the Center for International Forestry Research) examine how the commodities most often associated with large-scale land acquisitions—including plantation forestry and biofuels crops like jatropha, sugarcane, oil palm, and soybean—impact carbon stocks, biodiversity, and water consumption.

The chapter underscores that the carbon-saving qualities of biofuels should not be taken for granted; this is because carbon is actually lost during the land-use changes that precede biofuels production. However, biofuels systems have the capability of reducing carbon emissions, and so actual production can eventually "repay" the carbon debt incurred before production. Still, German and her coauthors argue that land conversions to oil palm production—which spawns extensive deforestation, a heavily carbon-emitting process—often lead to longer repayment periods (projected to be more than 900 years, in one documented case) than those experienced with other biofuels crops. The chapter also describes the devastating impact forest conversion to oil palm has had on animal species in Southeast Asia; in one case in Malaysia, it expunged as much as 60 percent of the area bird species. On the other hand, jatropha and rubber production have been found to leave the largest water footprints (that is, they consume the greatest quantities of water) of all the commodities analyzed in the chapter.

One can conclude from the data presented in this chapter that the most environmentally threatening large-scale land acquisitions may be those in Southeast Asia and sub-Saharan Africa, where most of the world's oil palm production takes place (the authors cite several cases of oil palm expansion in each region, some occurring in recent decades and others expected to commence in the future, all with 100 percent deforestation rates). By contrast, the major biofuel crops produced in Latin America are sugarcane and soybeans, which have triggered relatively little deforestation. The authors warn, however, that any type of land conversion can impact biodiversity and natural resource availability—and indirectly affect forests or other vulnerable land nearby.

Gary R. Blumenthal, of the agricultural consulting firm World Perspectives, Inc. (WPI), offers an unqualified defense of large-scale farmland acquisitions, suggesting that land deals can serve the interests of the most vulnerable and reduce hunger. How so? He argues that such investment "enables the full and efficient application of current technology," which entails less labor yet results in higher productivity levels. He notes that Zimbabwe's agricultural population per hectare of arable land is more than 56 times greater than that of the United States, yet American corn yields are 11 times those of Zimbabwe. That the efficient use of technology reduces the need for labor is a good thing, writes Blumenthal, because lower rates of labor per hectare mean better nutrition, higher education levels, and more health care for local communities.

Furthermore, the chief fact on the ground—a large, growing, and hungry world population—cries out for large-scale capital investment. "Using

smallholdings agriculture as a development policy is like promising an automobile to everyone in the world, but limiting construction to hand labor,"
he writes. "The principles of industrialization and mass production apply as
much to agriculture as they do to nonagricultural goods." Farmers do not
dispute such views, Blumenthal adds. Despite the negative connotation of
large-scale farming—"big is bad, while small is charming"—he notes that in
WPI surveys of farmers across the world, "nearly all aspire to become larger"
by expanding their acreages.

Responses to the Race for the World's Farmland

According to Blumenthal, financiers have strong incentives to invest in agriculture. And in a sector where demand is soaring and supply is dwindling,
financial returns are a chief motivation. "Capital flows to where it is rewarded the most," he writes, "and nothing attracts investment better than a
perceived market shortage."

However, says Blumenthal, historically the investment community has
avoided agriculture, owing to its fears about the passions and emotions
whipped up by outsiders' involvement in land. Only in the last few years,
when the commercial rationale became so compelling—thanks in large
part to the realization that agricultural investments can serve as a portfolio diversifier and hedge against inflation—has this situation changed, and
dramatically so. In 2009, droves of investors—hedge fund managers, agricultural industry executives, and chief financial officers of universities—
converged on a New York City hotel for Global AgInvesting 2009, "the first
investors' conference on the emerging worldwide market in farmland."[12] The
event has occurred each year since then; the 2011 conference, according to
its official website, globalaginvesting.com, featured more than 600 attendees
with a combined 10 million hectares under cultivation and $12.5 billion in
farmland assets.

Indeed, according to IFPRI's Ruth Meinzen-Dick and the University
of Minnesota's Helen Markelova, many deals are being negotiated at a
"rapid rate." Given this reality, they argue, policymakers and civil society can
no longer settle for making "blanket pronouncements praising or denouncing the deals," but must instead focus on what can be done to help host
countries "seize the opportunities and mitigate the risks" surrounding the
deals.

Their chapter proposes a series of questions to be asked about any
potential farmland transaction in order to help determine how beneficial it

would be for local communities, host governments, and investors alike. These questions focus on current land use (how and by whom the land in question is currently being used) and on land-tenure arrangements, or property rights. Do individuals have formal rights to the land, and does the government recognize these rights? Or do local groups have more informal "customary" tenure over the land (a status more easily exploitable by governments and investors)? What are the deals' terms—will the land be sold or leased? (The latter offers revenue streams and reversibility options, but short-term leases may not create incentives for long-term environmental sustainability.) Will there be enforcement provisions? To what extent will the expected benefits of the proposed deals be shared with locals—will farmers be able to participate in contracting arrangements, and will they have access to improved technologies? Will local communities retain any of the food produced on their land—particularly during food shortages? Will the land be able to withstand long-term intensive production? Finally, how involved are land users in the negotiations over these notoriously non-transparent deals? Transparency is essential, the writers insist, because "free, prior, and informed consent will create greater legitimacy" for land deals.

Meinzen-Dick and Markelova identify the qualities that can help ensure that foreign land acquisitions are "economically, socially, and ecologically sustainable." These include transparency, respect for land rights (including customary rights), benefits-sharing, and environmental sustainability. They single out efforts by the World Bank and UN to produce "codes of conduct" as especially encouraging developments, and they contend that wide dissemination of such codes would better prepare communities, host governments, and investors for "constructive negotiations." For these mechanisms to work, however, a variety of actors must participate. The international community must "push for adherence" to the code in both investor and host countries; host governments must monitor local people's rights; the media must "showcase" the better deals, "shame" the bad ones, and push for more transparency; and civil society must focus on "preventing unjust expropriation."

The code of conduct option has come under fire. Many detractors contend that since such codes serve a strictly normative purpose, they are toothless and thus incapable of inducing compliance on the part of host governments and investors. At a UN conference in October 2011, efforts to finalize guidelines on large-scale land deals failed, prompting the UN Special Rapporteur on the Right to Food to admit that such guidelines represent "an unresolved sticking point."[13] Still, negotiations were restarted in early

2012, and in March an agreement was reached on a proposed set of voluntary international guidelines on responsible land-tenure governance and access rights to land, forest resources, and fisheries. The guidelines were to be submitted to the UN's Committee on World Food Security for final approval later in the year.

An alternative approach puts more of the onus on host governments. Spieldoch and Murphy write that countries "ultimately need a national (and local) dialogue on what they want for and from their land." They recommend that host governments (with cooperation from investors) ensure that deals uphold the universal human right to food (a right enshrined in international legal conventions), and that land-investment guidelines incorporate the feedback, priorities, and needs of all affected groups and communities. Spieldoch and Murphy also advocate that land use be reviewed in light of demographic shifts. They point out that rural populations are projected to more than double by 2050 in some of the African countries most sought after by foreign land investors. "Getting a better grasp of the realities of both land use and availability will help craft appropriate policies," they conclude.

From the Farmland Frontlines: Regional Perspectives

Some critics contend that international responses to foreign land deals betray a level of ignorance about realities on the ground in host countries and local communities. So what are these ground realities? The next series of chapters offer accounts from four salient regions, written by people from—or intimately familiar with—each of these areas.

Africa

Africa is the biggest hotspot for overseas land acquisitions. Of the 203 million hectares of farmland cited by the ILC, 134 million are in Africa. While many of these acquisitions have occurred in the years following the 2007–8 global food crisis, the World Bank calculates that acquisitions totaled nearly 10 million hectares in just four African countries (Ethiopia, Liberia, Mozambique, and Sudan) during the relatively early period of 2004–9.[14] None of this is surprising when one considers that, according to the World Bank's 2011 study, of the world's 445 million hectares of unfarmed land "suitable for cropping, nonforested, nonprotected, and populated with less than 25 people per square kilometer," more than 200 million hectares are in sub-Saharan Africa (see Table 1-3).

Paradoxically, many African countries relinquishing their farmland are so acutely food-insecure that they depend on aid from the World Food Program (WFP). Ethiopia, for example, has received $116 million in WFP food aid—even while Saudi Arabia has grown grains on Ethiopian farms for Saudi consumption.[15] Meanwhile, Sudan has received "a billion pounds of free food" from international donors, yet has still managed to grow wheat for Saudi Arabia, tomatoes for the Jordanian Army, and sorghum—a Sudanese staple—for *camels* in the United Arab Emirates.[16]

However, there is another side to this story. In 2009, the head of Emergent Asset Management, one of the most active private investors in southern African land, informed the BBC that "we are not bringing in our own farm workers and then taking the food and exporting it." Instead, local communities will benefit from new farming techniques, seeds, technologies, and the "above-average wages paid by Emergent's local partner."[17] In 2011, IIED researchers managed to secure contracts for 12 land deals in Africa. They found that several contained beneficial terms for local communities—one in Mali applied international environmental standards, while several in Liberia contained explicit investor commitments on employment and train-

TABLE 1-3   Available Uncultivated* Land

Region	Total Area (in thousands of hectares)
Sub-Saharan Africa	201,546
Latin America and the Caribbean	123,342
Eastern Europe and Central Asia	52,387
East and South Asia	14,341
Middle East and North Africa	3,043
Rest of world	50,971
TOTAL	445,624

* Refers to land that is suitable for cropping and is non-forested, non-protected, and populated with less than 25 people per square kilometer.

Source: World Bank, *Rising Global Interest in Farmland*, 2011.

ing.[18] And several years after the Daewoo debacle, researchers discovered that land deals in Madagascar are emphasizing school building and clinic construction.[19]

Regardless of the nature of foreign land acquisitions in Africa, an essential fact remains: African land is highly contentious. "More so perhaps than on any other continent," writes Senegal-based agricultural-commodities exporter Chido Makunike, "so many livelihoods, and entire cultural and economic experiences, are directly tied to the land." These strong ties, he explains, "engender a strong sensibility about land that is poorly understood by many non-Africans." His contribution describes these sentiments about land in Africa, and argues that failing to understand them will make successful agribusiness projects in the region unlikely. For example, if foreign investors target what to them appears to be empty land but is in fact a community's ancestral burial ground, then "passion and resentment" will ensue.

Additionally, Makunike describes the large-scale agriculture model as "Africa-dismissive." Millions of smallholders are seemingly ignored, while capital, expertise, and sometimes even managers and workers are imported from overseas. He cites case studies from Sierra Leone and Mozambique, where investors' promised jobs to smallholders have not materialized, and from Ethiopia, where an Indian firm is using Ethiopian land to produce food for export that was previously used to raise Ethiopia's staple crop. The "presumption," according to Makunike, is that other than the land itself, "the African side has nothing to bring to the table." It is this "dismissive attitude" of foreign investors that not only prompts "worry and resentment" about land deals in Africa, but also "endangers their longevity and ultimate political and social viability."

Nonetheless, Makunike does not necessarily object to foreign investments in agriculture. On the contrary, he suggests that when local communities "can be shown and convinced" that the commercial use of land "would definitely and significantly improve community well-being," then the investment is a wise one. Makunike is cautiously supportive of contract farming, noting that it offers African smallholders income opportunities while giving them the flexibility to grow their own crops on the side. The biggest question is whether investors would have the patience to offer training and assistance to their smallholder partners—given that time-pressed investors "are used to having large groups of tightly controlled laborers who are hired and fired at will." If land deals are done right, concludes Makunike, local communities will see their interests "tied up with the success" of the investment—a tremendous benefit for the investor.

Asia

After Africa, Asia is arguably the most popular target for farmland investments. According to the ILC's 2012 report, publicly reported land deals in the region encompass 43 million hectares. Cambodia, Indonesia, and the Philippines have attracted particularly strong interest, and IFPRI has highlighted several proposed or finalized Asia-based deals in excess of 100,000 hectares.[20]

Investments in Asia differ from those in Africa in one notable respect: They are mostly intraregional in nature. According to the ILC, 75 percent of the land acquisitions in Southeast Asia have been made by investors hailing from elsewhere in Asia. By contrast, Asians, Americans, and Europeans are all involved in projects in Africa.

According to Raul Q. Montemayor of the Federation of Free Farmers Cooperatives, Inc. in the Philippines, "agribusiness opportunities abound in Asia"—a region home to growing populations and rising consumption trends. Farmland investors win over Asian governments with promises of official development assistance, loans, and other perks.

However, Montemayor expresses great concern about the "rapid encroachment on small farms" spawned by foreign land acquisitions in Asia. He reports how a Cambodian corporation, in partnership with foreign investors, has cleared land previously used for local food crops and livestock grazing; more than 1,000 families have been affected and smallholders speak of having lost their land without being compensated. He writes as well about the fears of unrest sparked by a Saudi firm's acquisition of 1.2 million hectares in Indonesia's Papua province, an area embroiled in separatist insurgency. Small farmers have precious little to gain financially from leasing their land to foreigners, according to Montemayor. He insists that "even a low-technology farmer" working his modest two-hectare plot could "easily generate" the two dollars per day offered as rental payments by foreign firms in the Philippines.

Montemayor offers recommendations for how international land investments can better benefit local landowners, rural communities, and Asian host countries generally. Strikingly, each of his proposals focuses on local initiatives; he says little about the role of international players, and nothing about an international code of conduct. He calls on host governments to develop clear policies on foreign land investment that take into account "the overriding interests of the country"—from food security to the environmental sustainability of land and natural resources. He also underscores that foreign investors must "strictly adhere" to relevant host-country rules and regulations, with repercussions if they fail to do so. He insists that locals be held to these rules as well, given that "most of the excesses and abuses" surrounding land deals are perpetrated by host-country militaries and politicians. Back in the 1980s and 1990s, he writes, local "goons" in the Philippines terrorized targeted investment areas, forcing settlers to flee and "making them easy prey for opportunists" ready to lease the settlers' land.[21] Finally, he recommends that legal assistance be provided to local landowners and users to ensure that they are not snookered into signing one-sided contracts.

Latin America

Africa and Asia have netted some of the largest deals, but investors are also fixated on Latin America, where, based on ILC figures, 19 million hectares have been acquired. According to an Argentinian study, foreigners own 11 percent of productive land in that nation.[22] This region, combined with the Caribbean, contains 123 million hectares of available cultivable land, says the World Bank; only sub-Saharan Africa boasts more. Additionally, investors are attracted to its nutrient-rich soil, adequate water supplies, livestock-producing capabilities, and advanced agricultural technologies.[23]

Bastiaan P. Reydon and Vitor B. Fernandes assert that foreign land investment is prolific throughout the region, and especially in land-abundant Brazil. The authors, both based at the University of Campinas in São Paulo, focus much of their chapter on this country, where, they write, FDI flows into the agricultural sector equaled $421 million between 2005 and 2007—a figure surpassed only by China and Malaysia. Brazilian law imposes limitations on foreign land ownership, the chapter explains, and a legal decision affirmed these restrictions as recently as 2010. Yet foreign acquisitions have proceeded nonetheless—including a $7 billion long-term deal inked by China in 2011 to grow 6 million tons of soybeans per year in one small town. More than 4 million hectares of land—and nearly 35,000 rural properties—are registered under foreign ownership.

Reydon and Fernandes suggest that poor land regulation and shoddy governance help fuel the high levels of foreign investment in Brazilian land. Half of Brazil's 850 million hectares are not registered with the official land registry, while irregularities, fraud, and corruption afflict both the official registry and the various notary offices that register land unofficially. The authors conclude that Brazil should better regulate land acquisitions instead of trying to "repress or prevent" them altogether. Land speculation is natural in capitalism, so "it is up to the state to regulate it, and to society to establish governance over it to forestall further harm."

Central and Eastern Europe Countries (CEEC) and the Former Soviet Union (FSU)

Though not as extensively as in Africa, Asia, and Latin America, land acquisitions also occur in Central and Eastern Europe and the former Soviet Union. After the Soviet Union collapsed in the early 1990s, foreign investors (most of them private) rushed to claim formerly state-owned farms—and this process has continued today. Such interest is understandable; Blumenthal notes that the nutrient-rich surface soils of the FSU are highly appealing to investors. Additionally, according to the World Bank, Eastern Europe and Central Asia contain 52 million hectares of available and cultivable land, with Kazakhstan, Russia, and Ukraine the most abundant. Still, even with this robust investment activity, one hears relatively little about land hunts in this part of the world. According to Carl Atkin of KinnAgri Limited, an international agribusiness management and consultancy firm, this is because such activities are long-standing, strongly encouraged in local settings, and therefore less controversial. While certain smallholder groups are opposed, "they tend not to be very well-organized, visible, or significant."

Atkin surveys investment types and the farmland investment climate across the CEEC and FSU. One group of financiers seeks real estate investments, and targets EU countries because of the legal and fiscal stability and well-developed property rights found in these nations. The other group focuses on operational farming investment, which involves "accessing large areas of land at relatively low cost," typically through leasing, and most often in Russia and Ukraine. Atkin is generally optimistic about investment prospects in the region. He notes that Europe is blessed with ample water resources and hence solid productivity potential. Furthermore, both the CEEC and FSU have strong infrastructure (in terms of roads and ports), and enjoy close access to markets in Europe and Asia.

Atkin acknowledges investor challenges as well, especially foreign ownership restrictions (including Poland's, which forbid foreign ownership until 2016 and are rooted in historic fears about Germans "buying up vast tracts of cheap land"). Quality management is a problem in the meat and milk sectors; many FSU states do not meet EU import standards on animal health and welfare. The global financial crisis has also presented challenges. Atkin notes that some investors are shifting away from Ukraine and other hard-hit countries, and more toward the CEEC and South America, which are perceived as more economically stable.

Soul Searching about Soil Searching: The Stakes

Atkin also offers his thoughts on the investment climate for farmland worldwide, and is largely sanguine. Investor advantages include not only the demand-supply scenario (population growth, dietary shifts, and the thirst for biofuels collide with limited land availability, rampant water shortages, and deficiencies in agricultural technology), but also the fact that agriculture is more "recession-proof" than the general economy. According to Atkin, this is because food expenditures are relatively inelastic, and "the fundamental production of commodities" for the very poor will be little affected by economic downturns—particularly relative to "higher-end food services and retail."

Long-Term Implications

Such an assessment suggests that large-scale international investment in agriculture may continue, if not intensify, in the years ahead. Such large, sustained investments over time could have major consequences, not just for individual smallholders and land users, but for entire host societies and countries.

Meinzen-Dick and Markelova point out that land converted from smallholder production to plantation agriculture will not likely revert to its original users, "and within a generation farming skills may be lost." Such land transfers therefore have "profound and long-term implications" for the structures of rural societies. They also discuss the harmful effect large land deals could have on the "wider sociopolitical and economic context" of host countries. Granted, to this point Madagascar is the only contemporary case where a land deal has contributed to widespread political instability. However, the factors at play in many host countries—land, food insecurity, and poverty—make up a combustible mix that could easily explode into conflict. In countries such as Pakistan, where violent, extremist anti-government movements have mastered the ability to exploit land-based class divisions, the risks are particularly high.

Examples already abound of land deals threatening or sparking unrest. Makunike writes of protestors in Sierra Leone blocking access to a Belgian investment site. In Kenya's Tana Delta, locals speak of being forcibly evicted in order to accommodate investor plans for a sugar plantation, and vow to fight back "with guns and sticks. . . . It will be war. The day is coming."[24] In Uganda, people have already retaliated. In April 2011, a mob killed an Indian man while protesting an Indian investment firm's decision to chop down a rainforest to make more space for sugarcane production.[25]

Several contributors also underscore that the long-term risks of large-scale land acquisitions do not apply only to host countries and investors. Montemayor contends that due to local demand, population growth, and projected climate-change effects along the Mekong River, Southeast Asia on the whole—a major rice-producing region—could conceivably become a net rice importer if foreign investors continue to export products they grow on local cropland. Hallam points out that third parties could be impacted by changes in global trade volume and price variability when a large food importer obtains its food outside the market.

Such observations raise larger long-run questions: Does non-market food production portend shocks for global market supply and consequent price rises? What could be the implications for poor food-importing nations (such as those in West Africa) that cannot afford to invest in agriculture abroad if supplies continue to be removed from the market and food prices once again rise precipitously? Strikingly, negotiations for land overseas have continued even after world food prices stabilized after 2008—an indication that wealthy food importers are willing to eschew global trade to meet food needs. One must consider how waning faith in the international food market could affect global food security prospects in the years ahead.

These long-term risks amplify the need for greater attention to and discussion about foreign land acquisitions. The world may be experiencing a land rush, but it is also caught up in a rush for information about this topic—and supply is limited. The pages that follow are meant to help reduce this shortfall.

Chapter 2

Are We Learning from History?[1]

DEREK BYERLEE

Underlying the recent worldwide focus on foreign "land grabs" is an assumption that these acquisitions constitute a new phenomenon—one brought about by a perfect storm of booming food and agricultural commodity markets and acute land (and water) scarcity. These new developments, we are told, have triggered a scramble for foreign land in the name of food security. This chapter argues that, in fact, rising foreign investment in farmland during commodity booms is nothing new. History provides many lessons for today's upsurge in investment.

Given the breadth of the subject, this chapter is necessarily restricted in coverage. Although overseas acquisition of land is an ancient affair dating from Roman times (consider the large estates established in North Africa to provision Rome), the emphasis here is on market-driven investments, dating from the first era of globalization in the second half of the nineteenth century. Then, as now, rapid industrialization (at that time in Europe, North America, and a bit later, Japan) produced growing consumer incomes and rising demand for food and industrial raw materials, in a context of sharply reduced transport costs and liberalization of trade, foreign investment, and international migration. These factors combined to induce companies from the North to invest overseas to supply growing markets, especially for tropical products such as sugar, rubber, and tea.

Given the focus of this book, this chapter's emphasis is on investments involving large-scale acquisitions of land for crop production (nonagricultural acquisitions, such as for mining and other purposes, are excluded), whether through outright purchase, leasing, or government concessions. I emphasize issues related to land rights, governance, and agrarian structure, even though labor rights have dominated much of the historical debate. Foreign (overseas) is broadly interpreted to include transnational investments within today's constellation of countries—that is, it includes investment by imperial powers in their colonies. I especially focus on Britain and the United States, historically by far the largest sources of foreign investment in agriculture. However, I also recognize that many large land-related investments were (as now) national in origin, although many of the same drivers applied and the outcomes were similar.

Framework for This Review

Two broad categories of foreign agricultural investments can be identified. First, investments may focus on downstream activities in the value chain, sourcing raw materials from independent farm operations through contracts or by purchasing in spot markets. This has in fact been the dominant business model and has become more common over time. However, since it does not involve direct land acquisition, it is not central to this chapter. Second, foreign companies may invest directly via a stand-alone farming company or as part of a vertically integrated company. Within this second type of investment, two further categories can be distinguished: (1) plantation agriculture, usually producing a single perennial crop with large amounts of manual labor and closely tied to processing, and (2) large-scale, mechanized farming of annual crops under corporate management, employing relatively little labor.

At the outset, it is important to emphasize that large-scale farming based on corporate management is the exception in agriculture. Throughout the world, family farming depending largely on family labor and managers has been and continues to be the dominant organizational form. It is also important to recall that by far the largest historical "land grabs" have been made by family farms associated with settlement and colonization by European migrants to temperate areas (almost everywhere, settlers trampled on the land rights of indigenous people).[2] However, settlers received little foreign investment directly, because capital for land clearing and land improvement was generally created through family labor. Nonetheless, land for many settler schemes was acquired through private companies that obtained access to large tracts of land and subdivided it, often with a strong element of speculation (see Box 2-1).[3]

Six commodities account for the great bulk of foreign investment involving large land acquisitions over the past 150 years—sugarcane, tea, rubber, bananas, palm oil, and food staples. They all continue to be important today, with two of them—sugarcane and palm oil—receiving a new life as biofuels feedstocks.

Technical characteristics are important in determining a commodity's suitability for being produced in a large plantation system (see Table 2-1). Classic plantation crops are often grown in large production units due to the combination of three factors: (1) large economies of scale in processing; (2) the requirement for close coordination between production and harvesting, due to the need to process quickly after harvest to avoid loss of quality; and (3) a low share by weight of the processed product relative to the raw material, which favors production close to the mill.[4] Tea, sugarcane, and oil palm are classic plantation crops. Although bananas are not processed, they

---

BOX 2-1
Private Investment in Land Companies

Up to the early 1900s, much colonization and even conquest was in the hands of private companies. These companies' main assets were lands vaguely designated to agriculture through subdivision for settlement programs. Much of this land was held for speculation, but also for exploiting natural resources such as timber. Examples were the New Zealand Company, the Natal Land and Colonization Company in South Africa, the Mexican Land and Colonization Company, and the Santa Fe Land Company in Argentina. In 1913 there were 130 British companies of this type holding 25 million ha of land, largely in Africa and Latin America, but also in North America and Oceania. This compares with 746 companies that held 5.6 million ha engaged directly in agriculture through plantations, and 40 companies that held 14.2 million ha for ranching. A further 11 companies held 2.7 million ha through railway concessions, most of which would eventually be sold off for settlement.

These companies acquired land through a variety of means. These included the disposal of public land (as in Argentina), direct purchases from indigenous peoples—albeit often from highly unequal negotiating positions (as in New Zealand), disposal of reputedly unused communal lands (as in Mexico under the Porfirio Díaz regime), and brute force (as with the British South Africa Company in Zimbabwe). Few of these companies endured, and many went bankrupt.

TABLE 2-1   Key Characteristics Favoring Large-Scale Production for Selected Crops

Characteristic	Sugar	Tea	Rubber	Bananas	Oil Palm	Grains
Coordination between harvesting & processing	H*	H	L	H	H	L
Low percent of processed product to raw material	H	M	L	M	H	L
Investment in processing and infrastructure	M–H	L–M	L	M	M	L–M
Investment up front for production	M	H	L–M	M–H	M	L
Year-round labor	M	H	H	H	M	L
Relative price risk	L	M	H	M	M	L
Need for tight quality control	L	H	L	M	L	L

* H = high, M = medium, L = low (all in relative terms)

require close coordination of harvesting and shipping—thereby favoring large-scale production.

Other factors listed in Table 2-1 may also favor large-scale farming models. However, note that production of grains has almost no characteristics that favor large-scale farming. Indeed, small-scale family farming generally has the edge here. This is because of the difficulties of supervising hired labor in geographically dispersed production, the flexibility in employing family labor in seasonally varied tasks on and off the farm, and the advantage of farmers' intimate knowledge of local climatic and soil conditions. Hundreds of studies attest to the efficiency of family farming; not until quite recently, as explained below, do we see the entry of foreign investors into food-crop farming.[5]

Historical Snapshots of Six Commodities

Sugarcane

By 1850, sugar was the most important agricultural product in international trade. Sugarcane had attained notoriety as the crop that had spearheaded

the slave trade back in the seventeenth century. In some of the major producer nations, such as Brazil and Cuba, slaves were still the basis of the
industry. Even where slavery had been abolished, it was replaced by indentured labor shipped around the world, largely from India. Labor recruitment
and working conditions continued to be poor in this system. Thus the history of sugarcane is dominated by discussion of labor rights; relatively little
attention has been paid to land issues. In fact, the initial sugar-producing
areas—Madeira for the Portuguese and Barbados for the British—were
uninhabited immediately prior to their becoming major producers of the
commodity.

Land issues came to the fore when sugar production for export was
introduced into more densely populated areas of Asia. In the late nineteenth
century, Java (in present-day Indonesia) was the world's second-largest sugar
exporter. Prior to 1870, under Dutch colonial regulations, villages were
forced to allocate one-fifth of their land to sugar and other cash crops in
lieu of paying land taxes.[6] This system was relaxed after 1870, when sugar
companies entered into contractual arrangements with communities to rent
land during the off-year rice rotation, and to provide wage labor. By 1939,
over a half million hectares (ha) were devoted to this system in Java, which
seems to have been a definite improvement over the earlier involuntary
supply of land and labor, though elements of compulsion remained in order
to organize the needed land in contiguous blocks.[7] In Taiwan (part of the
Japanese empire until 1945), Japanese sugar companies used government
subsidies to purchase land outright for production, but where this was done
under duress, violent protests by local communities resulted.[8] Ironically,
much of this land was rented back to smallholders to produce sugar under
contract.

After the emancipation of slaves, British Caribbean sugar producers
went into decline. By 1900 American sugar interests dominated the industry,
investing heavily in the Spanish-speaking Caribbean, Hawaii, and the Philippines. Hawaii presents an interesting case. There, around 1850, the governing royal family chose to move from a semi-feudal system of land tenure to
an arrangement providing full individual titles to indigenous land users and
their chiefs. The elite, who received most of the land but were cash poor,
sold their land to private interests, with five American sugar companies eventually taking over most of the land. The largest, the Hawaiian Commercial
and Sugar Company, amassed 200,000 ha.[9] Although land was legitimately
acquired, the capture of water rights was highly questionable. These powerful sugar interests were one factor leading to the annexation of Hawaii by
the United States in 1898.

Up to about 1900, the area of a sugar plantation required to meet mill capacity was quite small and most plantations were family-owned. This changed drastically after 1900 with a revolution in processing technology that provided huge economies of scale in milling. In Cuba, the area per mill expanded from about 200 ha in 1860 to 500 ha in 1904, and then to 3,250 ha in 1916 and 6,000 ha in 1929.[10] The story of sugar shifts at this point to one of increasing scale, with mill ownership moving from family operations to relatively large companies in the early twentieth century. This trend has continued to the present day; an average sugarcane-ethanol plant in Brazil today requires a supply area of 20,000 ha, and the most recent mills may require up to 70,000 ha, with a total investment of $1 billion or more. Today, sugarcane is also the only plantation crop that allows for the full mechanization of production operations (including harvesting), thereby largely solving labor supply problems.

These trends to larger milling scale gave areas with abundant land a comparative advantage in sugar production. After Cuba's independence in 1902, American sugar companies moved aggressively to invest in the young nation's sugar industry, eventually converting Cuba into the world's leading exporter. These sugar firms acquired large tracts of Cuban land, especially pasture and forest land in the east, aided by poorly defined rights for communal lands and by powerful company lawyers. Cuban American Sugar Company, for example, is reported to have obtained some 200,000 ha.[11] However, much of this land was rented out to contract tenants. Many contract farmers, both owners and tenants, became large farmers in their own right, leading to highly unequal control over land.

Very recently, foreign investment in sugarcane has received new impetus, thanks to the crop's strong ties with energy production. Energy companies from the North have been very active, but Brazilian and Asian companies have expanded their global reach as well. The world's largest sugar producer is now Cosan, a Brazilian company that sources from a huge sugarcane area of about 600,000 ha, with over half of this land under its own management.

Tea

Tea is the most labor-intensive of the crops covered in this chapter; today a tea plantation typically employs about two people per ha. It is also a relatively capital-intensive crop, requiring about $30,000 per ha to establish, with a payback period of about 13 years. For these reasons, and also because of its requirement for rapid processing within a few hours after harvest, black tea was historically produced on plantations.

Tea consumption took off with the industrial revolution in Britain, initially sourced from China through an East India Company monopoly. When this monopoly expired amid growing unrest in China, the British imperial government in India took a strategic interest in fostering tea production in northeastern India, where another tea species was indigenous. Initially the Assam Tea Company was the largest operation, but many other companies and individual planters entered the industry to meet rising demand. The industry faced high start-up costs, major infrastructural hurdles, and many failures, in part due to inexperience with tea production on this scale. Over time, with a desire for quality differentiation and branding, many of the major retail tea merchants, such as Tetley, integrated upstream into their own tea production.

Indentured labor was employed from other parts of India, and the rights of contracted workers were subjected to many abuses; death rates were high in the early years. Given the large amount of labor employed, labor rights and conditions have continued to be problems even today, although minimum-wage laws and labor standards have greatly improved.

The acquisition of land for tea in northeast India has been meticulously analyzed over a century. From 1840 to 1940, some 4.7 million ha were allocated. Rules for land acquisition were often quite good on paper, as land sales required prior surveys to demarcate forest lands not cultivated by communities (although undoubtedly used by them for other aspects of their livelihoods) and provisions for withdrawing concessions.[12] However, in due course a pattern emerged whereby during times of high prices, rules were relaxed and speculation became rampant, after which reviews and commissions tightened rules once again. With the expansion of plantations, demands from former immigrant plantation laborers for land, and local population growth, land competition increased and conflicts became more common in the twentieth century.

Sri Lanka entered the tea industry around 1870, eventually becoming the world's largest exporter. Estates were relatively small and many were owned and managed by individual planters, though some large, vertically integrated companies also entered the field, led by a firm owned by Thomas Lipton. As in India, labor abuses were pervasive, while land issues were relatively minor in the early years because tea farming had simply replaced diseased coffee plantations.

In Kenya, now rivaling Sri Lanka as the world's largest exporter, tea estates were established beginning around 1900. These were based on the plantation model, with both foreign ownership and individual settler planters. Although the tea area was quite small, land acquisition was linked to the settler model, with some 3 million ha of prime land reserved for Europeans, displacing African smallholders and eventually leading (in the 1950s) to the Mau Mau uprising, which centered around land conflict.

After their respective nations achieved independence (and even earlier in Kenya), the tea industries in India, Sri Lanka, and Kenya all underwent major structural changes to reduce foreign domination and to address ongoing labor problems. However, the trajectory of these changes has been different in each country, indicating how different policy contexts can lead to a variety of institutional models to promote both efficiency and equity.

At independence, India's government required majority ownership by Indians. The Tata Group, for example, took over Tetley (then the world's second largest tea company). In recent years, low prices, increasing minimum wages, and labor conflicts have threatened the profitability of Indian tea companies. Tata has addressed this by devolving ownership to employees. For example, in the state of Kerala, Tata devolved its plantations to the Kanan Devan Hills Plantations Company (KDHPC), where 68 percent of shares are now owned by employees.[13] Initial experience has been positive, with greatly improved labor relations and labor productivity.[14]

In Sri Lanka, after much debate, all plantations above a minimum size were nationalized in 1971. However, performance of the state-owned sector was poor, and Sri Lanka steadily lost competitiveness in world markets. The high management costs of state-owned plantations and high wage costs of unionized and increasingly militant labor eventually favored the emergence of independent private processors who contracted with smallholder producers. An important institutional innovation favoring this model was a government-brokered formula for establishing a price for raw tea delivered to factories based on the world price and quality norms. The transformation has been truly remarkable, with the production share of smallholders rising from 7 percent in 1960 to 60 percent in 2004.[15] By most measures, smallholders have proved more efficient than the remaining state-owned estates, though some very successful national private companies have emerged— especially Dilmah, the world's third largest tea company.

In Kenya, the pre-independence Swynnerton Plan was drawn up in the 1950s (Kenya became independent in 1963) to develop the African smallholder sector. The Kenya Tea Development Agency (KTDA), founded in 1964, has led the development of smallholder tea. With considerable backing from donors and multinational financial institutions, KTDA has supported smallholders and provided close supervision of production practices. Processing factories were initially managed by foreign tea companies, but were devolved to KTDA in the 1970s under smallholder ownership.[16]

KTDA was fully privatized in 2000 under the ownership of smallholder tea producers. With majority farmer equity, it now works with about 550,000 smallholders (holding an average of 0.4 ha) and 63 smallholder-owned factories. Today, smallholders account for 62 percent of national tea production, and the yield gap between smallholders and estates has fallen from 68 percent in 1980 to 18 percent today.[17]

Tea is a story of a remarkable transition from foreign-owned plantations to a robust smallholder sector (or one where workers are the majority shareholders). This transition, which has largely resolved both land and labor conflicts, reflects the efforts of a supporting government policy, innovative smallholders, and forward-looking companies.

Rubber

The nascent automobile industry stimulated a major new market for rubber in the early twentieth century. Rubber also became a highly strategic commodity due to its importance in wartime, especially during World War II, when the Allies' main source of rubber was captured by the Japanese.

In the early twentieth century, a price spike for rubber stimulated large inflows of foreign investment and rapid expansion of planted rubber through foreign-owned plantations in Southeast Asia (largely British, Dutch, and French, but also American-owned). Many family-operated plantations and small companies were not able to withstand the risks of operating in a highly volatile market and were taken over by vertically integrated tire manufacturing companies who wished to secure supply and their strategic interests. For example, Goodyear in Indonesia and Dunlop in Malaysia each had over 40,000 ha of rubber by the 1930s.

Except in Vietnam, expansion took place in low-population-density areas that required importation of labor. As with sugar and tea, rubber production employed indentured labor, largely Indian and Chinese, and similar issues of labor rights and conditions were widespread throughout Southeast Asia (though before 1910, workers harvesting wild rubber in the then-Belgian Congo and elsewhere suffered even worse abuses). In a recent comprehensive history of rubber, labor rights are mentioned dozens of times, yet land rights are not mentioned once.[18] In part this relates to the very low population density prevailing at the time in major production areas such as

Malaysia and the outer islands of Indonesia. Land grants were provided from forested areas that at the time were considered "wastelands," and the colonial government in Malaysia recognized and demarcated indigenous land rights.

Land rights associated with plantation rubber were more of a problem under French colonial rule in Vietnam, where virtually free land concessions encouraged land acquisitions well beyond needs, and conflicted with use by local communities.[19] This led, in 1927, to a French government commission of inquiry that suspended land concessions, followed by French legislation establishing powers of surveillance over all French colonies on matters of land concessions. However, implementation capacity was weak, and these regulations were soon relaxed or were not enforced under pressure from local companies.

Elsewhere, huge land concessions for rubber to Firestone in Liberia (400,000 ha) in 1925 and Ford Motors in Brazil (over a million ha) in 1932 were problematic.[20] In Liberia, land was granted at extremely low rates and with little regard to indigenous rights. Nonetheless, international attention to rubber in Liberia has focused more on labor rights and its enclave nature (what has famously been called "growth without development").[21] In Brazil, after two decades of technical failure and a nationalistic backlash against such a large land concession, Ford abandoned its effort. Another failure was an estimated investment of $1.75 billion (in today's dollars) by 85 US companies in rubber production in Mexico, a decision spurred by the 1910 price spike. These investments not only failed spectacularly (due to the use of an unsuitable plant species), but were also investigated for widespread investor fraud.

One of the unexpected developments at the time was the rapid emergence of smallholder rubber producers. Unlike other plantation commodities reviewed here, rubber could be processed on-farm through relatively simple methods. Despite colonial policies that favored estate production, it was quickly taken up by smallholders once the basic technology and infrastructure were in place. By 1940, half of Asian rubber was produced by smallholders, and today this share stands at over 85 percent.[22] Globally, rubber has emerged as a commodity that provides livelihoods to millions of smallholders and wage earners.

Today, traditional foreign investors such as tire companies retain only a small stake in rubber production, mainly Bridgestone-Firestone in Liberia. The major new investors have been from China, encouraged by Chinese government subsidies to stimulate production of this strategic industrial input. Chinese investors are rapidly expanding rubber production in Laos, Cambodia, and Cote d'Ivoire, and land conflicts have emerged in Cambodia. Given the strong record of smallholder production, it is not clear why Chinese investors have reverted to large-scale plantations.

Bananas

Foreign investment in bananas is a case where large companies, integrated vertically from farm to plate, created a market that had not previously existed. The trials and tribulations of the banana industry, led by the American company United Fruit (now Chiquita), made the sector the bête noire of foreign investment in Latin America in the twentieth century. This was largely due to United Fruit's massive acquisition of land in the Central American "banana republics."

Local producers and foreign investors in Central America and the Caribbean had been making small shipments of bananas to the United States since around 1880. At the turn of the century, the United Fruit Company saw an opportunity to popularize banana consumption by tapping into the land it had acquired in Costa Rica as part of an agreement to construct a railroad. Over the next few decades, United Fruit invested a billion dollars (in today's dollars) in establishing a fully integrated banana value chain, including port infrastructure, a railroad system, and a specialized shipping fleet.[23] Bananas initially favored large-scale production and vertical integration, due to the high up-front investment costs and the need to closely coordinate harvesting with shipping. The market was highly concentrated, with three companies controlling the bulk of the market. This structure remains in place today with the primacy of Chiquita, Dole, and Del Monte.

Although labor issues were important in banana production and labor unrest was common from the 1930s, land issues have dominated the history of banana production. Because plant diseases were a major problem in large-scale banana production, companies employed a highly land-extensive method of production that involved shifting cultivation every few years in order to control disease outbreaks. As a result, and probably also for purposes of maintaining market control and land speculation, the land areas controlled were sometimes as much as 20 times the area actually planted. Huge land concessions were mediated through private sales and government concessions at very low rates (for railroad construction as well as banana production). At its peak in 1935, United Fruit owned around 1.4 million ha of land in Central America—making it the largest farmland holder in the world at that time.[24]

Much of this land was forest in very sparsely populated areas, but still there were conflicts, in large part because existing land rights were poorly demarcated due to the high costs of land surveys and weak capacity for conducting them. Investment in infrastructure, population growth, and market development caused land prices to rise—leading to further competition for land and frequent land conflicts, as detailed in a number of studies from Honduras, Guatemala, and Ecuador.[25]

Not surprisingly, companies such as United Fruit—very large in relation to the relatively small economies of Central America—exerted considerable political influence. This came to a head in Guatemala in 1954, when a military coup backed by the US government overthrew an elected government that had introduced land reform legislation to take over unused land from banana companies. In 1975, United Fruit was also implicated in a bribery scandal to reduce export taxes in Honduras.

Facing growing labor unrest, increasing agitation for land reform, and pressure from international shareholders exposed to continuing bad press, the banana companies began a process of "vertical disintegration" in the 1960s.[26] This in time decreased the need for land. The changeover to a more disease-resistant banana crop variety also reduced the need for land. This led eventually to a divestment of land holdings, and by 1968 United Fruit's land possessions comprised "only" 80,000 ha.[27] Most bananas for export are now sourced through contracts with medium-sized growers.

Oil Palm

Oil palm is indigenous to West and Central Africa, where it was originally harvested for export to Europe for a variety of uses, such as soap. When demand expanded rapidly in the early part of the twentieth century, Lever Brothers (a predecessor of Unilever) sought land area to cultivate oil palm in Nigeria and Ghana. This was denied by the British West African colonial governments on the grounds that it would conflict with existing land users. Eventually, Lever Brothers obtained a concession of 140,000 ha in the Belgian Congo, and, working with the Belgian colonial government, was able to develop the technology needed to successfully cultivate the palm on large plantations. Not surprisingly, given the prior history of harvesting wild rubber in the Congo (marked by major abuses of human rights), labor rights rather than land rights constituted the main issue faced by Lever.

Beginning in the 1920s, oil palm technology was transferred from the Congo and cultivated on a small area by foreign companies in Malaysia and Indonesia. With declining rubber prices, Malaysia made a strategic decision in the 1960s to diversify its agriculture. It promoted a public-private research and development (R&D) partnership that greatly increased productivity of oil palm, building on technology from the Congo. Oil palm expanded rapidly, largely in former rubber areas but also in forest areas, and Unilever became one of the largest producers. After 1973, foreign companies were largely devolved to national ownership, and smallholder participation was actively promoted in the government.

With land and labor costs rising in Malaysia, the next phase of expansion (beginning in 1990) was in Indonesia, led by foreign investors from Malaysia and Singapore. In a situation of weak forest governance and poorly defined land rights, large investments have often sparked land conflicts, and deforestation has also been a major problem.[28] At the same time, Indonesian regulations on oil palm plantation establishments have required 20 percent smallholder participation as out-growers, and state programs have also provided direct support to smallholders. As a result, about 40 percent of the sector is now in smallholder hands. However, expansion of smallholder oil palm has not been immune to land problems, especially since many of the growers are immigrants from Java.

Under pressure from Western governments, the Indonesian government agreed to a moratorium on further deforestation in 2011, and Asian firms are now moving aggressively into Africa. They have acquired large land concessions in Liberia, Sierra Leone, and Gabon, among others. If these investments are strictly governed by the social and environmental commitments required for certification by the Roundtable for Sustainable Palm Oil, many of the problems with the earlier expansion in Indonesia could be avoided.

The oil palm industry is now one of the largest and most dynamic of the industries reviewed in this chapter. Over time, companies have consolidated and expanded into giant vertically and horizontally integrated firms (such as Sime Derby, with over 600,000 ha of plantations). UNCTAD lists eight of the 25 largest agricultural production companies in the world as being identified with oil palm. A telling statistic is that the value of exports of oil palm products from Malaysia and Indonesia now exceed the total value of *all* agricultural exports from *all* of sub-Saharan Africa, the region where the crop originated and where critical R&D for its initial cultivation was carried out.

Food Staples

While there is an enormous literature on foreign investment in plantation-type crops, there is very little historical record of foreign investment in food staples such as grains and oil seeds.[29] These latter crops were closely associated with colonial-era settlers' expansion of cultivated land areas in the New World, which came at the expense of indigenous groups. However, this was accompanied by very modest investments by the settlers themselves, and little foreign investment went directly into farming.

Direct foreign investment in the production of food staples has been largely associated with state-driven initiatives to ensure food security for the homeland. The most famous of these was the British groundnut scheme—a crash program by the state-owned Overseas Food Corporation in Tanzania (then a British colony) immediately following World War II to meet an acute shortage of vegetable oil in Britain.[30] The aim was to produce over a million hectares of groundnuts and other oilseeds within five years through major investments in land and in the associated infrastructure of a port, railway, roads, housing, security force, health, airstrips, and education. Some 2,000 European managers and skilled labor were employed along with about 15,000 African laborers, most of whom had to be recruited from other parts of the colony. Reports about this project, which was located in a very sparsely populated area, do not mention land conflicts—yet a scheme of this size must surely have deprived the communities in the area of some aspects of their livelihoods. The scheme ran into major labor problems, with a reported labor turnover rate of 20 percent per month. More importantly, it ran into colossal logistical and technical problems, with huge cost overruns as well as a cultivated area and yields way below targets. By 1955, when less than 10 percent of the target area had been planted despite over $1.5 billion (today's dollars) invested, financial losses were spiraling and the scheme was finally terminated.

This groundnut project is now widely cited as an example of the failure of large-scale farming in Africa. Isolation and difficult logistics in Tanzania contributed in part to this failure, but it is instructive to note that a parallel and less well-known effort targeting 100,000 ha in Queensland, Australia met the same fate.[31] These efforts demonstrated not only the folly of state schemes in the name of food security, but also the lack of faith in small-holders. As an ironic footnote, one study has calculated that if the colonial government in Nigeria had removed export taxes on groundnuts, the supply response from Nigerian smallholders would have been sufficient to meet Britain's needs for vegetable oil at the time.[32]

An even more grandiose state-driven scheme was Nikita Khrushchev's Virgin Lands program in the 1950s to plow up the steppes of Central Asia (mainly in Kazakhstan).[33] The original goal of bringing 13.5 million ha into cultivation was reached by 1954, and from 1954 to 1960 another 42 million ha were brought into production. Most of this land was classified as "virgin lands," though in reality pastoralists used these areas extensively. State farms established for the purpose ranged up to 70,000 ha. Large investments were also made in roads, housing, schools, and other infrastructure. Like the groundnut scheme, the Russian project experienced huge logistical and technical problems. In the absence of suitable technologies, weeds and soil erosion became major problems, while cost overruns due to poor logistics were rampant. In one year, for example, 32,000 combines were out of commission, leading to a failure to harvest 1.5 million ha. Eventually, with the advent of dry years and low yields, much of the area was abandoned—and with lasting damage to the environment. In the early 1960s, dust storms caused by wind erosion from this area affected cities as far away as Eastern Europe.

Later, state-led efforts in Africa to encourage private large-scale farming ran into a similar fate. Building on earlier colonial experiences in Sudan, the World Bank in the 1960s financed a 250,000-ha scheme to produce grains and oilseeds on "uninhabited land" in the country through large-scale mechanized farms. Following the 1970s food crisis, these farms expanded rapidly as Sudan (with financing from the Gulf states) sought to transform itself into the breadbasket of the region. About 80 percent of these farms are over 1,000 ha, and two very large farms with over 100,000 ha are joint investments between the government of Sudan and foreign governments. In total, about 5.5 million ha of land have been converted through the scheme (unofficial estimates are much higher). However, yields have remained extremely low (at about 10 percent of potential), natural vegetation has been destroyed, and land has been degraded to the extent that farms are often abandoned. Land rights of traditional users (both small-scale farmers and pastoralists) have been ignored, and encroachment by mechanized farms has been blamed for rising conflict in the area.[34]

In Kenya and Tanzania, large-scale mechanized wheat production has been introduced in areas that have traditionally been prime grazing grounds of pastoral people, especially the Maasai. The experience of the Canadian International Development Agency of introducing large-scale mechanized wheat farming on 40,000 ha in the Hanang Wheat Complex of Tanzania has been extensively reviewed in terms of technical and financial performance, but also in regards to the effects on local pastoral communities. After major CIDA investments, wheat production has been marginally profitable, but this does not account for the loss of livelihoods of the pastoralists and increasing conflicts over land use. Through litigation and negotiation, displaced pastoralists have attempted to arrive at a benefit-sharing agreement with wheat farmers, though with limited success. Wheat production in this project is now deemed unprofitable, and has been declining.

There are very few historical examples of corporate for-profit ventures into food-crop farms. The best known are the "bonanza farms" established in Minnesota and the Dakotas by railroad companies around 1900 through land grants for rail construction, which were financed by domestic and international bond holders.[35] These land grants, as elsewhere, presumably ignored the rights of indigenous groups or were negotiated through asymmetric land-sales agreements. The newfound ability to mechanize harvesting, combined with strong markets, encouraged these rail companies to invest in large-scale farms in order to demonstrate the potential of the land. However, these farms of up to 25,000 ha were short-lived, as rising land prices, labor problems, and dependence on one crop gave the competitive edge to more-flexible and diversified family farms.

Given this background, the post-1990 rise of corporate farms for food crops in Latin America, Russia, Ukraine, and Kazakhstan is a surprising phenomenon. These farms, which initially depended largely on domestic investors but have increasingly tapped global capital markets for expansion, are unprecedented in size; the largest one now runs up to a million hectares of cropped land, with revenues of over a billion dollars. The recent interest by corporate investors and investment funds in very large grain farms reflects a number of factors. Developments in technology—such as large machinery, zero tillage, GMOs (genetically modified organisms), and information and satellite technology—as well as innovations in business models have facilitated companies' management of very large farms. Indeed, experiences in Latin America and Eastern Europe have shown that with these innovations, corporate farms can overcome diseconomies of scale and be globally competitive in grains. Nonetheless, true "superfarms" have emerged only where there is not a level playing field for family farmers due to imperfections in input, financial, and product markets that favor large operations.

Lessons Learned from the Snapshots

The preceding snapshots reveal how the six commodities have demonstrated different historical trajectories and development outcomes. Yet several common elements emerge with respect to main drivers and impacts.

History Repeated . . . to an Extent

Foreign investment in agriculture in land-abundant regions is not new, reflecting patterns that have occurred over a century and a half of globalization.

First, investments have always been very cyclical, with spikes during times of high commodity prices. Foreign investments have also been subject to cycles of prevailing doctrines — globalization (up to World War I) followed by growing protectionism (up to World War II), and then strong nationalism followed by a further period of liberalization over the past two decades. Investments have also been amplified when, episodically, strategic concerns of the "home government" led the latter to take measures to ensure supplies of food and industrial raw materials.

Second, foreign investment has always been largest in the classic plantation crops (sugarcane, tea, bananas, and palm oil); their economies of scale in processing translate into large-scale production operations. Several industries, especially sugar, have seen major increases in economies of scale in processing, further promoting this trend. However, other factors have also sometimes encouraged large-scale operations. In particular, on frontier land, investment and risks in establishing a new crop were high, requiring considerable up-front financing to put in infrastructure, await tree maturity, recruit labor from outside, and develop technology (often from scratch for species that were being cultivated for the first time).

Third, and not surprisingly, given the high risks of new crops in new areas and the vagaries of world markets, failure rates were often very high. In some cases in the past, failures led to almost complete abandonment of an industry, such as rubber in Mexico. In other cases, bankruptcy or heavy debt burdens provided the opportunity for corporate consolidation through horizontal and vertical integration that allowed risks to be dispersed. However, even giants such as United Fruit ultimately ran into financial difficulties. While it is too early to gauge the fate of today's large-scale land-related investments, research published by the World Bank suggests that foreign investors are not making much profit off their farm projects, especially in Africa and for new crops such as jatropha—findings discussed later in this book by Ruth Meinzen-Dick and Helen Markelova.

Still, past experiences differ from today's scene in a number of important ways. The high social cost of many investments is a theme running through this chapter, but in the past these social issues were much more frequently related to labor rights than to land rights. Even when high death rates were brought under control, harsh labor practices often prevailed well into the twentieth century. Yet on the other hand, almost every colonial power had some checks and balances. Labor inspectors were appointed early on, and abuses were frequently investigated through parliamentary and royal commissions that generally made recommendations intended to improve human rights and labor conditions. Over time, civil society and the press played larger roles in exposing rights violations. Cumulatively, these efforts have paid off, since labor rights in foreign-owned plantations are a relatively minor issue today.

Another new phenomenon has been the direction of foreign investment. Today South-South investment flows are generally more important than the North-South flows that prevailed up to the 1970s (the major exception being today's North-South investment in biofuel feedstocks). Over the past 30 years or so, most European and American companies that historically dominated investments have divested their agricultural and plantation units either to national investors (sometimes the state) or to a new generation of multinationals from the South. Many among this new generation of companies have expanded from a national and regional presence to very large multinational operations, such as the Asian companies Olam, Wilmar, and Sime Derby, which are considerably larger than their historical counterparts. However, large Northern companies such as Unilever and Chiquita have maintained a strong downstream presence in processing and marketing.

Finally, there have historically been very few examples of foreign corporate investment in production of food staples either in the South or North. Most of these have been state-led efforts, such as the groundnut scheme, and were massive failures. The emergence of large private farming companies focusing on food crops in some regions is a new phenomenon that is still not well understood or evaluated. These seem to be most successful in parts of Latin America, where strong public and private R&D systems have provided robust technologies, and where land markets are well developed. It is much less clear whether they will succeed in Africa, where technologies are less developed and land rights are poorly defined.

The Need for a Long-Term View

Historically, the types of investors and investment outcomes have been highly heterogeneous, ranging from the good to the bad and the ugly. Still, over the long term, this chapter demonstrates that many investment experiences look strongly positive, especially in sectors such as tea and rubber that have evolved a thriving smallholder sector. In some cases, such as with rubber that could be processed through simple methods, the smallholder sector took off despite discouragement from colonial governments. Once investors had put in place the infrastructure and technology, the inherent efficiency of smallholders for a labor-intensive crop gave them a competitive advantage. Colonial officials and investors, like many governments and investors today, consistently underestimated the power of the smallholder sector to innovate. However, by 1900 there was already a lively debate about the role of smallholders in commercial agriculture, and some colonial governments, notably in British West Africa, actively pursued a smallholder approach, albeit with amenable commodities, such as cocoa.

In other cases, the increasing transaction costs of managing a large labor force, rising labor standards, and the threat of expropriation in an increasingly nationalistic environment were major motivations for the withdrawal of companies from direct agricultural production. Strong donor and government support to smallholders in diverse cases such as tea in Kenya, sugar in Thailand, and palm oil in Indonesia enabled the emergence of a vibrant smallholder sector, either through collective ownership of processing capacity or through contracts with processors based on well-defined rules for sharing benefits, often mediated by governments.

In short, historical experience has shown the importance of providing a level playing field for smallholders. Where support services have been put in place, including research, extension, land-tenure security, and finance, a vibrant smallholder sector has eventually emerged to dominate the industry. This has not only alleviated land conflicts, but also promoted inclusive rural development.

The need for a long-term view is also the conclusion of a 2011 evaluation of the investments of the Commonwealth Development Corporation (CDC), an arm of the British government to promote economic development through support to the private sector. CDC invested nearly $6 billion from 1950 to 2000 in 179 agricultural projects in Africa and Southeast Asia. Evaluations judged that only 30 percent were even moderately successful in economic terms.[36] Among the successes were profitable ventures such as oil palm in Southeast Asia and tea in Kenya, both reviewed earlier in this chapter. However, many of the failing projects were restructured under new ownership, and in the long term 70 percent were judged to provide significant economic benefits.

Importance of Land and Land Rights

Historically, many investments took place at a time of much lower pressure on land, and in frontier areas of very low population density. Additionally, forests were simply not accorded the significance that they are now. As late as 1972, leading experts on appraising investment projects provided guidance on valuing land: "The social cost of land is given by its productivity in the best alternative use, and the existence of large areas of virgin jungle in Malaysia implies a zero opportunity cost."[37] Today, recognition of the value of forest land in the context of livelihoods, biodiversity conservation, and climate-change mitigation has greatly increased the cost of converting forest lands.

The amount of land held by companies in the past was also often not very large, in part due to much smaller markets for products than today, and in part because processing technologies demanded smaller-scale operations. In cases where land concessions were very large, such as the 20 million ha granted to German companies and planters in West Africa, concessions were quickly reversed after World War II.[38]

Surprisingly, land and other rights of indigenous peoples were often recognized by the middle of the nineteenth century. However, recognition was much more likely where land was already cultivated, and rights continued to be ignored for uses such as nomadic pastoralism and hunting and gathering. Land and forest rights for fallow land in long rotations for swidden agriculture (whereby forest land is cut and burned to make space for temporary cultivation) were also often not recognized in forested areas. Controversies in Africa today often revolve around the same set of rights.

There were also important differences across countries in recognition of land rights. Generally, there was much greater recognition in the British Empire than in those of the Portuguese and Belgians. In Britain, the Aborigines Protection Society, formed in 1836, campaigned well into the twentieth century to urge greater respect for land rights. However, in British settler colonies (such as Kenya and Zimbabwe) that were self-governing from their earliest stages of existence, vested interests of settlers resulted in strong pressures for access to land and secure labor by denying indigenous rights.

At the other extreme, in British West Africa (where there were few settlers), indigenous land rights were recognized early on; in 1911 colonial officials drew up the Nigerian Land and Native Rights Proclamation. The British writer Edmund Morel, whose fame had been established earlier when he exposed human rights violations in the Belgian Congo, was especially laudatory about this proclamation for its protection of rights (at least those of men). He said that "the West African is a landowner, [and] desires that he shall continue to be one under British rule, not with decreasing but with increasing security of tenure."[39] Nigeria barred foreign investment in farmland until after 1950, when a pre-independence government allowed some investors to establish plantations with out-growers.

Finally, poor land governance, weak land rights, and high levels of land inequality frequently enable "land grabbing" to occur during periods of high commodity prices, regardless of the type of investment. Take the Philippines in the early twentieth century. The American colonial government banned foreign investment in farmland, but American investments in sugar-milling contracting to local farmers in a context of high land inequality and weak tenure security left a legacy of agrarian conflict in sugar-producing regions. Similarly, the Yucatán peninsula of Mexico in the late nineteenth century developed an export-oriented agricultural system based on very large-scale, locally owned haciendas, which took over much of the communal land of indigenous groups in the area (see Box 2-2).[40]

Indeed, even where agriculture is dominated by small- and medium-sized producers, conflicts may result in the absence of well-defined property rights—as in the cocoa sector of Côte d'Ivoire (see Box 2-3).[41]

Conclusion

A major lesson from history is that we should focus less on foreign investments per se, and more on strengthening the governance of land and forest resources, both in terms of getting a strong policy framework in place and of building capacity to implement it. Surprisingly, in the past, at least some of the rules and procedures for land acquisition were often quite advanced (at least on paper) relative to today's practices. These included:

- Requirements for prior surveys to demarcate existing communities and local use (at least for cultivation)—India and Malaysia

Foreign investors have received the most attention in the land grab literature. However, the history of domestic investors in large-scale, export-oriented production indicates that the geographic origin of the investor is immaterial. For example, the international market for twine took off around 1880, after the invention of the mechanical binder to harvest wheat on the rapidly expanding US and Canadian wheat frontier. Mexico's exports of henequen (a fiber used for making twine) expanded from 9,400 tons in 1879 to 100,000 in 1910 and over 200,000 in 1916, accounting for over 80 percent of the global market.

Henequen was indigenous to Yucatán, Mexico, and already locally produced and exported in small quantities. The emerging market for twine stimulated an immediate investment boom in large-scale henequen production in the Yucatán by Mexican companies and families from 1880 to 1920. The associated invention of processing machinery to extract the fibers served to accelerate this expansion and to encourage large-scale production, since henequen is a classic plantation crop that requires immediate processing within a few hours after harvest. Local land rights were usurped by an 1894 law that converted a million hectares of *ejido* (community) land of the indigenous Mayan people into state lands—which were subsequently allocated to about 300 hacienda-owning families that typically held areas of 1,000–2,000 ha. Although Yucatán was transformed from one of the poorest states in the nation to one of the richest, income was very unequally distributed.

The Mexican Revolution of the 1910s sought to address these inequities through land reforms backed by strong state intervention in markets. However, the collective *ejidos* that took over many of the haciendas encountered serious management issues in the face of state oversight and a steadily declining market for twine. The decline was a consequence of a global depression, droughts in the US wheat belt, increased competition from other suppliers such as East Africa and Java, the invention of the combine harvester (which eliminated the need for twine), and later, the substitution of synthetics for remaining twine uses. An industry that once dominated the state of Yucatán and employed about half the population has now all but disappeared.

BOX 2-3
Small Is Not Always Beautiful: Cocoa and Land Conflicts in Côte d'Ivoire

Up until 2000, while Africa was losing market share in global agricultural trade, Côte d'Ivoire was regarded as a success story in promoting commercial agriculture, leading sub-Saharan Africa in its agro-based exports. Côte d'Ivoire became the world's largest cocoa exporter, thanks to its hundreds of thousands of small- and medium-sized producers. State policies encouraged immigration to meet labor shortages and low-cost access to forest land for cocoa expansion. Immigrant laborers in turn used easy access to forest land to establish their own cocoa farms in return for their labor. In two decades, some 10 million ha of forest land were converted to agricultural uses. The closing of the land frontier led to increasing competition for land between local communities and immigrant groups. In the face of poorly defined land rights and weak forest governance, this competition escalated into conflicts that subsequently precipitated a tragic decade-long civil war along ethnic lines.

- Ensuring land was priced to reflect its economic value—India
- Auctioning of land concessions—India
- Requirements for screening investors to weed out speculators—Vietnam
- Requirements for demonstrating investment on the ground within a fixed schedule (that is, land cleared and planted) in order to maintain concessions—northeast India
- Requirements for out-growers—Nigeria and Indonesia.

Still, even when enlightened rules were in place, implementation often left a big gap between intentions and reality. Part of the implementation challenge was due to lack of capacity, especially the capacity to carry out surveys prior to making concessions, and to monitor the progress of investments on the ground. Beyond capacity, pressure by investors on local officials often led to relaxing the rules or to looking the other way during times of high prices and rising demand for land. The detailed documentation of changes in rules governing tea concessions in Assam demonstrates this process at work over a century.

This finding has important lessons for the current set of principles for responsible agricultural investment being promoted by international organizations to govern the current global land rush. To be effective, they will require strong complementary efforts to raise awareness, build capacity, and monitor results on the ground. The steady improvement in labor standards over a century, and better enforcement of these standards, demonstrates that real progress is possible.

Chapter 3

Overview

DAVID HALLAM

In recent years, interest in international investment in agricultural land has surged. Purchases and leasings of agricultural land in Africa by various Gulf-state investors for food production in support of their food-security strategies have perhaps attracted the most attention. However, these are just some of a variety of actual or planned investment flows with different motivations. Countries outside Africa—Indonesia, Malaysia, Pakistan, and Kazakhstan, for example—are also being targeted, while additional major investments have been made or are being planned by Chinese, Korean, Indian, and Malaysian investors. Investment companies in Europe and North America are also exploring opportunities. They are motivated by potentially high returns due in part to higher food prices, and especially where biofuels feedstock production is a possibility.

A main driver of this interest in international investment in food production appears to be food security, as well as a fear arising from recent high food prices and policy-induced supply shocks that have made dependence on world markets for foods supplies or agricultural raw materials more risky. At the same time, a number of developing countries in Africa are making strenuous efforts to attract such investments to exploit "surplus" land, consequently encouraging international access to land resources whose ownership and control in the past have typically been entirely national.

Not surprisingly, this apparently anomalous situation—food-insecure, least-developed countries in Africa selling their land assets to rich countries to produce food that is in turn repatriated to feed the rich countries' people—has attracted substantial media interest. It has also attracted international concern more generally, including attention at the G8 Agriculture Ministers' Meeting in April 2009, and more recently at the G20 Seoul Summit in November 2010. This latter forum requested that the Food and Agriculture Organization of the United Nations (FAO), the International Fund for Agricultural Development (IFAD), the United Nations Conference on Trade and Development (UNCTAD), and the World Bank "develop options for promoting responsible investment in agriculture."[1] This request was reiterated by the G20 in 2011.

Some argue that these investments could mark the beginning of a fundamental change in the geopolitics of international agriculture. Certainly, complex and controversial issues—economic, political, institutional, legal, and ethical—are raised in relation to food security, poverty reduction, rural development, technology, and access to resources, especially land. On the other hand, the low level of investment in developing-country agriculture, especially in sub-Saharan Africa, has been highlighted for decades as a matter of concern and identified as a cause of the slowdown in agricultural yield growth and the consequent upward pressure on price levels. Therefore, any possibility of additional investment resources from whatever source cannot be dismissed out of hand. The focus needs to be on how these investments can be win-win, rather than on accusations of neocolonialism.

Recent Investment Trends and Patterns

There are no detailed data on the extent of such investments. Available foreign direct investment (FDI) data is not sufficiently detailed to determine just how much investment in agriculture there has been and what forms it takes. It is therefore difficult to say with any precision whether the recent investments are a totally new development or a continuation of existing trends. However, the *World Investment Report* for 2009 (published by UNCTAD) has a focus on agriculture, and country case studies conducted by FAO, UNCTAD, and the World Bank provide some more-detailed information regarding the extent, nature, and impacts of investments in particular countries. Anecdotal information is available from the media, although the accuracy of much of this is questionable. Some information is available from the investors themselves and from those developing countries receiving inward investment, although few details are divulged, given the sensitivity surrounding these investments and the need for confidentiality.

On the basis of the information available, a number of observations can be made regarding recent trends and patterns.[2]

- International investments in agriculture rose significantly in 2008 and 2009. However, they actually declined in 2010, according to UN data. Additionally, the number of actual implemented investments appears to be fewer than the number being planned, discussed, or reported in the media. The World Bank projects that actual farming has commenced with only 20 percent of announced deals.
- The main form of investment is the purchase or long-term leasing of agricultural land for food production.
- Land investments can be large scale, with many involving more than 10,000 hectares and some more than 500,000 hectares.
- The amount of land in developing countries acquired by foreign interests in recent years is estimated to number in the millions of hectares, but land under foreign control remains a relatively small proportion of total land areas in host countries. Foreign investment in agriculture still accounts for a very small percentage of total FDI flows in most developing countries—less than 2 percent in Africa.[3]
- Major investors include the Gulf states, China, South Korea, India, and Malaysia.
- The main targets for investment are countries in Africa, but also Pakistan, Kazakhstan, Cambodia, and Brazil, among others.
- Investors are primarily from the private sector, but governments and sovereign wealth funds are also involved.
- Private-sector investors are often investment or holding companies, rather than agro-food specialists. This means that necessary expertise for managing complex, large-scale agricultural investments needs to be acquired.
- Since private-sector investors are often funded by government or sovereign wealth funds, it is frequently difficult to separate the private sector from the public sector and therefore to judge the extent of public-sector involvement.
- Sovereign wealth funds seem to be playing a lesser role than originally presumed, although they do appear to have diversified their portfolios to include investments in developing countries and in agriculture.
- In host countries, it is governments that are engaged in formulating investment deals.

- Recent investments emphasize the production of basic foods, unlike FDI in agriculture in the past.
- Investments include the production of animal feed to meet the rising demand for livestock products.
- More traditional FDI continues—in horticulture and flowers in East Africa, for example—but now emphasizes various forms of joint ventures, such as contract farming.
- There are some signs of a shift away from Africa, and of a search for greater local involvement, through joint ventures—as was the case with FDI in the past.

Investor Motivations

The motivation for these investments depends on whether the investor comes from the private sector or a government. Private-sector investments can represent portfolio diversification for financial returns. Biofuels production is also an important objective. Still, as noted earlier, a core motivation is food security. Investors seek enhanced food security through investment in countries that do not face the land and water constraints suffered by investor countries.

While there is currently a preoccupation with acquiring land, since the titled ownership of assets is seen as most secure, there are many arguments against this from the point of view of the host country. It is also not clear if it is even necessary or desirable for the investing country. The acquisition of land does not necessarily provide immunity from sovereign risk, and can provoke political and economic conflict. Other forms of investment, such as contract farming and out-grower schemes (when smallholders produce and sell to a bigger farm or processing facility), can offer just as much security of supply, and are discussed later on. It is interesting to note that some of the features of the current round of land investments appear to be contrary to trends in FDI more generally, which seem to favor looser contractual arrangements rather than the actual acquisition of major assets. Indeed, as observed in the preceding chapter, there is a strong historical precedent for investor support of contract arrangements with smallholders.

In any case, land investments are only one strategic response to the food-security problems of countries with limited land and water resources. Therefore, discussion of these investments needs to be set in the wider context of broader strategic debate about food-security problems. There are a variety of other mechanisms to improve food security—including the creation of regional food reserves, financial instruments to manage risk, bilateral agreements including counter-trade (barter arrangements), and the improvement of international food market information systems—under active discussion. At the least, investments could simply target much-needed infrastructure and institutions that currently constrain developing-country agriculture, especially in sub-Saharan Africa. This, together with efforts to improve the efficiency and reliability of world markets as sources of food, might enhance food security for all concerned by expanding production and trade possibilities.

Host Country Motivations

Lack of investment has been identified as a fundamental cause of the stagnant production and low productivity of developing-country agriculture. FAO estimates that in order to double food production by 2050 (a target that must be attained to feed growing populations and to ensure a basic right to food), developing countries need an additional $83 billion per year in investment.[4] Public investment resources are limited by budgetary pressures, and official development assistance to agriculture has been declining over many years. The private sector in developing countries tends to have little capacity to fund investment. International investments therefore have a potentially important role to play.

At the same time, a number of countries are enthusiastically seeking to attract such investments to exploit "surplus" land that is allegedly unused or underutilized. However, selling, leasing, or providing concessional access to land raises questions about how the land concerned was previously being utilized, by whom, and on what tenurial basis. In many cases, the situation is unclear due to ill-defined property rights (including informal land rights based on tradition and culture). While it is true that much land in sub-Saharan Africa is currently not utilized to its full potential, "surplus" land overall does not necessarily mean land is unused or unoccupied. Its exploitation under new investments involves reconciling different claims.

Changes in use and access may involve potentially negative effects on food security, and raise complex economic, social, and cultural issues. There is substantial evidence of such negative effects arising in other contexts as well—large-scale biofuels feedstock production, for example. These effects, in the context of both food security and biofuels, are taken up in detail elsewhere in this volume. What bears mentioning here is that the presence of such effects demands, at the least, consultation with those with traditional rights to the land in question, suggesting the need for alternative arrangements for investments. More generally, issues are raised by the shift in terms of access to land from traditional and historical to market-based.

One reason land may not be used to its full potential is that the infrastructural investments needed to bring it into production are so immense as to be beyond available national budgetary resources. International investments might bring much-needed infrastructural investments from which all can benefit, but at the same time inadequate infrastructure may deter international investors.

On the other hand, international investments are seen as potentially providing a variety of developmental benefits, which are described below. Whether these potential developmental benefits are actually realized is a key concern in the current discussion.

Impacts of International Investments

Benefits to the host country are a major concern. The essential question involves the extent to which benefits from land investments spill over into the host-country domestic sector in a way that produces a synergistic relationship with existing smallholder production systems and other key food-production players. Benefits should, in theory, arise from capital inflows, technology transfers leading to innovation and productivity increases, infrastructural provisions, quality improvement, export earnings, the upgrading of domestic production, income and employment creation (including for local input and service suppliers), and possibly an increase in food supplies for the domestic market and for export. Indeed, investments in agriculture should be able to boost food security.

Crucially, these benefits will not materialize if investments result in the creation of an enclave of advanced agriculture in a dualistic system with traditional smallholder agriculture—particularly if the smallholders cannot attain this advanced agriculture. Studies on the effects of FDI on agriculture show that such benefits do not always come about.[5] These studies catalogue concerns over highly mechanized production technologies with limited employment-creation effects; a dependence on imported inputs and hence limited domestic multiplier effects; the adverse environmental impacts of production practices such as chemical contamination, land degradation, and depletion of water resources; and limited labor rights and poor working conditions. At the same time, there is also evidence of longer-run benefits in terms of improved technology, product quality, and sanitary and phytosanitary standards. In considering the question of benefits, it is therefore important to take a longer-term view.

Additional political and ethical concerns are raised in cases where the host country is food-insecure. While there is a presumption that investments will increase aggregate food supplies, this does not imply that domestic food availability will increase—notably in cases where the food produced is repatriated to the investing country. Food supplies could even decrease in countries where land and water resources are commandeered by investment projects at the expense of domestic smallholders. Extensive control of land by other countries can also raise questions about political interference and influence.

The impacts of such investments are not necessarily confined to the two parties involved. Indeed, third countries may be impacted through any resulting changes in international trade volume and price variability. Such a scenario could arise when a major importer secures food supplies outside the market.

Research into the nature and impacts of recent foreign investments has tended to rely on case studies, usually at the country level.[6] As would be expected, investments are problematic if they involve large-scale land acquisitions in situations where local land rights are not clearly defined and governance is weak. Case studies catalogue a lack of transparency in land transfers, no consultation with local stakeholders, and no recognition of their rights. Land transfers have involved the displacement of local smallholders and the loss of grazing land for pastoralists, negative impacts on livelihoods, and no compensation. There are also instances of environmental damage arising from excessive water demand for large-scale production of crops such as oil palm and sugar.[7] Such large-scale monoculture also limits biodiversity. These findings highlight the need for social and environmental impact assessments of any investment project involving large-scale land transfers. At the same time, there is evidence of some potentially positive effects of foreign investments. One study notes that the Marakala sugar project in Mali (funded in part by South Korea) is expected to generate 5,000 jobs directly, and up to 20,000 indirectly (albeit against the displacement of 1,600 smallholders).[8] According to another report, investments in Ghana are estimated to have created 180,000 jobs between 2001 and 2008.[9] (However, while investments may lead to significant employment creation, this benefit needs to be balanced against the loss of traditional livelihoods when smallholders are displaced.) Additionally, foreign investments are not always environmentally damaging: investors in floriculture in Uganda, for example, have introduced more environmentally friendly production methods.[10]

Governments cite technology transfer as an important reason for seeking to attract foreign investment. However, the evidence is mixed. There are indications of technology spillovers in Morocco, Egypt, and Uganda, but less so in Senegal. The UNCTAD *World Investment Report 2009* concludes that the technological contributions of transnational corporations to local communities have been limited, since technologies developed for commercial crops are not easily transferred to smallholder production of staples.[11]

The technology and production benefits of foreign investments to local food security would presumably be zero if crops are grown entirely for export to the investor country. It could even be negative if land, water, and other resources are taken out of production for subsistence or local markets. However, there is evidence of greater local availability of palm oil in Ghana, horticultural products in Senegal, and rice in Uganda as a result of foreign investments.[12] Clearly, it is difficult to generalize as to the benefits, or otherwise, of foreign investments. The case studies do not address all aspects, and they provide only a partial picture. Even within a country, the evidence from different investments can be conflicting, and a particular investment can have both positive and negative impacts. More research is needed.

Whether or not international investments lead to broader developmental benefits for developing countries depends crucially on the terms and conditions of the investment agreements, and on the effectiveness of the policy and legislative frameworks in minimizing risks.

Alternative Business Models

There are a number of alternatives to land purchasing or leasing that might achieve or even surpass the food-security objectives of investing countries.[13] Alternative business models—various contractual arrangements, for example—can offer just as much security of supply. It is interesting to note that in other contexts, vertical integration (whereby one firm takes control over upstream or downstream activities) tends to be based much more on such arrangements than on more traditional approaches (whereby firms simply buy upstream or downstream firms and undertake all these firms' activities). The development of East African horticultural production for export by European supermarkets is a case in point. Such looser arrangements are likely to be more conducive to the interests of the host country. However, even here, there will probably be questions as to the compatibility of the needs of investors with those of smallholder agriculture. This, in turn, raises questions about the potential to reduce poverty.

Determining the appropriate business model will depend on what products the investment is intended to produce, on the production system itself, and on what collateral investments—in infrastructure, for example—are needed. Investors may favor land purchases or long-term leasing where economies of scale are significant, or where major infrastructural investments, such as roads and ports, are needed. Where economies of scale are not significant, contractual arrangements may be just as acceptable to investors and possibly more capable of generating developmental benefits for local producers.

Mixed models are also possible. For example, there are instances of large-scale commercial units, often a privatized former state farm, owned and operated by an international investor, and participating in a symbiotic relationship with smallholders. The latter sell their output under contract to the central company, while receiving support in the form of agreed-upon sales, credit, and technical assistance. In essence, such mixed models feature both the traditional acquisition of a large facility and arrangements with local smallholders to supply additional production. Sugar investments in Tanzania are one example of such an arrangement, while the creation of a similar model based on so-called farm blocks is an objective of government policy in Zambia.

Policy Implications

If it is acknowledged that international investment might make a positive contribution to raising productivity in developing-country agriculture, then the question arises as to what policies might help maximize the positive contributions while minimizing the associated risks. Investing countries can provide policy incentives to encourage and target outward investment. However, the onus to attract investments to where strategic needs are the greatest, and to ensure that those needs are met, falls primarily on the host countries. Investment priorities need to be identified in a comprehensive and coherent strategy, and effective measures need to be devised to match capital to opportunities and needs. Domestic policy measures are also needed to ensure that local agriculture is capable of capitalizing on any spillover benefits of investments.

Host countries need to create an environment that is conducive to international investment and reduces perceived risks. Developing countries have made a great deal of progress in this respect in recent years, liberalizing entry conditions and establishing investment-promotion institutions to facilitate inward investment. Some participate in bilateral treaties and other international agreements and conventions for contract enforcement, arbitration, and dispute settlements (such as the Multilateral Investment Guarantee Agency). At the same time, national interests need to be preserved. Legal frameworks often favor the investor rather than the host country, and in particular investors' rights over those of host-country stakeholders. This highlights the need for strong investment contracts that reference host-country concerns. Clear and comprehensive domestic law is essential.[14]

Still, the lack of clear property rights, especially in regards to land, remains a deterrent to investment in some countries. Lack of adequate infrastructure may also deter some investors, although others see the very provision of infrastructure as a necessary component of their investments.

If the general developmental benefits of international investments are to be realized, then appropriate policy, institutional, and legislative frameworks need to be in place to guarantee them. Apart from the financial terms and conditions of the investment, provisions may be needed concerning the local sourcing of inputs such as labor; food security; social and environmental standards; property rights and stakeholder involvement; how much food to export and how much to retain in the host country; and the distribution of revenues.

No matter how successful developing countries are in attracting foreign investments, no positive developmental impacts will result if their agricultural sectors are not capable of capitalizing on the spillover benefits. Appropriate domestic agricultural and rural development policies need to be in place to ensure that local agriculture can benefit from new technologies and that local economies can respond to new demands for inputs and services.

Conclusions and Outstanding Issues

The decades-long lack of investment in global agriculture has been identified as an important underlying cause of the 2007–8 food crisis and of the difficulties developing countries have encountered in dealing with this crisis. Developing countries' capacity to fill the investment gap is limited, and the share of official development assistance going to agriculture has trended downward over the years to as little as 5 percent. Therefore, in general terms, the recent surge in interest in international investment in agriculture should be welcomed rather than condemned.

The much-publicized "land grab," involving the purchase or leasing of agricultural land in developing countries for food production, is just one form of investment, and one that is arguably least likely to deliver significant developmental benefits to the host country. While such investments should not be rejected in principle, there are considerable risks for host countries, and the investments raise complex and controversial issues—economic, political, institutional, legal, and ethical—in relation to food security, agricultural investment and development, and land tenure and transfer. It is important that any international investment bring development benefits—technology transfers, employment creation, upstream and downstream linkages, and so on—to the host country. However, these benefits are not automatic.

Given the global concern about large-scale land acquisitions, there are calls for international action to regulate them. In the absence of strong domestic legislation and equitable investment contracts, an international initiative—whether it be a voluntary code of conduct, guidelines, or statement of principles—could highlight host-country interests and also guide investors toward socially responsible investment.[15] There is broad political support for an international response that would highlight the need for transparency, sustainability, and the involvement of local stakeholders and recognition of their interests, and that would emphasize concerns about domestic food security and rural development. International organizations (and their member countries), the G8, the G20, and civil society groups have all expressed their support for such a measure. Admittedly, however, there are some differences in opinion as to what form this response should take. Some civil society groups are pushing for a complete moratorium on the deals, or at least something legally binding. Most of the world, however, wants only a voluntary, code-of-conduct-type arrangement.

FAO, the World Bank, UNCTAD, and IFAD are developing principles for responsible agricultural investment that respect rights, livelihoods, and resources along these lines. These principles, based on detailed research on the nature, extent, and impacts of foreign investments and on best practices in law and policy, are intended to distill the lessons learned and provide a framework to which national regulations, international investment agreements, global corporate social responsibility initiatives, and individual investment contracts might refer. The principles include the following:

1. Respect for land and resource rights. Existing rights to land and natural resources are recognized and respected.

2. Food security and rural development. Investments do not jeopardize food security and rural development, but rather strengthen it.
3. Transparency, good governance, and an enabling environment. Processes relating to investment in agriculture are transparent and carefully monitored, ensuring accountability by all stakeholders.
4. Consultation and participation. All those materially affected are consulted, and agreements from consultations are recorded and enforced.
5. Economic viability and responsible agro-enterprise investing. Projects are viable economically, respect the rule of law, reflect industry best practices, and result in durable shared value.
6. Social sustainability. Investments generate desirable social and distributional impacts, and do not increase vulnerability.
7. Environmental sustainability. Environmental impacts are quantified, and measures are taken to encourage sustainable resource use while minimizing and mitigating negative impacts.[16]

While there appears to be broad support for the aim of these principles, agreement on how to implement them may prove more difficult. There seems to be little political support for a rigorously enforceable legal instrument embodying these principles. There are already existing international instruments and commitments that address similar concerns, though in slightly different contexts. The first principle draws on the FAO Voluntary Guidelines on Governance of Land Tenure and Other Natural Resources, formulated in 2009. The Equator Principles of 2006 address some of the social and environmental issues referenced in the last two principles. The Organization for Economic Cooperation and Development Guidelines for Multinational Enterprises, issued in 2000, and various human-rights commitments, including the FAO's 2005 Voluntary Guidelines on the Right to Food, also provide models. Nevertheless, further development of these principles will require widespread consultation with all stakeholders, including governments, farmer organizations, nongovernmental organizations, the private sector, and civil society. Such a consultative process is inevitably lengthy, but without inclusive, comprehensive, and effective consultation, it is unlikely that anything workable will be achieved. Furthermore, such rigorous deliberations and negotiations bring to light the various pros and cons of these investments, thereby making all parties more aware of the concerns about them. In this way, the very process of developing such principles, guidelines, and voluntary codes can help promote more responsible investment behavior. Consider, for example, investors' heightened interest in contract farming in recent years—an arrangement with arguably fewer risks to local communities than large, plantation-style agriculture.

There is a continuing need to monitor the extent, nature, and impacts of international investments, and to catalogue best practices in law and policy to better inform both host and investing countries. Detailed impact analysis is needed to support national policy and international responses. Forms of investment other than land acquisitions (such as contract farming and other joint ventures) may be more likely to yield development benefits for host countries. The scope of such investments needs to be evaluated, and best practices promoted.

If FDI is to play an effective role in filling the investment gap facing developing-country agriculture, then there is a need to reconcile the investment objectives of investing countries with the investment needs of developing countries. Investment priorities need to be identified in a comprehensive and coherent strategy, and efforts must be made to identify the most effective measures for promoting the matching-up of capital to opportunities and needs.

Chapter 4

Social and Economic Implications

ALEXANDRA SPIELDOCH
AND SOPHIA MURPHY

In the wake of the 2007–8 global food crisis, food security jumped back to the top of the international policy agenda. Some five years later, policymakers show no sign of losing interest. Nor should they. Governments are nowhere near achieving the Millennium Development Goal of halving hunger by 2015. Instead, the incidence of hunger has continued to rise. Policymakers have universally agreed to boost investment in agriculture, reversing the neglect under which agriculture has languished for several decades. What form this investment should take, however, has proven highly controversial. Questions as to what kind of agricultural technologies to use; whether to focus on the production of food for local markets or commodities to trade; how to cultivate links to local, regional, and international markets—all of these issues are hotly contested.

Context

In the recent debate over how to achieve food security, one element has attracted more attention—and controversy—than any other: foreign direct investment in land. The year 2008 witnessed a truly extraordinary number of negotiations on the part of governments and private firms looking to sign agreements that would confer ownership of, or long-term leases on, land abroad. The phenomenon attracted a great deal of attention at the time. That attention has continued to the present day—and so has the investment. A 2011 estimate from Oxfam International suggests as many as 227 million hectares (ha) have come under contract since 2001.[1] This is an area roughly equivalent to the size of Western Europe (and more than twice the largest previous estimates). Not all of these deals have resulted in signed contracts. Many are still under negotiation, and some contracts fall apart because of adverse reactions in the countries where the land is located. Sometimes the land is cultivated and sometimes it lies fallow. Yet the trend continues, and by any calculation, the amounts of land involved are truly staggering.

From the start, multilateral institutions paid close attention to land investments. So did the media: early reports from the *Financial Times*, for example, brought attention to the South Korean company Daewoo's proposal to lease roughly half the arable land of Madagascar to grow crops to export back to South Korea. The coverage was not positive.[2] That deal, one of the most outrageous so far, eventually fell apart, and the administration that had given the deal its blessing lost control of the government. Given how much encouragement developing countries had had from bilateral and multilateral donors to seek out FDI, the less-than-positive reactions to the proposed investments from organizations such as the International Food Policy Research Institute (IFPRI) and even the World Bank were striking. In April 2009, IFPRI released a report titled "'Land Grabbing' by Foreign Investors in Developing Countries: Risks and Opportunities." The *World Investment Report 2009* (an annual report from the UN Conference on Trade and Development, or UNCTAD) focused on agriculture and agribusiness and included a review of land-lease and land-purchase agreements. Also in 2009, Olivier de Schutter, the UN Special Rapporteur on the Right to Food, proposed guidelines for land investments with human rights principles at their core.[3] The FAO commissioned several pieces of work and held intergovernmental meetings to review the issue, eventually starting a process to develop what are called the Voluntary Guidelines on Responsible Governance of Tenure of Land, Fisheries, and Forests (usually referred to simply as the Voluntary Guidelines, or VGs).

In 2011, the World Bank published an overview of the state of investments, stressing the importance of good public information and the need to enforce land rights.[4] The World Bank has also hosted negotiations on what it calls the RAI Principles (Principles for Responsible Agricultural Investment). This created a rival for the VGs, which generated considerable tension. Most civil-society organizations and a number of governments have been concerned that the countries that dominate decisions at the World Bank would somehow preempt a more widely shared negotiation under UN auspices, embodied in the Voluntary Guidelines process. By October 2011, however, it was clear that the VG negotiations, held under the auspices of the UN Committee on Food Security (CFS), would have precedence.[5] In March 2012, the negotiations were successfully concluded.

While only a weak mechanism from a legal point of view, the VGs cannot come soon enough. In the years since land investments appeared so dramatically on the international policy agenda, there have been shockingly few examples of projects that offer real benefits to local populations, or even to national host governments. There are few if any safeguards to protect the public interest of the countries whose land is leased or bought, nor any to protect the communities that live on the land where investments are taking place. The continually expanding literature on the subject—produced by academic institutions, nongovernment organizations, the UN, and various other sources—continues to confirm this overall conclusion.

Land investments touch on one of the most sensitive areas of economic, political, social, and cultural life. Giving a foreign entity the right to use the natural resource base—namely, soil and fresh water—was forbidden by law in many countries until recently, and is still tightly regulated. A number of issues stand out in this highly politicized area. Chief among them is the question of how to protect the rights of those most directly affected by the deals so that they are given not just a hearing, but also some control over any investment and the implementation of land agreements. Perhaps even more fundamentally, how will people, especially those living in countries with a history of colonial occupation, respond to foreigners leasing or buying their land?

The motivations for these foreign land investments are addressed in detail elsewhere in this book. The aim of this chapter is to focus on the troubling social and economic implications of these deals. In particular, it looks at how agricultural investments affect the people who live on or adjacent to the land in question, as well as how the investments affect national governments. Specifically, we focus on unequal power relations (particularly between the contracting partners and between host-country governments and their people); conflicting interpretations about land use; the scarcity of natural resources; and the potentially negative implications for women smallholder producers. We conclude with policy recommendations.

Unequal Power Relations

Fundamentally, there are significant risks for host countries because of the lopsided power relationships involved in virtually every one of the proposed deals. Many of the investors are large, well-established transnational firms such as Archer Daniels Midland, Cargill, and British Petroleum, or investment funds such as the Carlyle Group, which manages billions of dollars worldwide. Other investors are governments of wealthy countries (including Saudi Arabia, Qatar, Bahrain, South Korea, and China), or corporations acting with a rich state's blessing. Conversely, most of the host governments are poor, some (such as Sudan) are involved in wars, and others (Madagascar, Zimbabwe, and Pakistan) are politically unstable. Many are recipients of international food aid. Additionally, few preside over strong and independent democratic institutions. This is, of course, a risk for investing firms or countries, but it also raises questions about the authority of host governments to speak on behalf of the communities directly affected by land sales or leases.

The International Institute for Sustainable Development (IISD) produced a report in 2009 that reviewed land purchases and lease agreements in the context of bilateral and regional investment agreements, which have proliferated over the last decade.[6] IISD demonstrates how unequal power among parties can play out in creating unfair rules. Significantly, many existing bilateral investment agreements require host governments to treat the foreign investor exactly like domestic investors. Such accords also give investors the right to export all or almost all of what is produced. They allow host countries to limit exports in the midst of a financial crisis but not necessarily in times of food shortages, and further, they allow foreign investors to sue host governments for any lost profits. The rules are just not appropriate from a food-security perspective.

Within host governments, there are different levels of authority and competing political and policy interests that extend the inherently unequal relations all the way down to the community where the land is being taken. For example, it is quite possible that several ministries in the host government might be involved in negotiating a contract, while other ministries with an interest are excluded. Ministries that might have an interest include industry, agriculture, land, forestry, rural development, trade, finance, energy, women's affairs, health, and environment. Rarely are power relations among different ministries even approximately equal. Local and state authorities will definitely have a considerable stake in the deal, but may well be excluded from the negotiations. The local community itself is likely to have more than one view on the priorities for investment and the conditions that should be attached to any new economic development. Women generally have less access to information and less of a political voice than men. Additionally, there will be clear differences in views between landless workers and those with land, between larger and smaller landowners, and even within households—because men and women often have different stakes in the use of land and in any accompanying employment and commerce. All of this must be taken into account.

Conflicting Interpretations of Land Use

Sometimes farmland investments are supported because investors acquire the use of marginal or unused land. Yet deciding the best way to use the land is a political issue. What the government (or an official interpreting a satellite image) may categorize as wasteland might very well be meeting an important share of rural people's household needs—particularly the poorest households, and especially during times of economic shock, which many developing countries are now experiencing. Uncultivated land is used for grazing, as a source of wild foods and medicinal plants, and for access to water.

Members of networks such as the South Asian Network on Food, Ecology, and Culture have documented the importance of uncultivated land for families in India, Bangladesh, and elsewhere. A survey of 50 families in 10 Bangladeshi villages revealed that uncultivated food provides an average of 65 percent of the food (by weight) and 100 percent of the feed and fuel needs of the poorest households (those with no land), and 34 percent and 20 percent respectively for the better-off households (those who own some land).[7]

Disputes over land ownership have a long and violent history the world over. The legacy of land dispossession carries a powerful political charge related to national identity, reconciliation, justice, and the legitimacy of the state.[8] Moreover, the push for land acquisitions by foreign interests comes at a time when many countries are still struggling to implement agrarian reform, in some cases after brutal civil wars or the demise of confiscatory political systems such as apartheid in South Africa. Efforts to secure the passage and implementation of land policies and laws that are pro-poor, pro-farmer, and pro–food security are easily undermined by market-led approaches, especially when the terms of the contracts specify that foreign investors must have the same rights as local businesses.

Scarce Natural Resources

Natural resource degradation, particularly of common-property resources, is increasing food insecurity and undermining the livelihoods of the poor. The UN reports that land degradation affects more than 900 million people worldwide and as much as two-thirds of the world's agricultural land.[9] It is projected that as many as 1.8 billion people will live in regions facing absolute water scarcity by 2025, and that two-thirds of the world's people could be subject to water stress if trends do not change.[10] As a result of climate change, countries in sub-Saharan Africa could experience declines in yields of 20–30 percent by 2080.[11]

Efforts that restore agricultural land to ecological health would be a significant investment in a country's future prosperity and in the well-being of local communities. UNCTAD and the United Nations Environment Program have published a series of case studies on successful experiences with organic agricultural production in East Africa.[12] FAO has also published work in this area, as have many academics, including Jules Pretty at the University of Essex and Miguel Altieri at the University of California–Berkeley.

Industrial agriculture, however, which remains the dominant model for the large-scale investment in agriculture discussed here, uses large amounts of fresh water, depletes the soil of nutrients at unsustainable rates, and depends heavily on fossil fuels (for machinery, fertilizer, pesticides, storage, and transportation), which in most developing countries are an expensive import.

Impacts on Women Smallholder Producers

A number of the incentives offered by governments to attract foreign land investors reinforce the disadvantages of smallholder producers and, in particular, women, who lack bargaining power, resources, land rights, and access to markets. They are commonly discriminated against in both formal and customary systems of land tenure. Their ability to claim legal rights and participate in institutions and political activities is often curtailed, making their rights vulnerable to abuse. If the government or the community appropriates their land, they have little or no recourse.

It is also true that some women have found new opportunities for paid employment, as well as markets for their produce, with the arrival of new investors and new firms. For instance, contracts to grow horticultural products have created such opportunities. Yet other women have found themselves further marginalized, unable to meet the requirements that the new opportunities impose, and saddled with yet more work as their responsibilities multiply. To date, women farmers have yet to benefit substantially from contract farming because they lack land rights and other resources that could serve as a guarantee for reliable production. They also lack information and bargaining power, leaving them at a significant disadvantage in the value chain, with limited possibilities to take on more-prominent roles as buyers and sellers.[13]

In sum, governments and policymakers must proceed with considerable caution and forethought if they wish to avoid worsening poverty, and especially women's poverty. A study published in 2010 on large-scale acquisitions in Central Ghana highlights the possible hazards. Multiple companies have invested in jatropha production in this region, clearing land that had been used for yam cultivation and other minor food crops for local consumption. In this process, the investors did not consult with the households that were directly affected, and many people were involuntary removed from their lands. As a result, 75 percent of the families interviewed experienced a decline in their standard of living. Women were the hardest hit: they had fewer food crops available and less household income from their production. Also, a large portion of the acquired land consisted of forests where women traditionally obtained their medicine, fuel, wild fruits, game, shea nuts, and *dawa dawa* (a local spice). Loss of access to forest products reduced their income and their access to essential resources, reduced their food security, and increased the time they had to spend gathering firewood, a vital source of fuel.[14]

What Next?

In 2009, the FAO's David Hallam commented:

> Imagine empty trucks being driven into, say, Ethiopia, at a time of food shortages caused by war or drought, and being driven out again full of grain to feed people overseas. Can you imagine the political consequences? That's why proper legal structures need to be put into place to protect land rights, and why we should look at some form of international code of conduct.[15]

The fact that some of the countries targeted for investment receive food aid from the World Food Program (WFP) reinforces the probability of Hallam's scenario. Cambodia, Niger, Tanzania, Ethiopia, and Burma are all countries with completed or projected land deals, and they are all beneficiaries of WFP aid. These countries are home to millions of people who live with extreme levels of food insecurity. They all need to make significant investments in their domestic production as one part of reestablishing food security.

Government initiatives under multilateral and regional auspices may make land investment agreements more equitable and sustainable, but ultimately countries need a national (and local) dialogue on what they want for and from their land in order to increase their food security and to meet sustainable development goals. Then, they need to implement the recommendations from those dialogues. In 2009, the African Union (AU) published guidelines for such investments. According to the British newspaper *The Independent*, the AU's guidelines on land deals include "recommendations that new investors should promise to help with infrastructure, such as health facilities, agree to pay local taxation, and look at ways to get more involved on the food-processing side, which would create more local jobs."[16] If implemented, these recommendations would constitute a positive step forward.

Policy Recommendations

Here are some initial steps that can protect both human rights and ecological health:

Articulate a National Vision for Agriculture That Respects Human Rights

Government economic policies must be consistent with human-rights obligations, including the right to food. Such an approach would set the stage for a coherent regulatory framework for investment. The UN Special Rapporteur on the Right to Food's minimum human-rights principles are listed here:

1. All negotiations should be conducted in a fully transparent manner and with the participation of local communities.
2. Any shifts in land use can only take place with the free, prior, and informed consent of local communities concerned.

3. The rights of local communities should be safeguarded at all times through protective legislation at the national level.
4. Local populations should benefit from revenues generated from investment, and contracts should prioritize their development needs.
5. Labor-intensive farming systems, which create more employment, should be given priority.
6. Investment should respect the environment through sustainable production practices.
7. Investors should be obligated to respect labor rights and a fair wage for farmers in order to benefit local communities.
8. Investors should provide a certain percentage of crops to be sold through local markets as a means to increase the productivity and benefits to local producers.
9. Investors should undertake impact assessments of the potential risks and benefits based on local employment and incomes; access to productive resources by local communities; the arrival of new technologies; the environment; and access, availability, and adequacy of food.
10. Indigenous communities should be granted specific forms of protection to their rights to land.

Build Ecologically Sound and Resilient Farm Systems

Ecological sustainability is critically important. The International Assessment of Agricultural Knowledge, Science, and Technology for Development (IAASTD), signed by 58 governments, reflects a clear consensus among governments, academics, and nongovernmental organizations (NGOs) on the need to redirect agricultural science and technology to support small-scale farmers and local knowledge. This assessment makes clear that climate change is undermining many existing agricultural production practices and assumptions. The IAASTD reviews some of the available policy options to enable agriculture to adopt more climate-friendly practices. Investment in adaptive technologies must prioritize policies that give preference to the leadership of smallholder producers, including women; that emphasize the development and use of local seed varieties, as well as farmers' ability to save seeds; and that provide reliable access for small producers to local, regional, and global markets through collective engagement in agricultural value chains.

This approach received renewed support at the 37th session of the UN Committee on World Food Security, held in Rome in October 2011. There, a discussion of smallholder investment included the following recommendation, which surely applies to land investments as much as to any other investment: "Ensure that public investment, services, and policies for agriculture give due priority to enabling, supporting, and complementing smallholders' own investment, with particular attention to women food producers who face specific difficulties and need specific policies and support."[17]

Protect the Space for Local Priorities

Governments must ensure broad-based engagement, leadership, and accountability related to the design and implementation of the various guidelines on land tenure and investment. This should include NGOs and especially community-based organizations, farmers' organizations, and also affected populations that might not be represented by local associations, such as indigenous people and women. Human rights organizations say from experience that enacting good laws and ensuring they are implemented are two distinct things. This makes working with local communities and establishing norms for their involvement all the more important in order to understand local power relationships, get local community support for any policy changes, and consider best strategies to protect against abuses. It means enhancing the capacity for local leadership and alliances to influence decisions, as well as a commitment to facilitate meaningful participation through mandatory quotas, benchmarks, and indicators.

Understand the Complexities of Land Use and the Pressures on Land Availability

The International Land Coalition argues that two kinds of land ownership should be distinguished: land owned by the government (sometimes called crown land), and land for which clear ownership rights are conferred on individuals.[18] Crown land is rarely unused, but users are not likely to have a clear legal right to the land should the government decide to lease it out on a formal basis. Land held by individual title cannot be passed on without the owner's consent, but there are many examples from across the developing world where such consent is forced, whether because of underlying poverty and need, because of misinformation given about landholders' rights, or simply because the state has the power to force consent, even without the legal authority.

Meanwhile, the pressure on land is already great, and it continues to grow. Many developing countries face increases in populations, especially in rural areas, over the medium and long term. In Ethiopia, projections suggest that the rural population will grow from 70 million in 2006 to 183.4 million in 2050; in Madagascar, it is expected to grow from 18.6 million to 44.4 million; and in Tanzania from 38.5 million to 85.1 million.[19] These demographic patterns have major implications for land availability. Getting a better grasp of the realities of both land use and availability will help craft appropriate policies.

Consider How the Investment Fits with Broader Development Objectives

There continues to be fierce debate on the value of "free" market trade versus more regulated trade and investment. But on a number of related issues, some consensus is emerging. For instance, there is widespread agreement on the importance of agriculture and its contribution to broader—and relatively equitable—development in poorer countries. Agriculture is no longer viewed just as a sector associated with poverty, or as a sector to leave behind as a country develops. There is also growing agreement on the need for radically different approaches to natural-resource management in order to reflect the emerging scarcity of fresh water, on the need to address global hunger that has not gone away and is expected to grow, on the need for much more careful husbandry of genetic diversity in crops and domesticated livestock, and on the importance of restoring agriculture to solar-powered rather than fossil-fuelled energy use.

Conclusion

The 2007–8 food-price crisis signaled the need for a renewed commitment to investment in agriculture. Such investment should support the role of governments to reorganize their agricultural sectors more appropriately. This may well require stronger regulatory practices for taxation, local procurement and subsidies for small farmers, and marketing boards to establish a fair price for farmers. Communities need real choices about their future. Investments must serve the interests of the most vulnerable—not only those who can pay or who are well positioned to gain. Any investment in land must be linked to democratic processes that are based on public political debates and meaningful participation among all relevant stakeholders.

Chapter 5

Environmental Impacts[1]

LAURA A. GERMAN,
WOUTER M. J. ACHTEN, AND
MANUEL R. GUARIGUATA

This chapter reviews evidence surrounding the environmental impacts of large-scale land acquisitions. The environmental signature of these land transactions results from several factors, including scale and geographical distribution, the commodities involved, and the particular practices employed by investors for land clearing and cultivation.

Recent evidence on scale and distribution suggests a significant increase in land acquisitions in recent years, from an estimated annual expansion of land under cultivation of 1.9 million hectares (ha) per year from 1990 to 2007, to as high as 56.6 million ha in a single year (2008–9). This research reveals that Africa is the prime target of the global land rush, comprising an estimated 70 percent (39.7 million ha) of these deals, followed by Asia and Latin America. It is clear from this work that biofuels, food crops, and plantation forestry are driving these expansion trends, although in different proportions depending on the focus of the analysis, the region, and the time period assessed. While it is often difficult to assess the relative influence of biofuel, food, and feed markets for multipurpose feedstock, it is evident that biofuels are the primary driver of large-scale land acquisitions in Africa, and that biofuels account for increasing proportions of land expansion associated with common starch, sugar, and oilseed crops (an estimated 43 percent globally).[2]

Uncertainty and Confusion Surrounding Environmental Impact Debates

A high degree of uncertainty characterizes debates about the environmental impacts of recent large-scale land acquisitions. On the one hand, developing countries are seen as having an advantage with regard to the area of agro-ecologically suitable and uncultivated/available land—and particularly in Africa and South America, believed to have the largest areas of such land available.[3] In Asia, nearly all suitable land is classified as agricultural or forested land, suggesting that future expansion will come at the expense of one of these land uses. However, definitions can obscure important land uses from view. Land classified as available ("marginal," "degraded," "idle," "abandoned," "unproductive," or "unutilized") often has important economic uses for the poor, and may provide critical environmental services. Ambiguous definition of such concepts leaves them open to interpretation, and thus to the cultural and philosophical biases of decision makers.

Additionally, one must question the assumption that governments can channel investors to truly degraded or unutilized land by simply zoning areas according to their suitability and availability. A study in the Philippines, for example, found both populated and agriculturally productive lands in areas designated as "marginal."[4] Additionally, targeting marginal land may reduce returns on investment, suggesting that powerful incentives or regulatory instruments (both of which are largely absent today) are required to encourage investors to target land that truly is marginal.

One more source of confusion surrounds the promotion of biofuels as a "green" alternative to fossil fuels, whose combustion results in large net CO_2 emissions. A key justification for the shift to biofuels as an alternative energy source is the climatic benefit anticipated to accrue from these fuels, whose combustion (by releasing gases sequestered through cultivation) should reduce greenhouse-gas (GHG) emissions. This promise of greener energy has led to the inclusion of biofuels in alternative energy targets in many industrialized countries, notably the United States and European Union (EU) member states, and in a growing number of developing countries, notably Brazil. However, recent publications quantifying the climate effects of biofuel feedstock cultivation suggest that this benefit cannot be taken for granted. GHG emissions associated with land-use change often generate significant carbon "debts," postponing the net climate benefit of many biofuels for considerable periods (this concern is discussed in detail later in this chapter). Fossil fuel usage in cropping, processing, and marketing push biofuels further away from carbon neutrality.[5]

This chapter seeks to shed light on these debates by summarizing what is known about the environmental impacts of large-scale land acquisitions. Drawing on published data and secondary sources to define the scope of analysis and distill evidence, we synthesize what is known about the environmental impacts of a selection of key commodities driving agro-industrial expansion and large-scale land acquisitions in key eco-regions of the global South. Following a brief introduction to the methodology, we summarize evidence on land-use changes associated with large-scale land acquisitions and the implications of these shifting land uses for various environmental variables. We conclude with a discussion of mechanisms for strengthening the governance of environmental impacts.

Methodology

To carry out this review, it was necessary to clearly define the scope of analysis. This included the identification of both focal eco-regions for large-scale land acquisitions and the key crops or commodities implicated in these processes. For this purpose, we triangulated the information on the crops and eco-regions associated with the recent surge in large-scale land acquisitions from several recent synthesis reports with data on recent agricultural expansion from the FAOStat database.[6] Where FAOStat data suggested significant agricultural expansion for crops or eco-regions not captured in the synthesis reports, we conducted literature and online searches to distill whether expansion of the crops in question was associated with industrial-scale production (plantation agriculture), or reported to be associated with the "land grab" phenomenon. We also included select crops that do not register as significant based on global statistics on agricultural expansion, but which are nevertheless known to be tightly associated with the recent wave of large-scale land acquisitions.

Once a list of focal crops and eco-regions was identified, we conducted literature reviews to identify documented evidence on land-use changes. The implications of these land-use changes for three environmental variables (carbon stocks, biodiversity, and water use) strongly associated with land-use change and attributed to plantation agriculture were then assessed based on published data.

Two caveats are in order. One is that not all crops implicated in the recent wave of land acquisitions are covered in this chapter, owing to space limitations and insufficient evidence of environmental effects. Single- and multiple-purpose biofuel crops are given more attention than other commodities because of their significance in driving land acquisitions, and because of the attention given by the scientific community to understanding their environmental impacts in recent years.

The other caveat is that the documented evidence (regional reviews or case studies) on land-use change associated with selected commodities does not necessarily derive from transactions in land that would be a manifestation of the recent "land grab" phenomenon. They are nevertheless included because they represent trends associated with commodities and eco-regions featuring prominently in these land acquisitions.

Identification of Focal Eco-Regions and Crops

The findings of a 2011 World Bank study and a 2012 International Land Coalition report reveal that Africa is the prime target of the global land rush (accounting for between 48 and 66 percent of area expansion in the 2000s, and about 70 percent during the dramatic surge in land-related investments between October 2008 and August 2009), followed by Asia (between 21 and 40 percent in the 2000s) and Latin America (about 9 percent).[7] Our search therefore focused on these three regions.

The World Bank's 2011 report on large-scale land acquisitions, analyzing the global expansion of areas under production in the 1990 to 2007 period, notes that the growth of harvested area was narrowly attributable to a few key crops. The Bank found plantation forestry to be leading global land-use change, followed by soybean and maize (at 37.1 million ha, 32.9 million ha, and 27.3 million ha, respectively).[8] Other food and multipurpose crops such as rapeseed, rice, oil palm, sugarcane, and sunflower were found to account for between 4 and 12 million ha each. The report attributes the expansion in oil crops to higher consumption of cooking oil in Asia, greater use of soybeans as feed, and the production of biodiesel in the EU. The expansion of maize was attributed to the increased production of bioethanol in the United States and to the increased demand for maize as animal feed in Asia, while the expansion in rice was attributed to population growth in Asia and changing patterns of consumption in the Middle East and North Africa.

To explore the extent to which these patterns have continued beyond 2007, as well as their spatial distribution, we analyzed crops driving land-use change globally in the 2000 to 2010 period. While tree plantations, soy, and maize continue to account for the bulk of area expansion, a host of other crops have also entered the picture, as indicated in Table 5-1.

It is important to note that the pace of expansion for these crops has increased dramatically between the period profiled by the World Bank and the last decade, with tree plantations increasing from an average of 2.2 million ha per year in the 1990–2007 period to 4.9 million ha per year from 2000 to 2010. Similarly, the expansion rate of soybean increased from 1.9 to 2.8 million ha per annum, and maize from 1.6 to 2.5 million ha per annum.

To decide whether each of these crops would be included in our analysis of environmental impacts, we next explored the extent to which these land-use changes are associated with large-scale (as opposed to smallholder) production and linked to the "land grab" phenomenon. The World Bank's 2011 report finds that 78 percent of soybean expansion has been on large-scale farms, while approximately half of the expansion in area under oil palm, sugarcane, and maize may be attributable to large plantations. The 2012 International Land Coalition report, which focuses on key categories of commodities behind large-scale land deals in the 2000–2010 period, identifies biofuels at the forefront of the land rush (37.2 million ha, or 40 percent of the area acquired), followed by food crops (11.3 million ha, or 25 percent) and forest concessions (8.2 million ha, or 11.5 percent). Given the prominence of multipurpose feedstock (soybean, oil palm, sugarcane) and tree plantations in both land-use change analyses and land grabs, the environmental impacts of these commodities were featured in our analysis.

While the bulk of sunflower and rapeseed expansion was also found to occur on commercial plantations, these are left out of the analysis as the area of expansion does not overlap with those regions where land grabs are most intense. Based on literature searches and a review of sites dedicated to profiling the land-grab phenomenon, the expansion of beans in South Asia and cow peas in West Africa were found to be largely driven by smallholders, and thus eliminated from our analysis. Vegetables were also excluded because expansion was heavily concentrated in China, where area expansion is driven largely by domestic investments. Jatropha and rice are included due to their documented importance in driving land acquisitions in Africa, despite their lesser prominence (or absence) in analyses driven by global datasets.[9]

TABLE 5-1   Top Ten Crops Driving Global Land-Use Change, 2000–2010

Change, 2000–2010 (in million hectares)

Commodity	World	Central Africa	ESA*	North Africa	West Africa	C America & Caribbean	South America	Southeast Asia	South Asia	Central Asia	East Asia	Europe	North America	Other
Tree plantations	49.38	0.10	0.43	0.78	**1.15****	0.38	**3.76**	**2.80**	**3.02**	0.01	**22.74**	**4.01**	**8.47**	1.73
Soybeans	28.02	0.01	0.36	0.01	-0.20	0.09	**22.00**	-0.07	**2.82**	0.06	-0.80	**1.63**	**2.12**	-0.02
Maize	24.82	**1.37**	**2.91**	0.07	**2.18**	0.54	**1.74**	**1.50**	0.89	0.03	**9.44**	0.40	**3.74**	0.00
Beans, dry	5.92	0.51	0.68	-0.02	0.16	0.31	-0.82	0.84	**4.81**	0.03	-0.41	-0.15	0.09	-0.11
Rapeseed	5.85	0.00	0.03	0.00	0.00	-0.01	0.09	0.00	-0.54	0.30	-0.12	**4.17**	**1.63**	0.30
Oil palm	4.97	0.00	0.00	0.00	0.39	0.14	0.11	**4.28**	0.00	0.00	0.01	0.00	0.00	0.04
Sugarcane	4.44	0.02	0.21	0.00	0.05	-0.51	**4.24**	0.11	-0.09	0.00	0.51	0.00	-0.06	-0.04
Vegetables	3.50	0.02	0.41	0.27	0.12	0.07	0.01	0.30	0.67	0.02	**1.66**	-0.06	0.00	0.00
Cow peas	3.01	0.09	0.13	0.20	**2.56**	-0.01	0.01	0.02	0.00	0.00	0.00	0.00	0.01	0.00
Natural rubber	1.92	0.04	0.00	0.00	0.06	0.03	0.04	**1.42**	0.06	0.00	0.26	0.00	0.00	0.00

* ESA = Eastern and Southern Africa

** Boldface denotes subregions with at least a million hectares for any given commodity.

Source: FAOStat.

When searching for evidence of land-use change for the crops selected for inclusion in this study (jatropha, maize, oil palm, rice, rubber, soybeans, sugarcane, and tree plantations), we found that evidence was highly uneven. In recent years, assessments of land-use changes and related environmental impacts (such as greenhouse-gas emissions and biodiversity) have focused a great deal on crops that can be exclusively or optionally used for biofuel production, like jatropha, oil palm, sugarcane, and soybeans, and less on rubber and rice. And while maize has been the subject of analysis of land-use change, it is largely in the context of indirect effects of production in the United States and effects on world food prices—which fall outside the scope of our analysis. Our search therefore has generated a patchy set of relevant evidence for these latter commodities, necessitating a heavy reliance on less-scientific evidence of land-use change examples.

This chapter focuses on those crops for which scientific evidence is more grounded (jatropha, oil palm, soybean, sugarcane, and plantation forestry), and minimizes discussion of those for which scientific evidence is limited (maize, rubber, and rice). Unfortunately, this restricts our ability to discuss the wider environmental impacts associated with land-use change across a larger variety of crops. In an effort to provide some window into the environmental effects of land expansion involving the production of maize, rubber, and rice, Appendix II of this book features some representative tables, based largely on media reports. They are meant to be illustrative only and should not be taken as comprehensive in coverage.

Land-Use Changes Associated with Large-Scale Land Acquisitions

This section reviews how the crops tied to the land-grab phenomenon, and emphasized in our analysis, are driving land conversions.

Jatropha

Jatropha is a small perennial tree originating from Central America, but currently cultivated globally. Jatropha gained much attention in 2003 when the Indian government's planning commission declared it one of the focal crops for biodiesel production. It has been promoted as a drought-resistant crop that can simultaneously reclaim wastelands, foster rural socioeconomic development, and produce renewable fuels. As jatropha is a toxic plant, it is mainly promoted for its fuel use. Unless detoxification is employed, no food or feed applications are possible.

The stated benefits of jatropha production—wasteland reclamation, development, renewable fuels—resulted in significant investments (private and public), triggering land conversions all over the world. Particularly during 2007 and 2008, jatropha cultivation rapidly expanded based on its claimed ecological adaptability and its perceived potential to generate high yields under limited management. Although jatropha was initially promoted for introduction to (semi-)arid and degraded lands (and indeed in several cases this has happened, including on degraded land in India), a range of land-use conversions have occurred (see Table 5-2). Jatropha has converted agricultural land used for food crops and cash crops (as in Brazil, Mexico, Ghana, Zambia, and the Ivory Coast) and pastureland (as in Mexico). Furthermore, there are cases where jatropha was established in natural woodlands (India, Brazil, Tanzania, and Zambia) and secondary forests (Mexico). Such changes arguably undermine jatropha's environmental sustainability claim.[10]

The reviewed scientific literature illustrates that jatropha is indeed being introduced globally (with land conversions occurring in South Asia, South and Central America, and Africa), but it is also clear that detailed information on which land-use types are converted to jatropha is often scarce.[11] This is probably due to the fact that the conversions are rather recent and thus poorly documented.

Oil Palm

Unlike jatropha, oil palm is an oil crop primarily used for the food industry, although it is suitable and is used for biofuel production as well. Oil palm is well adapted to the humid tropics, and is mainly produced in Malaysia and Indonesia. According to FAOStat, together these countries host about 9 million ha of oil palm plantations. However, since 2005, 52 projects have acquired 3 million ha for oil palm cultivation across sub-Saharan Africa—with most of this area having been acquired since 2009.[12] Oil palm–driven land expansion has been heavily criticized for deforestation and the conversion of carbon-rich peatland, with important consequences for biodiversity and both above- and below-ground carbon losses.

Table 5-3 summarizes documented evidence of oil palm conversions in Southeast Asia and Africa. Many of the cases show a high degree of direct

TABLE 5-2 Evidence of Jatropha-Related Land-Use Change Available in Literature

Subregion/ Country	Period	Expansion (in hectares)	Land-Use Change	Source and Year
South Asia/ India	2005	250	100 percent in woodland	*Global Change Biology Bioenergy*, 2011
South Asia/ India	*		100 percent in degraded grassland	*Applied Energy*, 2010
South America/ Brazil	2007	76	100 percent in woodland	*Global Change Biology Bioenergy*, 2011
South America/ Brazil		6,720	95 percent established in pasture, 2 percent in cropland, 3 percent in natural vegetation	*Environmental Science and Technology*, 2010
C America, Mexico		2,350	100 percent established in secondary woodland	
C America, Mexico			25 percent established in secondary forest, 25 percent in fallow land, 50 percent in permanent cropland	*Ecology and Society*, 2011
C America, Mexico			5 percent established in secondary forest, 29 percent in pasture, 66 percent in agricultural land	
Africa/Ghana		780	46 percent established in a mix of open and closed woodland, 23 percent in permanent cropland and 31 percent in fallow land	*Ecology and Society*, 2011
Africa/Zambia			24 percent established in mature woodland, 61 percent in permanent cropland, 15 percent in fallow land	*Ecology and Society*, 2011
Africa/Zambia		500,000		Center for International Forestry Research, 2012
Africa/ Tanzania			Jatropha establishment in woodland	World Wide Fund for Nature Tanzania, 2009, and *Energy Policy*, 2011

TABLE 5-2   continued

Subregion/ Country	Period	Expansion (in hectares)	Land-Use Change	Source and Year
Africa/ Ivory Coast			Jatropha-converted cotton fields	*Global Change Biology Bioenergy*, 2009
Africa/ Madagascar		450,000		Center for International Forestry Research, 2012
Africa/ South Sudan	2008–2011	600,000	100 percent to be established in forest (oil palm & jatropha)	Center for International Forestry Research, 2012
Africa/Ghana	2005–2010	1,100,000		Center for International Forestry Research, 2010
Africa/ Madagascar	2005–2010	900,000		Center for International Forestry Research, 2010
Africa/Tanzania	2005–2010	640,000		Center for International Forestry Research, 2010
Africa/Zambia	2005–2010	600,000		Center for International Forestry Research, 2010
Africa/ Mozambique	2005–2010	500,000		Center for International Forestry Research, 2010

* Blank cells indicate that data is not available.

deforestation (constituting about 40 to 100 percent of plantation expansion). This deforestation includes the conversion of secondary, primary, and peatland rainforests. One report highlights three oil palm case studies with forest and/or peat conversions comprising between 88 and 99.5 percent of the expansion area, and conversions of agricultural land constituting between 0.5 and 12 percent.[13]

TABLE 5-3   Evidence of Oil Palm–Related Land-Use Change Available in Literature

Subregion/ Country	Period	Expansion (in hectares)	Land-Use Change	Reference
SE Asia/ Indonesia	1982–1999		70 percent established in forest	Center for International Forestry Research, 2009
SE Asia/ Malaysia	1990–2005	1.8 million	55.5 percent established in forest	*Trends in Ecology and Evolution,* 2008, and *Conservation Letters,* 2008
SE Asia/ Indonesia	1990–2005	4.4 million	38.6–68.2 percent established in forest	*Trends in Ecology and Evolution,* 2008, and *Conservation Letters,* 2008
SE Asia/ Indonesia		8.09 million	46 percent established in forest	*Conservation Letters,* 2009
SE Asia/ Malaysia	1980s–2010	6,244	100 percent lowland tropical rainforest	*Ecology and Society,* 2011
SE Asia/ Indonesia	1982–2006	5,495	48 percent established in lowland tropical primary rainforest, 43 percent lowland tropical secondary rainforest, and 9 percent in agricultural land	*Ecology and Society,* 2011
SE Asia/ Indonesia	1989–2009	5,266	84 percent established in tropical peatland forest, 4 percent in swamp, 12 percent in agricultural land	*Ecology and Society,* 2011
SE Asia/ Indonesia	1990–2008	20,855	96 percent established in lowland tropical primary rainforest, 2 percent in tropical peatland forest, 1 percent in swampland, 0.5 percent in agricultural land	*Ecology and Society,* 2011

TABLE 5-3 continued

Subregion/ Country	Period	Expansion (in hectares)	Land-Use Change	Reference
SE Asia/ Peninsular Malaysia		2 million	On average, 10 percent established in peatlands	*Proceedings of the National Academy of Sciences* (USA), 2011
SE Asia/ Borneo, Malaysia		2.4 million		
SE Asia/ Indonesia		3.9 million		
Africa/ DR Congo		0.1 million	100 percent to be established in forest	Center for International Forestry Research, 2010
Africa/ South Sudan	2008–2011	0.6 million	100 percent (oil palm & jatropha) to be established in forest	Center for International Forestry Research, 2012
Africa/ DRCongo	2010	0.47 million		Center for International Forestry Research, 2012
Africa/ Liberia	2009	0.31 million		Center for International Forestry Research, 2012
Africa/ Gabon	2010	0.05 million	100 percent to be established in forest zone	Center for International Forestry Research, 2012

Soybean

Soybean is an annual crop which can be used for food, feed, and fuel purposes, and is mainly cultivated in South America. Between 1990 and 2010, the area under soybean cultivation in this region expanded from 17.7 million to 46.2 million ha.[14] According to FAOStat, Brazil and Argentina are the main soybean-producing countries, with 23 million ha and 18 million ha, respectively.

As Table 5-4 indicates, there has been relatively limited direct deforestation caused by soybean expansion, despite the crop's establishment in areas with high forest and woodland cover (3.5–8.4 percent of the expansion area). Indeed, one report, having monitored deforestation between 2000 and 2006 in three Brazilian regions (Mato Grosso, Rondônia, and Pará),

TABLE 5-4   Evidence of Soybean-Related Land-Use Change Available in Literature

Location	Period	Expansion (in hectares)	Land-Use Change	Reference
S America/ Brazil	2000–2004	1.7 million	3.2 percent established in Amazon and 5.2 percent in Cerrado	*Journal of Environmental Management*, 2010
North Brazil			6 percent established in Amazon and 6.2 percent in Cerrado	
South Brazil			0 percent established in Amazon and 4.2 percent in Cerrado	
S America/ Brazil	2001–2004		Soy expansion triggered 0.5 million ha deforestation in Amazon	*Proceedings of the National Academy of Sciences* (USA), 2006
S America/ Brazil	2005–2010		8 percent established in Amazon and 92 percent in permanent cropland	*Ecology and Society*, 2011
S America/ Brazil	anticipated		Expansion will occur in degraded pasture	*Ecology and Society*, 2011
S America/ Brazil	2010–2020	10.8 million	3.5 percent of expansion will be established in forest, 83 percent in pasture, 9 percent in cropland	*Proceedings of the National Academy of Sciences* (USA), 2010
S America/ Argentina	2000–2005	4.7 million	32 percent established in cropland (wheat, corn, sunflower, sorghum), 27 percent in pasture, 19 percent in savannah, and 22 percent in forest	*International Journal of Life Cycle Assessment*, 2009

was unable to establish a statistical relationship between deforestation and soybean expansion.[15] Rather, the bulk of the expansion has occurred on pasture and annual cropland. However, there are indications that soybean production has shifted to forest frontiers more recently.[16] Additionally, there are concerns about indirect deforestation effects (see Box 5-1).[17]

BOX 5-1
Indirect Land-Use Change

Indirect land-use change refers to displacement of current land-use systems by a subsequent land use, which in turn results in land-use change in new areas. For example, if sugar expansion results in the displacement of cereal cultivation, and cereal farmers make up for the shortfall by bringing previously uncultivated land into cereal production, then this would be considered indirect land-use change. In the event that farmers respond by intensifying cereal production on lands already dedicated to cereal production, or in the event that sugar expands in formerly forested areas, it is often assumed that there is no indirect land-use change. Economic uses of forests, however, are also often displaced to new areas.

Sugarcane

Like oil palm and soybean, sugarcane is a multipurpose crop, used as both a food and a fuel crop, and mainly produced in Brazil. The land conversion triggered by sugarcane is similar to that caused by soybean, albeit under very distinct biophysical and policy contexts. Sugarcane expansion has been found to trigger relatively limited direct deforestation effects (0 to 4.9 percent of expansion areas; see Table 5-5). In Brazil, sugarcane has been introduced mainly in pastures and on cropland. Modeling experiments have found that future sugarcane expansion in Brazil will cause little direct deforestation (much of this expansion is projected to be in pastureland, with the remainder converting agricultural land). However, as with soybeans, indirect effects could be significant, with a predicted 5.2 million hectares of indirect deforestation.[18]

Plantation Forestry

Tree plantations amount to an estimated 7 percent (264 million ha) of the total global forested area, with only five countries (China, USA, Russia, Japan, and India) comprising about 53 percent of this area. According to FAO forestry resource data, between 2000 and 2010, the area of planted forest increased by about 5 million ha per year, most of which occurred in areas originally devoid of forest cover. The Asia-Pacific region accounts

TABLE 5-5   Evidence of Sugarcane-Related Land-Use Change Available in
Literature

Location	Period	Expansion (in hectares)	Land-Use Change	Reference
S America/ Brazil	2005–2008	1.06 million	4.9 percent established in Cerrado, rest in pasture and non-sugarcane crops	*Nature Climate Change*, 2011
S America/ Brazil	2005–2008	1.8 million	53 percent established in pasture, 44.6 percent in annual crops, 0.3 percent in forest	Center for International Forestry Research, 2012
S America/ Brazil	2003–2010	4.3 million	69.8 percent established in pasture, 26.2 percent in annual crops, 0.6 percent in forest	First World Sustainability Forum, 2011
S America/ Brazil	1996–2006		No direct deforestation, no conversion of food crops, mainly converting pasture	*Mitigation and Adaptation Strategies for Global Change*, 2009
S America/ Brazil	1996–2006		Sugarcane-reduced forest area by 12 percent, conversion mainly from pasture	*Mitigation and Adaptation Strategies for Global Change*, 2009
S America/ Brazil	1996–2006		Sugarcane converted 84,000 ha forest (2.2 percent of deforestation)	*Energy Policy*, 2011
S America/ Brazil	2007–2008	352,000	69 percent established in pasture, 12 percent in soybean, 4.9 percent in corn, 8.3 percent in orange, 0.6 percent in coffee, 3 percent others, 2.2 percent in new land	*Energy Policy*, 2011, and *Global Change Biology Bioenergy*, 2011
S America/ Brazil	2007–2008	9,000	31 percent established in pasture, 68 percent in soy, 1.3 percent in new lands	*Energy Policy*, 2011, and *Global Change Biology Bioenergy*, 2011
S America/ Brazil	2007–2008	609,000	66 percent established in pasture, 18 percent in soybean, 5 percent in corn, 5 percent in orange, 0.4 percent in coffee, 4 percent others, and 1.4 percent in new land	*Energy Policy*, 2011, and *Global Change Biology Bioenergy*, 2011
S America/ Brazil	2010–2020	5.7 million	No direct deforestation anticipated; 93 percent established in pasture, 7 percent in agricultural cropland	*Proceedings of the National Academy of Sciences* (USA), 2010

for an estimated 54 million ha of forest plantations, with India having 33 million ha (60 percent of the regional total), followed by Indonesia and Thailand. Tropical Africa reports a total of 4.6 million ha of forest plantations—the largest share being in Nigeria at 0.7 million ha, followed by Sudan and Madagascar. However, with at least 1.2 million ha of large-scale land deals approved for forestry projects in Mozambique alone in the last few years, it is clear that these figures fail to reflect rapidly changing realities on the ground in Africa. Meanwhile, in tropical Latin America and the Caribbean, which account for an estimated 8.8 million ha, plantation areas are concentrated in Brazil (5.6 million ha), followed by Venezuela (0.86 million ha), and Peru (0.64 million ha).[19]

Globally, according to FAO, about 75 percent of the area of planted forests consists primarily of native species; however, these are predominantly monocultures in industrial-scale plantations, and thus not equivalent to native forest per se. Yet in reality the story differs depending on the regional context. Across eastern and southern Africa, the percentage of exotic (nonnative) species out of the total planted forest area is 99 percent, and 97 percent in South America. By contrast, across South and Southeast Asia, the value is 16 percent, and for North and Central America, even lower (3 percent). A closer look at land-use changes associated with plantation expansion in Africa and South America is therefore needed to get a complete picture of the environmental impacts of tree plantations. Meanwhile, across the tropics, fast-growing monocultures (such as *Eucalyptus* and *Pinus*) dominate lumber- and fiber-production plantations. According to one study, teak, a high-value hardwood species, is also attracting substantial investment.[20]

Globally, FAO reports that the area of planted forest has steadily increased, adding more than 3.6 million ha from 1990 to 2000, 5.6 million ha from 2000 to 2005, and 4.2 million ha from 2005 to 2010. When dividing these trends between afforestation (which involves previously nonforested land) and reforestation (involving areas previously forested) for the period of 2000 to 2005 (see Table 5-6), afforestation is the predominant trend in Africa and South and Southeast Asia, while for South America, expansion has been driven primarily by reforestation. According to FAO definitions, the conversion of natural forests to tree plantations does not constitute deforestation. However, this process clearly affects important environmental indices such as biodiversity, carbon stocks, and hydrological functions linked to vegetation. This may result in an underestimation of the actual environmental and land-use change effects of tree plantations.

TABLE 5-6   Land-Use Changes Associated with Forest Plantations
for Selected Regions, 2000–2005

	Afforestation		Reforestation	
Location	Expansion (ha/yr)	% increase	Expansion (ha/yr)	% increase
E and S Africa	4,552	87.7	6,070	42.4
S and SE Asia	37,478	89.0	46,796	12.8
Central America	–1,152	–57.1	572	24.1
South America	–1,151	–6.2	93,451	189.0

Source: FAO, Global Forest Resources Assessment 2010.

Environmental Consequences of Land-Use Change

This section examines the carbon debts and biodiversity impacts associated with observed land-use changes, as well as water consumption patterns (footprints) associated with key crops.

Carbon-Stock Changes

Land-use conversions generally go hand in hand with carbon-stock changes. By removing vegetation in order to introduce new vegetation, the amount of carbon stored in the biomass (above and below ground) changes. For example, land-use conversions from forests to annual crops will trigger a loss of carbon stored in the aboveground biomass of that land. Land-use change can also trigger changes in soil carbon stocks (forest soil will accumulate more carbon and respire less than soil under permanent tillage). Land-use conversions can trigger both carbon-stock decreases (as with forest to annual cropping) and increases (as with reforestation).

Because biofuel crops are mainly promoted and cultivated to reduce fossil-energy dependency and greenhouse-gas emissions, numerous studies have assessed the carbon-stock implications of land conversions to biofuels. Although biofuel systems generally do reduce GHG emissions, land-use change prior to biofuel feedstock production can lead to carbon debts, which can negate the carbon balance for prolonged periods and, as such, postpone net greenhouse-gas reductions.[21] Nonetheless, because biofuel systems trigger reductions in greenhouse-gas emissions, they are able to "repay" the carbon debt caused by the land conversion necessary to establish biofuel crop cultivation. Therefore a repayment time can be calculated for biofuel crops (or for the biofuel application of multipurpose crops).

While less assessed and discussed, conversions to food, feed, or fiber crops can also trigger carbon debts. Unlike biofuels, these commodities cannot repay their debt because these products have no CO_2-emissions reduction potential. Due to lack of available data, no such examples are discussed below. We restrict our analysis to biofuel-related carbon debts and their respective repayment times.

JATROPHA

In Brazil, the conversion of *Caatinga* woodland leads to direct carbon debts that are expected to be repaid by jatropha biodiesel production and use in 10–20 years.[22] In Tanzania, the conversion of *Miombo* woodland generates carbon debts that are estimated to be repayable in 76 years.[23] And the conversion of *Prosopis* woodland and degraded grassland in India is expected to cause a small carbon debt, repayable by sequestration in jatropha biomass alone within five years.[24] Carbon debts associated with indirect land-use change for forests and woodlands are hard to find in the literature, given the (often erroneous) assumption that these areas have no existing economic uses that would be deflected to other areas.

In cases where jatropha converts pasture and cropland, carbon debts associated with both direct and indirect land-use changes have to be accounted for. Such situations in Ghana, Mexico, and Zambia have resulted in total carbon debts (those associated with direct *and* indirect effects) higher than those cited for Brazil, Tanzania, and India above, with repayment times estimated as high as 629 years.[25] In one of these cases, jatropha yields were found to be too low to allow for biodiesel production to have any greenhouse-gas-emission reduction potential (due to the failure to provide adequate technical support to smallholder farmers)—and hence, carbon debts associated with land conversion cannot be repaid.

OIL PALM

As Table 5-3 illustrates, oil palm triggers considerable deforestation, and the crop's conversion of peat forests triggers particularly sizable carbon debts. Repayment times under these circumstances may reach an estimated 918 years when peat emissions occur over a 50-year period.[26] By contrast, repayment times for carbon debts incurred on non-peat forests may range from

59 to 85 years.[27] When palm oil is not used for biodiesel production and instead enters the cooking oil market, the carbon debt caused by the land conversion is the same, but is not repaid.

Soybean and Sugarcane

Several studies have focused on the CO_2 implications of land conversions to soybean and/or sugarcane in Brazil. One examines the conversion of *Cerrado* woodland and grassland in Brazil into sugarcane and soybeans. The conversion of woodland to sugarcane was found to generate nearly twice the carbon debt as grassland to soybeans. When used for biofuel production (sugarcane bioethanol and soybean biodiesel), repayment times were estimated at 17 and 37 years, respectively.[28]

Another study looks at future expansion of the two commodities in Brazil, concluding that nearly 11 million ha of soybean expansion would create debts repayable in 35 years, and nearly 6 million ha of sugarcane would generate a debt repayable in just four years. However, taking into account expected indirect land-use change effects, total repayment times would increase to 246 years for soybean biodiesel and 46 years for sugarcane bioethanol.[29]

Biodiversity Impacts

Land conversions of any type may have both direct and indirect effects on local habitats and plant and animal species. This section reviews what is currently known and documented about these effects.

Jatropha

As indicated in Table 5-2, jatropha results in the conversion of different types of land uses. Cutting woodland will have more significant biodiversity implications than greening degraded land. However, to our knowledge, no detailed studies on how jatropha affects biodiversity are currently available in the scientific literature.

Oil palm

Compared to jatropha, the impact of oil palm on biodiversity is much more apparent and documented. Indeed, in the year 2000, according to one study, oil palm expansion in peat swamp forests led to a biodiversity decline of 1 percent in Borneo (equivalent to the loss of four species of forest-dwelling birds), 3.4 percent in Sumatra (16 species), and 12.1 percent in peninsular Malaysia (46 species). Reforestation of these cleared peatland forests, the study estimates, would enhance biodiversity by up to 20 percent.[30]

The actual impact on specific animal species is also profound. Research has shown that the conversion of tropical lowland rainforest (such as in Malaysia) into oil palm directly influences the abundance of ant species. Oil palm plantations in the country, this research finds, can sustain only 5 percent of the ground-dwelling ant species present in the forest.[31] Another study shows that forest conversion to oil palm in peninsular Malaysia eliminated 48 to 60 percent of the prevailing bird species.[32]

TREE PLANTATIONS

Tree plantations are usually less biodiverse than natural forests. Yet the absolute or relative magnitude of this contrast varies as a function of many factors. One such factor is the preexisting vegetation prior to plantation establishment, whether natural or modified forest, degraded or abandoned agricultural land, or land that was never forested. Which tree species are involved, the management objectives and intensity, plantation age, and position in the landscape are all factors shaping biodiversity impacts of plantations. Furthermore, there is often a trade-off between the yield of monoculture tree plantations and their environmental (and social) impacts.[33]

SOYBEAN AND SUGARCANE

Given that the land-conversion profile of both soybean and sugarcane mainly involves pasture and cropland, one might expect that direct impacts on biodiversity are rather minimal. However, researchers have concluded that such conversions can trigger indirect effects in Brazil's *Cerrado* and Atlantic forest regions, and in the Amazon. These regions are highly biodiverse, are under continuous pressure, and (despite admirable efforts in Brazil to protect these areas) are vulnerable to conversion. Given how vulnerable they are, further expansion of agricultural commodities on pastures and cropland nearby will lead to more deforestation, habitat loss, and loss of biodiversity.[34]

Water Footprint

Table 5-7 depicts the total water footprints (blue-, green-, and gray-water footprints)[35] of the commodities covered in this chapter and in Appendix

TABLE 5-7   Water Footprints (WF, in cubic meters per ton of production) of
Selected Commodities

Commodity	Location	Total WF	Source and Year
Jatropha oil	Brazil	3,222	*Proceedings of the National Academy of Sciences* (USA), 2009 (study minimum)
Jatropha oil	(study average)	7,347	*Proceedings of the National Academy of Sciences* (USA), 2009 (study average)
Jatropha oil	India	21,729	*Proceedings of the National Academy of Sciences* (USA), 2009 (study maximum)
Jatropha oil	Egypt	2,544	*Proceedings of the National Academy of Sciences* (USA), 2009
Maize	Spain	407	*Proceedings of the National Academy of Sciences* (USA), 2009 (study minimum)
Maize	(study average)	1,100	*Proceedings of the National Academy of Sciences* (USA), 2009 (study average)
Maize	Nigeria	3,783	*Proceedings of the National Academy of Sciences* (USA), 2009 (study maximum)
Maize	The Netherlands	153	*Ecological Economics*, 2009
Maize	USA	308	*Ecological Economics*, 2009
Maize	Brazil	664	*Ecological Economics*, 2009
Maize	Zimbabwe	3,363	*Ecological Economics*, 2009
Maize	(global average)	1,222	UNESCO, 2010
Palm oil	Brazil	1,502	*Ecological Economics*, 2009
Palm oil	Thailand	3,420	*Agricultural Water Management*, 2011
Palm oil	(global average)	4,971	UNECSO, 2010
Rice (paddy)	(global average)	1,673	UNECSO, 2010
Rubber	(global average)	13,748	UNESCO, 2010
Soybean	USA	979	*Ecological Economics*, 2009
Soybean	Brazil	602	*Ecological Economics*, 2009
Soybean	Zimbabwe	1,360	*Ecological Economics*, 2009
Soybean	Italy	1,442	*Proceedings of the National Academy of Sciences* (USA), 2009 (minimum)
Soybean	India	7,540	*Proceedings of the National Academy of Sciences* (USA), 2009 (maximum)
Soybean	(study average)	2,521	*Proceedings of the National Academy of Sciences* (USA), 2009 (average)
Soybean	USA	974	*Global Change Biology Bioenergy*, 2011

TABLE 5-7 continued

Commodity	Location	Total WF	Source and Year
Soybean	USA	715	*Global Change Biology Bioenergy*, 2011
Soybean	USA	1,134	*Global Change Biology Bioenergy*, 2011
Soybean	USA	902	*Global Change Biology Bioenergy*, 2011
Soybean	USA	761	*Global Change Biology Bioenergy*, 2011
Soybean	USA	1,037	*Global Change Biology Bioenergy*, 2011
Soybean	(global average)	2,145	UNESCO, 2010
Sugarcane	Thailand	312	*Agricultural Water Management*, 2011
Sugarcane	USA	153	*Ecological Economics*, 2009
Sugarcane	Brazil	128	*Ecological Economics*, 2009
Sugarcane	Zimbabwe	160	*Ecological Economics*, 2009
Sugarcane	Peru	108	*Proceedings of the National Academy of Sciences (USA)*, 2009 (study minimum)
Sugarcane	Cuba	524	*Proceedings of the National Academy of Sciences (USA)*, 2009 (study maximum)
Sugarcane	(study average)	248	*Proceedings of the National Academy of Sciences (USA)*, 2009 (study average)
Sugarcane	(global average)	210	UNESCO, 2010
Eucalyptus (newsprint)	Brazil (subtropical)	406	UNESCO, 2010
Eucalyptus (newsprint)	Brazil (tropical)	441	UNESCO, 2010
Eucalyptus (newsprint)	China (subtropical)	2,045	UNESCO, 2010
Eucalyptus (newsprint)	China (tropical)	1,840	UNESCO, 2010
Eucalyptus (printing & writing paper)	Brazil (subtropical)	497	UNESCO, 2010
Eucalyptus (printing & writing paper)	Brazil (tropical)	540	UNESCO, 2010
Eucalyptus (printing & writing paper)	China (subtropical)	2,501	UNESCO, 2010
Eucalyptus (printing & writing paper)	China (tropical)	2,250	UNESCO, 2010

II, enabling a comparison of water consumption across different commodities. The measure includes both water-use efficiency of the crop (biomass produced per volume of water consumed) as well as water consumed in the processing of the final product.

Looking at global averages on a per-ton basis, sugarcane is shown to consume less water, on average, than maize, soybean, palm oil, and *Eucalyptus*. Yet it is also clear that water use for any given commodity varies significantly by location, as is the case for jatropha oil produced in Egypt and India. Looking at water-use impacts of different commodities by country, it is clear that for Brazil, on a per-ton basis, the water footprint of sugarcane ranks best, followed by those of soybean, maize, oil palm, and finally jatropha.[36] Research on water footprints of different tree species also highlights the relative performance of producing specific end products. Water footprints for printing and writing paper, for example, tend to be higher than for newsprint.

It is important to note that there are measures of hydrological impact other than water footprints, and these can produce very different findings. Concerns regarding the negative impacts of fast-growing tree plantations on surface and groundwater supplies stem from concerns over absolute water consumption, which is better represented by a measure emphasizing total water consumed per cropped area rather than per unit of biomass. Crops with high water-use efficiency can also, with rapid plant growth and high biomass production, result in higher volumes of water consumed per unit of area. In certain circumstances, such highly efficient crops can exert greater absolute impacts than crops with lower water-use efficiency.

Furthermore, the net hydrological impact on the ecosystem will result from a host of factors, including land-use change, water-quality changes associated with sedimentation and run-off, and differences in water availability. Higher water consumption in a water-rich environment may be less harmful than lower consumption in areas where water is scarce, for example. Thus, while the water footprint is a useful metric, it is not the only relevant measure of hydrological impacts.

Hydrological impacts of tree plantations are contingent on a number of additional factors. If grasslands are afforested, runoff may decrease up to 44 percent, whereas on reforested land, runoff on average may decrease by up to only 31 percent; these reductions may be more prominent during the dry season.[37] Location can also be an important determinant of the water footprints of different tree species. Comparative studies in South Africa suggest that *Eucalyptus* tree plantations use more water than *Pinus* tree plantations, whereas the opposite has been reported in Australia.[38] In general, fast-growing tree species tend to be more water-demanding than slow-growing ones, and young planted forests have greater water use than older ones. Initial soil conditions may also influence local outcomes; in heavily compacted soil, afforestation may in fact increase groundwater recharge due to improved infiltration.[39]

Governance of Environmental Impacts

There is an urgent need to explore mechanisms for governing land-based investments in the global South, so as to leverage their potential as an engine of economic growth while avoiding unnecessary social and environmental costs. Yet all too often, concern for deforestation and other environmental impacts is assumed to be universal, and the desirability of forest conservation taken for granted. Indeed, evidence suggests that policymakers and planners are preoccupied with economic-development imperatives, and by the desire to leverage investment while minimizing social disruption (such as by avoiding areas under cultivation). This often results in the explicit targeting of (often biodiverse) forests and grasslands for investment. Thus, a calculus that focuses exclusively on the ecological benefits of forest and environmental protection will tend to fall on deaf ears.

Research can help to shift the cost-benefit calculus by replacing narratives that uncritically inflate the potential benefits of large-scale land acquisitions while minimizing their costs with evidence-based analysis of both costs and benefits (trade-offs) in specific locations. However, political will is a necessary precondition for ensuring environmental protection in the context of economic or rural development models designed to stimulate commercial scale investments. In countries where the political will to regulate forest conversion (whether endogenous or induced by exogenous pressures) combines with good regulatory oversight, it is possible to balance plantation expansion with environmental controls. Brazil is illustrative, as it is the one case where significant success has been achieved in regulating deforestation in the context of agro-industrial expansion.[40] Three key factors contributed to this success: government policies restricting the percentage of landholdings that could be deforested, the monitoring of compliance through remote-sensing technologies, and a soy industry moratorium. According to the Brazilian Forestry Code of 1965, 80 percent of all landholdings must be set aside as "legal reserves" in which native vegetation must be preserved. The government began monitoring compliance in 1988 and has achieved significant reductions in deforestation. From 2006 to 2010, for example, Brazil halved the rate of deforestation in the Amazon relative to preceding years. The Soy Moratorium is a pledge among major soybean companies to refrain from trading soybean produced in areas of the Brazilian Amazon deforested after July 2006. It is the outcome of a well-organized, civil-society-led pressure campaign and industry-led initiative.[41] While it is difficult to differentiate the relative effects of the moratorium and government policies, an article analyzing deforestation in the 2009–10 crop year found only 6,300 ha of soy grown in areas deforested during the moratorium period, accounting for only 0.25 percent of deforestation.[42]

However, despite these successes, the Soy Moratorium has largely failed to address indirect land-use change effects, accounting for some of the negative biodiversity impacts observed for sugarcane and soybean. Equally worrying, agribusiness interests seem to be eroding this political commitment, as suggested by legislative changes introduced to the Forest Code in 2011.[43] In some ways this is not surprising, for while Brazil's experience illustrates the promise of regulating direct deforestation in the context of agro-industrial expansion, a far more common scenario—seen in so many different geographical contexts—involves the active targeting of forest lands and weak enforcement of environmental regulations.

For countries with limited political support to minimize the ecological costs of agro-industrial expansion, or with limited capacity to guide sector development in more ecologically benign trajectories, to what extent can other complementary governance instruments play a role in achieving these aims? Market-based instruments to govern social and environmental practices of producers and financiers are proliferating and hold some promise as mechanisms for bolstering or complementing domestic environmental controls. The proliferation of certification schemes to enhance the sustainability of the growing biofuel industry,[44] voluntary codes of conduct for agricultural investment, sustainability reporting schemes, industry-wide or financier-specific responsible-investment policies, and industry-wide or company-specific sustainability and corporate social-responsibility policies for upstream industries[45] are important examples.

These schemes may provide complementary controls on the social and environmental practices of investors by encouraging their compliance with internationally recognized principles or standards, making compliance with national laws mandatory (thus bolstering domestic regulatory capacities), or placing conditionalities on finance. However, their current reach is limited by several factors, including their voluntary nature (and thus limited coverage of economic operators and investments), the quality and specificity of the standards, and the lack of independent verification of compliance (with the exception of certification). Industry-wide and company-specific codes of conduct are undermined by their tendency to emphasize broad principles rather than quantifiable, outcome-oriented performance measures, and by the failure of their sponsors to take adequate steps to implement the codes and make their efforts transparent.[46] A 2011 review of responsible-investment instruments in the biofuel sector found that the vast majority of investors either lack responsible-investment policies or have adopted policies that are insufficiently robust. And where these responsible-investment policies do exist, they tend to lack independent monitoring and compliance processes.[47]

These deficiencies, however, mask the potential for hybrid arrangements that build on the complementarities of different governance instruments. The publication of sustainability criteria, in conjunction with a policy mandate to ensure minimum levels of renewables in the fuel mix for the transport sector in the EU, sets a powerful incentive to biofuel producers to ensure the sustainability of their practices. The rapid proliferation of sustainability schemes to meet the sustainability requirements of the EU Renewable Energy Directive, and evidence that existing standards are changing in response to EU sustainability criteria, illustrate the strong potential of market requirements to shape sector performance.[48] However, the potential of such hybrids between public policies and market-based certification and verification will depend on the scope and specificity of market requirements, the degree of multi-stakeholder involvement in designing and verifying compliance with certification standards, and the prevalence of alternative markets setting the performance bar lower than the EU.

Hybrids between producer-country environmental regulations and market-based certification also hold the potential to strengthen compliance with national laws and thus bolster domestic regulatory capacities. Three of the seven voluntary schemes approved by the European Commission to verify compliance with the Renewable Energy Directive, for example, make compliance with national laws and international agreements general requirements for operators. Yet the potential of such a hybrid arrangement to effectively govern the environmental impacts of company practices will rest on the number of economic operators certified and on which standard they choose. Making certification a precondition for investment in a country and selecting "high-performing" standards as options for compliance can be expected to significantly ratchet up the environmental and social performance of investors. Admittedly, however, this may be politically infeasible during the early stages of sector development, when host-country governments often assume a supportive over a regulatory role in order to attract and sustain investment.

Conclusion

This chapter suggests that the commodities both implicated in the recent wave of large-scale land acquisitions and driving global land-use change include multipurpose crops (food-feed-fuel) and large-scale tree plantations. This expansion is driven by multiple end markets, including those for food, feed, fuel, and fiber, and is highly location-specific. And while the impacts of this phenomenon on greenhouse-gas emissions, biodiversity, and water availability for other uses are clearly significant, these impacts vary considerably based on a host of factors, including commodity selection (and for carbon debt repayment, whether the commodity is intended for fuel or other end uses), geographical location, spatial distribution, management, and governance conditions.

Given the highly uneven data on land-use change for different commodities and the geographically spotty data for those crops for which more robust data do exist, this analysis should not be interpreted as the full story. Further analytical work and monitoring is needed to produce a clearer picture of the global environmental hotspots associated with large-scale land acquisitions and of the effectiveness of instruments employed to govern environmental impacts.

Chapter 6

Investors' Perspectives

GARY R. BLUMENTHAL

In recent years, elevated prices for food crops have attracted the attention of investors. Many of these money managers have little experience in the sector, but they share a fascination with the profit potential when fast-rising demand growth collides with inadequate agricultural production systems and concurrent environmental limits. The icing on the cake is that commodities can serve as a hedge against inflation while contributing to portfolio diversification. The result is that agricultural commodities have become a new investment asset class.

In fact, it has not always been this way. Until recently, investors shied away from farmland. This chapter traces the evolution of investor views on agriculture; underscores the advantages and necessity of investor-driven, and oft-criticized, large-scale agricultural production; and describes the various considerations financiers must take into account in order to produce successful farmland investments.

Historic Investor Disaffinity for Farmland

Historically, the investment community has had little interest in the food and agricultural sector. According to an analysis in the *European Review of Agricultural Economics*, food processing captured just 10 percent of global investment in manufacturing between 1998 and 2004.[1] This historical lack of interest has occurred despite the fact that the food and agricultural sector employs over half of global labor, and comprises a significant share of both gross domestic product and per capita income.

What has typically scared investors away from agriculture is that it comprises perhaps the largest social issue confronting governments everywhere. The elephant in the room is the huge excess of labor devoted to agriculture. In fact, only a fraction of the world's farmers would be needed if current technology—which investors can provide—were fully applied.

Perceptions of Large-Scale Farming

Another reason investors may have held back is that the large-scale farming they prefer—which emphasizes cutting-edge technology and less labor—is so often maligned. For example, opponents complain that large farms displace small farmers, promote monoculture, and harm the environment. Yet such criticism is deeply misplaced. Consider that countries with higher rates of agricultural labor per hectare of land incur poorer nutrition, lower education levels, and a lack of health care. For example, according to data provided by the World Resources Institute (WRI) and the UN Food and Agriculture Organization (FAO), countries with high intensities of agricultural labor (mainly in sub-Saharan Africa and much of Asia) also have undernourished populations. Conversely, across Europe and North America, where agricultural labor intensities are low, people are better nourished.[2]

Additionally, well-executed investments generate benefits that extend far beyond profits for the investor. These include jobs, local community investment, access to markets and goods, and tax revenues. Productivity also soars. Figure 6-1 depicts the clear benefits to yields when labor-per-land rates are low. To take some country-specific examples, FAO data indicate that Zimbabwe's agricultural population per hectare of arable land is more than 56 times greater than the United States, and China's 251 times as much, yet US corn yields are nearly double that of the Middle Kingdom and 11 times that of Zimbabwe.[3]

Fortunately, the advantage of scale is an emerging epiphany. It is even showing up in the views of the Indian Council of Agricultural Research (ICAR), an agency of the usually populist Ministry of Agriculture. At a July 2011 conference, ICAR's director-general described the profitability problem in agriculture by saying that "it is not farming, but the scale of holding

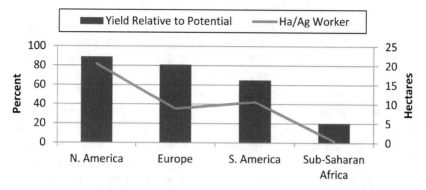

FIGURE 6-1   Yield Relative to Potential: Average for Four Major Commodities.
Source: World Bank Policy Research Working Paper No. 5588, March 2011.

that is not remunerative."[4] ICAR has acknowledged that India's average of 0.92 hectares per farmer makes agriculture inefficient.

Yet despite evidence that large-scale agricultural production delivers more food at a lower cost, it continues to bear a negative connotation. This is particularly true in rich countries, where food security is less of a concern. The common prejudice is that big is bad, while small is charming. The European Union has established a high-level commission to investigate competition in its food-supply chain after small farmer complaints about the market power of large retailers. The Obama administration has carried out a series of public hearings investigating the market power of large agribusinesses. And Washington's "Know Your Farmer, Know Your Food" initiative, spearheaded by the US Department of Agriculture (USDA), seeks to strengthen local and regional food systems by, among other things, encouraging small farmers and farmers' markets.[5]

Several skeptical members of the US Senate complained in a 2010 letter to the US Secretary of Agriculture that the USDA effort is narrowly aimed at "small, hobbyist, and organic producers . . . propping up the urban locavore markets whose customers generally consist of affluent patrons. . . ." Since less than 2 percent of farms generate over half of all US commercially used production, they complained that these "feel-good measures are completely detached from the realities of production agriculture."[6] However, the larger problem is that the whole marketing scheme is based on duping consumers into thinking that food from small and local producers is somehow fresher, safer, and environmentally friendlier without any basis in fact. It bears mentioning that the "organic" label came out of a political demand made by organic growers to Congress. Organic standards are based on recommendations from the organic foods industry itself via USDA's National Organic Standards Board, which is housed in the agency's Agricultural Marketing Service, and not in the Animal and Plant Health Inspection Service (APHIS) or any other science-based entity.

Small may be charming to the outsider, but in multiple surveys of farmers conducted by World Perspectives, Inc., in the United States and around the world, nearly all aspire to become larger. If you ask farmers—as I have—how many acres they would want to farm if capital were not a problem, they repeatedly give answers that exceed what they currently farm—two times the acreage for rice, three for corn and soybeans, and five for wheat. Importantly, advances in seed and the size of planting and harvesting equipment make large-scale production the competitive benchmark.

Moreover, scale has important implications in a rapidly globalizing world. For decades Japan has protected its small farms (their average size is 1.8 hectares) from import competition. The much larger and more important industrial part of the economy would benefit from Japan joining the Trans-Pacific Partnership trade negotiations—but this will require the government to undertake policies that enable shifts to larger farms. Toward that end, Tokyo has established a task force to look into the assistance needed to encourage larger farms with younger operators. According to Japanese press reports in 2011, the government is creating a 200- to 250-ha farm in Miyagi Prefecture with support from major technology companies, and major food retailers are forming alliances with farmers for larger-scale produce farms.

Fighting against Scale

The emerging investor interest in agriculture is viewed as exploitive and abhorrent by some critics, who claim it will worsen the condition of the poor. Anteneh Roba of the International Fund for Africa is typical of those who envision an investment approach that is very different from what made American agriculture successful. He admits that Africa has long suffered from "pestilence, famine, disease, and hunger," but then, contradicting himself, warns that intensive factory farming will ruin a traditional agricultural system that has "sustained Africa for millennia." He argues that "industrial agriculture is inherently less efficient at producing food than smaller sustainable farms," and that "sustainable farms require more workers and create more jobs. . . ."[7]

Such statements prompt one to recall a comment made by the American economist Milton Friedman decades ago. While visiting a Chinese canal project in the 1960s, Friedman was told that workers were using shovels instead of power equipment because it required more workers. He famously replied, "Then why don't you just give them spoons instead of shovels to create even more jobs?"[8] Of course, that is the problem: Agriculture currently supplies most of the jobs in poor countries, but its inefficiency concurrently starves too many people. Moreover, it squanders human talent on small, repetitive tasks at a time when the accumulation of knowledge and technology enables productivity and accomplishment in a wide range of pursuits. But the effort to keep out private investment capital, also known as divestment campaigns, is defiant when it comes to such facts. According to the nongovernment group GRAIN, a coalition of similarly minded groups successfully lobbied the California state teachers' pension fund to cut its planned investment in commodities by more than 90 percent.

Opposition to outside investment in agriculture—particularly investment associated with foreigners—is not new, and has long incited xenophobic reactions. Consider some of the laws that have been enacted in the United States: The Alien Land Act of 1887 was against European purchases in new territories, while the Agricultural Foreign Investment Disclosure Act (AFIDA) of 1978 required foreign investors in US farmland to register with the USDA. While fully permitted today, foreign farm ownership must still be registered under the AFIDA. At any rate, only about 1 percent of US land is owned by foreigners, mostly forest land historically controlled by Canadians. Even with a completely open investment system, the vast majority of farmland exchanging hands today in the United States is occurring between farmers.

Many countries are like the Ukraine, which remains highly restrictive of foreign ownership of farmland. In December 2011, Argentina's Senate voted 62 to 1 to prohibit foreign nationals from holding title to more than 2,500 acres, and limits the total farm area controlled by aliens to 15 percent. Other countries, like Pakistan, have invited foreign investment in their agricultural sectors in an effort to help fight double-digit food inflation, but have received only a modest response from international financiers.

As host of the G20 agriculture ministers meeting in June 2011, the French initially proposed a policy restricting the purchase or leasing of farmland in developing countries. After too many countries objected, the G20 settled for endorsing the work of various multilateral institutions. The main initiatives, which are discussed elsewhere in this book, are the World Bank–led Principles for Responsible Agricultural Investment, and the UN-led

Voluntary Guidelines for Responsible Governance of Tenure of Land, Fisheries, and Forests.

Much Ado about Nothing

In reality, despite recent investor interest in farmland, there is, at least as of yet, relatively little international private investment in large-scale agricultural production. A 2010 study prepared for the Organization for Economic Cooperation and Development (OECD) estimated current private capital investment in farmland and infrastructure at about $14 billion.[9] The following year, FAO Director General José Graziano da Silva described the purchase of farmland by rich countries in poor countries as "qualitatively important," but so far unimportant on a quantitative basis.[10]

To be sure, the general boom in commodities has been a bonanza for those developing countries with something to sell (that is, those exporting primary commodities). According to the UN, foreign direct investments in these developing countries ramped up between 2005 and 2008, with the aim of capitalizing on the global supply/demand situation (see Figure 6-2). Notably, however, most of this investment has gone into nonagricultural enterprises like Nigerian oil drilling, Chilean copper mines, and Jamaican bauxite pits.

As much as agricultural development agencies like the FAO would like to see outside capital flowing into developing-country agriculture, the agency concludes that "domestic and international corporate investment in agricultural production is marginal and contributes little to farm-level capital formation." It reports that such acquisitions comprise "no more than 1 percent of the arable land in the countries involved, a small amount in the global context."[11]

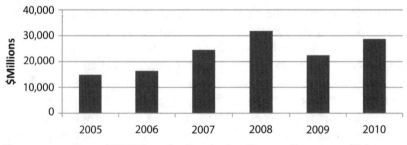

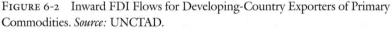

FIGURE 6-2　Inward FDI Flows for Developing-Country Exporters of Primary Commodities. *Source:* UNCTAD.

Investors have plenty of reasons to avoid agricultural production. These include high levels of risk, near-universal government interference in the sector, unclear property rights, and difficulties recovering capital investments involved in disputes. And then there is all the news ink being spilled about so-called land grabbing, with defenders of the poor decrying "agrarian colonialism."

Yet herein lies the irony. The FAO has estimated that developing countries will need $80 billion in new investment each and every year in order to reduce food insecurity. Given the fiscal position of most rich countries, the money will have to come from the very private-sector investment that is so strongly discouraged.

Reasons to Invest in Agriculture

Given the considerable obstacles, why should financiers bother to look to farming? There are in fact compelling reasons, both financial and policy-based.

Commercial Rationale

In 2008, the commodity price spike and associated warnings of food shortages drew the attention of many outside investors to the agriculture sector. From the money manager's viewpoint, large-scale agriculture (which involves large farming projects) enables the full and efficient application of current technology, and thus results in higher productivity rates (refer back to Figure 6-1). Additionally, as mentioned earlier, agriculture provides a hedge against inflation, and contributes to portfolio diversification. Furthermore, some investors envision real-estate value appreciation on an increasingly populated planet, and still others consider agricultural investments to be the perfect antidote to their otherwise glass-and-steel-encased urban lives.

Given the fundamental supply-and-demand situation, commercial investors can certainly visualize the financial returns possible. An already-malnourished world population will grow 50 percent larger, and hundreds of millions will rise to middle class status—with a commensurate increase in demand for animal-protein products. Surplus commodity stocks have declined, and food prices are forecast to stay above historical levels.

Meanwhile, land is limited and available prime production land is technically becoming scarcer. Capital flows to where it is rewarded the most, and nothing attracts investment better than a perceived market shortage. The converse occurred during the extended bear market in agriculture from 1996 to 2002. During that period, the industry was unable to attract either capital or talent. Instead, the information technology sector grabbed all of the money, talent, and headlines, while agricultural economists repeatedly warned that food-stocks-to-use ratios—the buffer against supply shocks such as drought—were declining rapidly.

Public Policy Rationale

Commercial investors also pay attention to what policymakers say and do. The G8 agriculture ministers meeting in Treviso, Italy, in April 2009 emphasized the "global challenge to reduce food emergency," warning that the lack of food could become a global security issue. The G8 specifically called for increased investments in agriculture from both public and private sources.

Crop demand, driven by demographics and increased wealth, is further increased by biofuels policies. Policymakers have actively primed biomass-based energy with both mandates and subsidies (nearly half the increase in demand for corn in recent years has been due to ethanol). Policymakers also warn that climate change will increase the need for biomass production. So long as the supply of food crops is undermined by their diversion for use in biofuels production, their demand will remain high.

Key Considerations for Agricultural Investors

Nonetheless, just because investors are won over by commercial or policy incentives does not mean they will gladly dive into farmland projects. There are several factors of agricultural production of importance to investors, all of which are weighed carefully prior to investors committing themselves to any investments. These are physical capital, financial capital, human capital, and geopolitical risk.

Physical Capital

Investors in real estate are fond of two adages about land: "They don't make it anymore," and "location, location, location." Concurrently, those in agriculture contend that trade in food is really trade in water, since the latter is fundamental to the former's production. Livestock-friendly areas constitute a third important component of successful agricultural production. All three elements are discussed in detail below.

First, more than any other sector, the success or failure of agriculture depends greatly upon where it takes place. Land is a necessary asset for meeting food and fuel demand, but it is also a limited asset; only a small percentage of the world's land is considered arable today. Additionally, as any agronomist will point out, not all soil is equally productive; different soil types befit different types of agricultural production. If land costs were undifferentiated, a commercial land investor would seek to acquire mollisol areas (that is, areas with naturally nutrient-rich surface soils that run deep with organic matter). Mollisol areas—which include parts of North and South America and portions of the former Soviet Union—will involve lower costs in terms of nutrient supplementation (such as fertilizer use).

However, in areas where market forces have been allowed to price land fully, the relative natural productivity of the soil is likely already capitalized into the land value. This means that a commercial land buyer must calculate the long-term cost of nutrient soil supplementation, the resulting yield (productivity), and thus the financial return for each potential soil type and its respective cost of acquisition.

Because soil type affects requirements for both mechanical and chemical energy (for example, natural gas used to produce ammonia as a precursor for inorganic nitrogen supplementation), poorer soil areas have tended to go fallow during times of high energy costs and/or low agricultural commodity values. However, energy and agricultural prices have more recently become intertwined, making marginal soil areas more economically viable, or profitable. Still, the ambition is to reduce cost relative to return. Therefore, many investors aspire for agronomic areas viable for the production of a valuable legume (such as soybeans) that naturally contributes to the binding of nitrogen in the soil, consequently reducing the requirement for costly supplementation with inorganic fertilizers.

The second critical physical asset for competitive agricultural production is water—a heavily consumed and increasingly precious resource. In sub-Saharan Africa, North Africa, and Southwest Asia—regions with high levels of population growth—more than 60 percent of surface water is allocated to human uses, with the majority going to agriculture. The UN report *Water in a Changing World* forecasts that half the world's population will be living in areas of acute water shortage by 2030.[12]

From the context of water availability, udic areas can offer suitable land for agriculture. These are regions that benefit from well-distributed rainfall and soils that store moisture at levels equal to or in excess of the amount lost to evapotranspiration, and can be found in the eastern United States, the rainforest areas of South America, Western Europe, China, and west central Africa. Ustic areas—found in parts of North and South America, equatorial and southern Africa, Europe, and Australia, and in much of India—may also be favorable for agriculture. Such land is characterized by moisture that is limited, but present during times and conditions suitable for agricultural production.

To be sure, water is transportable. With global climate change and associated water scarcity threatening future food production, there is an increased focus on irrigation. Regular and evenly distributed rainfall is not necessary to have a productive agricultural area like California's Central Valley. Irrigation enables farmland in semi-arid Idaho—with an average annual rainfall of less than 12 inches—to be valued at almost as much as farmland in Tennessee, which gets average annual rainfall amounts of nearly 50 inches.

What is notable is how extensively irrigation has been deployed in the two most populous countries of the world, China (55 percent irrigated) and India (90 percent irrigated), whereas in the world as a whole, only around one-third of arable land is being irrigated. Because irrigation systems have typically been expensive relative to the cost and value of the resulting agricultural production, deployment has usually been the result of government initiatives. And as governments are scaling up their planning for vast agricultural projects that will require extensive irrigation, businesses around the world are scaling up to manufacture the equipment; farm equipment manufacturer John Deere reportedly made acquisitions in 2008 to become the world's third-largest irrigation company.

Finally, since the number of people worldwide who under-consume protein exceeds the number of people who are hungry, investors are keen to look at the relative competitiveness of livestock-producing areas around the world. Livestock production systems are broadly distributed around the globe, though those considered concentrated animal feeding operations (CAFOs) are more pronounced in the United States and Europe, and are rapidly growing in China. There is also an increasing number of CAFO operations in Brazil and Argentina.

Livestock production is area-intensive, and requires land for pastures or for feed production. Since most agricultural land is presently fully utilized, the places considered likely for supporting increased future livestock production are generally forested areas—hence the concern that increased animal protein production will lead to more environmental destruction.

Financial Capital

Financial capital is important for any economic endeavor, and agriculture is a particularly capital-intensive industry. Moreover, capital and access to capital are not evenly distributed. Many businesses operate while utilizing borrowed capital. The greater the debt liability of a company relative to its assets, the larger the risk.

According to US Department of Agriculture data, US agriculture has a debt position (debt-to-asset ratio) of just 10.3 percent, which means it is flush with financial liquidity. By contrast, many agricultural producers in developing countries have very little access to credit, regardless of their equity position, and thus find it hard to make investments in their own business. Thus capital is a prime factor of production that the agricultural investor brings to the bargaining table.

Human Capital

Developing countries often assert that their advantage in production agriculture is an abundance of low-cost labor. However, in many cases technology trumps labor—the success of the Industrial Revolution being the broader case in point. This is the reason why economic growth calculations produced by the OECD utilize total factor productivity, which takes into account total outputs not caused by traditionally measured inputs. The cost of labor is relative to the cost and availability of technology, which varies by agricultural commodity or product.

As noted earlier, agricultural systems are generally the least efficient—meaning they produce the lowest amount of usable biomass per hectare—when the area per agricultural worker is lowest. Ironically, global and national policies are largely geared toward preserving the current volume of labor per hectare. Instead, investors assess human capital on the basis of three factors: cost relative to available technology, education, and entrepreneurship (culture).

Geopolitical Risk

The rule of law is extremely important to investors, and they must often weigh the geopolitical risk to their investments. Generally, investments in countries with the greatest geopolitical risk hold the potential for the greatest long-term gains or losses, while surer bets but lower returns can be found in less geopolitically risky countries. For example, farmland in the United States is already largely developed, has good transportation access, is very expensive, and has relatively small returns. Conversely, many poor countries have poor infrastructure, and land delivers suboptimal returns because of a lack of investment. If an investor successfully develops the land in such nations, there will be huge returns as the land's capacity is optimized. At the same time, given that the rule of law is often poorly developed in such countries, typically there are also high levels of risk.

In January 2012, the Association of Foreign Investors in Real Estate, with support from the University of Wisconsin's School of Business, issued an assessment of the emerging countries most desirable for commercial real estate acquisitions. The BRIC countries (Brazil, Russia, India, and China), and developing states closely associated with rich countries (Mexico because of its proximity to the United States and NAFTA, and Turkey because of its proximity to EU states and potential EU accession), were considered the most attractive.

Pursuing general real estate investment is quite different from pouring capital into agricultural land. Farmland with relatively low geopolitical risk (as in the United States or Europe) is already highly capitalized. Thus, investors in agricultural land must look at agronomic values as well as geopolitical risk. In its 2011 study of large-scale farmland investments, the World Bank used the Global Agro-Ecological Zoning methodology to find the best areas for farmland investment. The Bank's conclusion was that the most optimal countries are those with low-density populations and large areas of undeveloped arable land. The seven countries that best fit these parameters were Sudan, Brazil, Australia, Russia, Argentina, Mozambique, and the Democratic Republic of Congo.[13]

The Need for Caution

Since risk analysis is a key part of the due diligence required of all investors, the following four factors should be carefully weighed in addition to the four previous elements:

Volatility

Prices for undifferentiated agricultural commodities have fallen, but some economists argue that current price volatility is more the norm. Indeed, it is important to note that the entire history of commodity prices illustrates this volatility. The sector's volatility, including longer periods of low prices than high prices (the trough preceding the recent boom lasted 19 years, and the one before that lasted 11 years), is one of the factors that discouraged the interest of general investors in the past. Only in more recent times have sophisticated investors come to recognize that commodities add diversity to their portfolios and serve as a hedge against inflation.

Asset Depreciation Risk

Annual land value growth for 2010–17 is forecast at 3 percent, which is better than passbook savings but far below what investment bankers were previously promoting. Additionally, while commodity price fluctuations can be hedged, there is no formal farmland risk-management tool. Moreover, farmland asset-value decreases impose longer-term losses rather than one-off events. Land is less liquid, so losses must be endured.

Historical Experience

Anyone who has been around agriculture for a few years is understandably skeptical about the assertion that "this time it's different." The claim of a new era for agriculture is not new. A similar period of high agricultural commodity prices in the 1970s prompted investment in large-scale farms in both rich and poor countries. At the time, US Agriculture Secretary Earl Butz told farmers to "get big or get out," and he encouraged them to plant "from fence row to fence row."[14] However, it all came crashing down in the 1980s. The Commodity Research Bureau's grain index had hit a historic high of 330 in 1981, but plunged to below 160 by 1987. US farmland values declined by 30 percent or more, bankrupting many farmers. It took over 20 years for farmland price levels to recover.

Politics

The same policymakers beckoning the foreign investor can turn on the metaphorical dime if they sense strong objections from the people. Land, after all, is fraught with political conflict. Former FAO Director-General Jacques Diouf has wisely described foreign purchases of farmland as "a political hot potato."

Conclusion

Historically, agricultural land has represented a particularly difficult realm for the investor. The Swing Riots of 1830—when farm laborers protested, among other things, the use of horse-drawn threshing machines in Britain— were the agricultural equivalent of the riots led by the Luddites, the British textile artisans who in the early nineteenth century responded violently to the technological advances sparked by the Industrial Revolution.

Meanwhile, turning land over to foreign hands is undeniably controversial. Simeon Mitropolitski of the *International Real Estate Digest* has written that if you ask Russians what was worse, killing five million Ukrainian farmers in the 1930s or selling Alaska to the United States in 1867, you shouldn't be surprised by the answer. "For the Russians," he explains, "the selling of Alaska was a real crime because selling the land was selling their souls."[15]

And yet meeting the food requirements of a larger and wealthier world population requires scale and capital investment. Using smallholdings agriculture as a development policy is like promising an automobile to everyone in the world, but limiting construction to hand labor. The principles of industrialization and mass production for increasing productivity apply as much to agriculture as they do to nonagricultural goods.

In sum, investors have historically been wary of farmland—a sentiment that lingers today despite the new wave of corporate interest in agricultural production. Yet with public coffers depleted, private financing is essential for helping reduce global food insecurity. To encourage such investment on a greater scale, we must see it for what it is—relatively modest interventions to feed and employ the poor—and not for what is merely feared—a rapacious assault that is being waged on, or will be waged on, livelihoods and property.

Chapter 7

Improving Outcomes

RUTH MEINZEN-DICK AND
HELEN MARKELOVA

Large-scale acquisitions of agricultural land have become a hot and widely discussed issue, fueled by numerous media reports as well as increasing attention by the research and practitioner community since 2008. This trend has been associated with the image of wealthy food-importing nations that have the capital to invest in agriculture, but sparse land and water resources to produce enough food on their own. Biofuels expansion and speculative investment by domestic as well as foreign investors have also played a major role. These farmland deals, whether in the form of purchases or leases, have many economic, social, and political implications for both investor and host countries. The conjunction of land, food, and money has produced both strong interest in this topic and an emotive debate about whether these represent much-needed investment or a neocolonial "land grab."

However, a polarized debate on whether the deals are good or bad generates more heat than light. Instead of blanket pronouncements, what is needed is a careful examination of each case in terms of the social and environmental implications. In this chapter we discuss the nuance needed to go beyond the polarizing talk, and identify the elements that must be in place for land deals to enjoy beneficial as well as sustainable outcomes.

As Derek Byerlee's chapter in this book discusses in detail, foreign investment in, and acquisition of, land in other countries is not a new phenomenon.[1] However, the current wave of land acquisitions has a different scale, new drivers, and a new set of players. In the postcolonial era, the private sector was seen as the main actor in land acquisitions, generally buying land from private landowners in host countries. While private investors remain major actors today, many of the new deals are between governments (or sovereign funds), or involve governments backing private investments.[2] Moreover, although much of the attention has been on foreign investors, local elites also play a major role in that they are acquiring land, either by themselves or through joint projects with foreign investors.

The emergence of investor states represents more than just the appearance of a new actor; it is also indicative of the new drivers behind the land acquisitions. While the private sector has traditionally invested under the motivation of maximizing profit, often focusing on tropical commodities rather than on basic staple crops, food-security concerns are an important factor in many of the new investments, especially those by governments. Agricultural production constraints, growing demand, diminishing availability of arable land and water, bottlenecks in storage and distribution, and a lack of confidence in world food trade all culminated in the food-price crisis of 2007–8, and in increased concerns about the availability and price of food, even in relatively wealthy countries.[3] Yet the prospect of exporting staple foods from developing countries—where there are significant numbers of food-insecure people—raises questions about the deals, especially those occurring in countries where food aid is also being supplied.

In addition to food-security concerns, energy security is another driver of the recent land deals. With oil reaching over $100 a barrel in 2007–8, many countries have been seeking alternative sources of energy to increase long-term energy security and reduce oil imports. Governments in China, India, Brazil, the United States, and the European Union have enacted a number of mandates for the use of agrofuels in transportation fuels, guaranteeing a profitable agrofuels market and encouraging the private sector to invest in this area, and even providing financial incentives such as subsidies and tax breaks.[4] Both the food- and energy-security drivers have created a heightened focus on two types of crops: staples (wheat, maize, and rice) and agrofuels (such as jatropha), as well as crops like oil palm and sugarcane that can provide either food or fuel.

Proponents of these land deals claim that there is an abundance of arable land to be used for agriculture, and "unused" or "unproductive" land to be used for agrofuels cultivation.[5] However, in many cases these lands are already being used or claimed under customary or informal arrangements, even though these uses and claims are not always formally recognized by governments. This is especially the case in Africa, where up to 90 percent of land is under customary tenure: formally held as state land but used by communities, often for generations.[6]

In addition, even though the amount of arable but uncultivated land that is potentially available for expanded crop production is estimated to be about 445 million hectares,[7] half of these reserves are found in just ten developing countries, five of which are in Africa.[8] The availability of marginal and abandoned lands may increase this number, but there are often substantive reasons behind this availability, presenting real limitations for crop or agrofuels cultivation. For example, such land could suffer from inadequate water resources, inaccessibility to markets, or ecological unsuitability. Upon closer examination, many of these lands are also being used by rural communities for important livelihood activities such as animal grazing and the collection of fuelwood, biomass, and fruits.[9]

Opportunities and Threats

Proponents of large-scale investment in agricultural land point to a number of potential opportunities for both investors and host countries. However, there are concerns that this "win-win" outlook is unfounded and that such investments may not lead to agricultural development or benefit the host countries and their poorest citizens. This section considers the opportunities presented by the land deals as well as the threats they pose for the livelihoods of the communities where the deals are, or will be, happening.

The Promises of Agricultural Investment

Certainly the agricultural sector in the developing world requires more investment than is presently allocated. Such countries need an influx of capital and technology to stimulate rural economies, and in the face of domestic fiscal constraints, large-scale foreign investment appears to be an attractive means of acquiring such resources.[10] Many of the deals include provisions for infrastructure such as ports or roads, which are of interest to host governments and can be regarded as a benefit to the host country as a whole. There is evidence that increased investment in food and agrofuels production in the rural areas of developing countries can have important benefits for their economies, particularly in terms of boosting and modernizing the agricultural sector and reviving rural economies.[11]

Such revitalization would be important not just for domestic economies, which would benefit from the incoming capital, the development of new industries (such as agrofuels), and greater food availability, but also for rural communities by generating new farm and off-farm employment and opportunities for livelihood diversification.[12] In addition, investors would bring in new agricultural technologies, which many of the developing countries would not otherwise be able to develop or obtain due to low levels of spending on the agricultural sector.[13] In addition to the direct spillovers such as technology transfers, the benefits promised by some investors include the rehabilitation and upgrading of rural infrastructure (such as roads and bridges), the construction of new health facilities and schools, and even local capacity-building, all of which could contribute to increased yields and incomes, and thus, long-term poverty reduction. Finally, keeping in mind recent food-price crises, one could argue that the global economy could also benefit from such agricultural investments, because increased production would result in better world food-price stability.

The Danger Signs

Despite the potential opportunities that large-scale land acquisitions may present to host countries and rural communities, there are plenty of warnings that they may also be detrimental to the socioeconomic development of these countries. For example, many of the alleged major benefits, especially payments and infrastructure investments, go to the domestic economies at large, and investor companies are often granted general subsidies and tax breaks on such transactions. In order to assess the net benefits or losses for the livelihoods of resource-dependent communities, one must consider not only the benefits that may accrue to local people in terms of employment or increased output prices, but also any losses for people who were deriving their livelihoods from the land being leased or purchased.

In many cases, the question of possible benefits for local populations depends on the security of land tenure. If existing land users have secure land tenure and can negotiate with outside investors, then there is at least some compensation. Even in these cases, however, there are concerns about whether local landowners are adequately informed about fair prices or about the full implications of selling their land, and about their being subjected to undue pressure to transfer their land.[14] In Latin America, such sales are leading to high levels of land concentration in some countries. The experience of Central America during the coffee boom of the late nineteenth century, when land privatization policies led to the concentration of land in few hands, provides a cautionary tale.[15] Current commercial pressures on Latin American land have led to higher levels of land concentration than in the early 1970s, prior to agrarian reform.[16]

However, in cases where local communities' land tenure is not secure (such as when land is officially designated as state land and its users have only customary rights to it), negotiations are between the government and investors. Local people may have little say in the deals, and little compensation if they are forced off their land. This lack of attention to existing users who do not necessarily have formally recognized claims to land has already resulted in many evictions and contributed to landlessness and impoverishment, with documented cases of dispossession in countries ranging from Indonesia to Ethiopia and Peru.[17] Moreover, the lands often allocated for such use are those designated as "underutilized," but of crucial importance for mobile populations and women. Without formally recognized rights, these groups face a higher risk of displacement.[18]

In addition to unrecognized rights to resources, local resource users have low bargaining power and virtually no presence in the negotiations over land deals. Even though local and international civil society and media have been advocating on their behalf, the playing field remains very uneven—local consultations are not held, and deals are made without the informed consent of the resource users. As Alexandra Spieldoch and Sophia Murphy discuss elsewhere in this volume, women, in particular, are very often left out of the discussions over land deals, with little recognition of their rights, needs, and interests.[19] Even if some form of compensation is agreed upon, it becomes difficult to monitor investor compliance with the agreed terms of compensation and other proposed benefits for affected communities. The rapid pace at which many of these deals are being completed does not allow the time necessary to establish sound governance mechanisms, especially because of the international forces (such as high global food prices and increasing energy demands) at play.[20]

Shifts in climate patterns, demographic changes, and higher agricultural prices have raised the value of arable land (and water) everywhere, making the expected returns to land even higher.[21] This has increased both domestic and international competition for land, making it even easier for smallholders to lose their landholdings to more powerful actors. Those with better access to financial resources, whether large international corporations, foreign governments, or even domestic businessmen, are better able to secure access to land, further eroding the poor's access to resources.[22]

The place of smallholders in meeting future global food demand will be determined to a large degree by who is successful in gaining or retaining the rights to the land used for agricultural production. Land converted from smallholder production to plantation agriculture is unlikely to be transferred back to its former users, and within a generation farming skills may be lost. The transfer of extensive land areas to large mono-cropping systems therefore has profound and long-term implications for the economic and social structures of rural societies, and may significantly reduce the livelihood options of local land users.[23]

As discussed at length in this book's environmental impacts chapter, the ecological sustainability of land and water resources used in the deals is another important concern, especially considering the relatively short-term orientation of many investors versus the long-term outlook needed in considering the environmental impacts of land uses.[24] Large-scale intensive agricultural production can threaten biodiversity, carbon stocks, and the availability of land and water resources. Land that is perceived as "unused" is often in long-fallow cultivation cycles because its tropical soils are unsuitable for sustained intensive cultivation.[25] If the land is already marginal, more cultivation may lead to further degradation.[26] Moreover, irrigating these large plantations may divert water from local users or from environmental flows.[27]

Critically, large-scale land acquisitions may have a negative effect on the wider sociopolitical and economic context of the host country. There are documented cases, such as the Daewoo Logistics Corporation's (ultimately unsuccessful) plan to lease 1.3 million hectares of land in Madagascar, where negotiations over deals contributed to political instability and internal social conflict.[28] These types of acquisitions touch on the already politically contentious issue of land allocation and land rights, so they carry a possibility of exacerbating existing tensions. Besides, many of these developing countries are already net importers of food and receive large amounts of food aid. For example, the country with the largest World Food Program presence is Sudan. However, Sudan is also the site of some of the larger land deals and is letting investors export food crops grown in the country.[29] This raises concerns about the implications of land acquisitions for the internal food security of host countries, given that high-quality land may be diverted from local food production, livestock grazing, and other livelihood activities of local communities.[30]

Finally, World Bank research shows that large-scale investors are not necessarily more productive than smallholders. In many cases they are unable to develop much of the land they acquire, or cannot make a profit on the land that they are farming. The reasons for this include investors' lack of knowledge of the local environment; an underestimation of the complexity of farming; difficulties in establishing large-scale technologies in heterogeneous local environments; and the high costs of land clearance and of establishing necessary infrastructure. In addition, the volatile prices of oil and agrofuels, coupled with the difficulties of getting produce to market where there is inadequate infrastructure, have decreased returns to large-scale farming, especially in remote and "undeveloped" areas. As a result, many investors anticipate their greatest profits not from agricultural production, but from rising land prices. Their incentives are therefore to acquire land as cheaply as possible and hold it, without necessarily putting it into production. In the meantime, small-scale farmers and pastoralists who had been using the land have lost their livelihoods, and overall production may actually decrease.[31]

Beyond Polar Positions: Questions for Large-Scale Land Acquisitions

There are two major competing narratives that prevail in discussions about large-scale acquisitions of agricultural land. One is a "beneficial investment" narrative concerning investors bringing needed investment (and, in some cases, improved technology, farming knowledge, or rural infrastructure); generating employment; and increasing food production. The second is a "neocolonial land grab" narrative concerning investors expropriating local land with little local input, and growing crops that are exported directly— even when local people do not have enough to eat. The widespread media stories and growing debate over these two narratives have played an important role in drawing attention to the issue.

But the time has come to get beyond blanket pronouncements praising or denouncing the deals, and to look more closely at the specifics of each case. Because investors are negotiating deals, often at a rapid rate, the focus of policymakers and civil society needs to shift to what can be done to ensure that host countries and local groups can seize the opportunities and mitigate the risks associated with the deals. Asking the following questions about any deal can help assess the extent and distribution of benefits, and can provide the key to the long-term sustainability of the investments, which in turn can help investors, host governments, and local people alike.

Current Land Use

The starting point is to look at how the land is currently being used, including for agricultural production, pastoralism, or biodiversity conservation. Who are the current users? Are they communities or individuals? What other vital resources like water and forests are being used in conjunction with the land? If the land is fallow, then why is this so—is it unsuitable for agriculture, or is it being left alone for reasons of conservation? Is this land being used for purposes other than agriculture? A realistic comprehension of these questions is the foundation for understanding who will be affected, and for ensuring that the net benefits of investor involvement are not overestimated.

Land Tenure Arrangements

It is essential to look at current users' property rights. Are these individual or communal rights, and are they recognized by the state and outside investors? Are there any indigenous groups using the land under customary tenure, and if so what are their livelihood sources? Situations of customary tenure are especially prone to land expropriation in a manner that is considered legal under statutory law but illegitimate by local people. If the land is under private ownership, then existing users are more likely to have a say in the arrangements and to derive a benefit. In some cases indigenous people are especially disadvantaged; in other cases they may be better organized and have stronger land rights than more recent migrants or other poor households. Whatever the situation, if local rights are not respected, then there will be resentment and protests are likely to arise.

Proposed Land Use and Livelihoods

A realistic assessment of proposed investment patterns on the land is needed to gauge the likely scale of benefits from large-scale land acquisitions. And it is not only the scale of benefits that matters, but also the way the benefits will be shared. Therefore, it is important to ask if there are opportunities for smallholders to participate (such as through smallholder contract farming), and whether improved technologies will be shared with local farmers. Will the new land uses generate more and better livelihoods (through employment, contract farming, and increased local agricultural output prices), and will they generate more income than the income from previous sources?

Food Security

Food and energy security in investor countries is driving much of the current wave of foreign land acquisitions, but it is critical to look at the food-security situation in host countries and surrounding regions as well. Will the food produced on the land be exported (all or in part), or sold domestically? What happens if there are food shortages in the host country, and especially in the food-producing region? Exporting food while local communities go hungry not only harms local people, but is also likely to cause unrest, thereby undermining the sustainability of land deals.

Ecological Conditions

Understanding local ecological conditions is necessary in order to assess whether proposed productivity increases are achievable and sustainable, and whether they will impose positive or negative externalities. Why is land currently not under intensive cultivation? What are the production constraints? How realistic is it to expect that the investors' injection of capital and knowledge will spark sustainable production increases? Will there be land degradation over time, as usually happens when tropical forests are cut for cultivation? If irrigation is brought in, does that take water away from local communities? Is the irrigation likely to be sustainable, or will it lead to salinization over the long term? Will farming practices reduce biodiversity? The latter issue is a particular concern in forest areas, whereas the diversion of water is a particular concern in dryland areas. Environmental costs need to be weighed against any projected productivity increases, because such costs not only undermine the long-term sustainability of the farms in question, but can also cause harm to others outside the area of the land deal.

Transparency

One major problem with many of the large-scale land acquisitions is that they have been shrouded in secrecy, which creates suspicion and precludes local participation. It is important to ask in each case about the extent to which existing land users are informed about and involved in negotiations over the land deals. What compensation or share of benefits do they get? Free, prior, and informed consent will create greater legitimacy for land deals.

Terms of Agreement

The nature of the contracts and agreements shapes the distribution of benefits between the investors, the host government, and local people. Is the land sold or leased to investors? Leases, unlike sales, offer reversibility of arrangements and a revenue stream each year, rather than a lump-sum payment. However, short-term leases may not create a strong incentive for investors to consider long-term environmental sustainability. Are there other investments such as infrastructure development (like roads, bridges, and information and communication technologies) built into the terms of agreement? What revenues do the state and local people receive from sales, rentals, or infrastructure investment, and what tax relief or other incentives are offered to investors?

Enforceability

Agreements are one thing; delivering on them is another. Therefore it is important to consider what enforcement provisions are included in the contract. Who will monitor compliance and enforcement? What measures will be used as enforcement mechanisms? Are there arbitration or conflict-management institutions accessible to local people (who often lack the resources to challenge large companies in court)? Enforcement is especially problematic when there are large power asymmetries between investors, host governments, and local people, so credible measures are a necessity.

The Way Forward

Examining each of these factors can help policymakers, practitioners, researchers, and journalists to move beyond blanket pronouncements. Additionally, media coverage and civil-society campaigns to showcase the land deals that are relatively beneficial—and to shame those that are not—can help show investors that it is in their long-run interest to ensure that their investments are not just legal, but also legitimate. The next step beyond stopping bad deals is to try to ensure that all future large-scale investments in agricultural land are mutually beneficial. This requires the inclusion of the following elements:

- Transparency in negotiations and inclusion of all affected groups (including women).

- Respect for existing land rights, including customary rights (held under customary arrangements, as individuals or clans or tribes) and common property rights (jointly managed by community members under formal or informal arrangements).
- Sharing of benefits with local people, through employment, contract farming, and other mechanisms such that livelihoods are enhanced, not lost.
- Environmental sustainability of new production systems (as well as of new roads and infrastructure) to ensure that benefits continue to the next generations.

Ongoing efforts to develop an international code of conduct for large-scale acquisitions of agricultural land, as exemplified by negotiations over the UN-led Voluntary Guidelines on Responsible Governance of Tenure of Land, Fisheries and Forests, and over the World Bank–led Principles for Responsible Agricultural Investment, can provide an important mechanism for ensuring that these farming projects are economically, socially, and ecologically sustainable. (An agreement was reached on the Voluntary Guidelines in March 2012.) Widespread dissemination of these guidelines and principles will help prepare local people, host governments, and investors for constructive negotiations. It would be naïve to think that a code of conduct would level the power asymmetries, but even having such a code to appeal to can help in negotiations. Additionally, it will be important for the international community to push for adherence to such a code in investor countries as well as host countries, and for host governments to monitor and safeguard local people's rights.

However, international and national government structures alone are not sufficient. There will remain an important role for the media to ensure transparency on land deals, for researchers to document outcomes, and for civil society to keep pressure on investors, all in order to prevent unjust expropriation. Just as we need to look beyond blanket pronouncements about large-scale land acquisitions, we also need to look beyond simple prescriptions for their governance, and to engage with multiple types of institutions in order to foster sustainable and mutually beneficial increases in agricultural productivity.

Chapter 8

Regional Perspectives: Africa

CHIDO MAKUNIKE

Large-scale commercial farming in Africa such as that being contemplated and executed by many international investors today is not a new phenomenon on the continent. The economic component of colonization by European powers often included farming plantations. Sometimes this involved the growing of tropical crops for export back to the mother country. At other times, cash crops were grown for general export to raise money for the colonial project.

The introduction of colonial plantations left a mixed legacy in Africa. The positive aspects include the introduction of well-adapted new crops (such as maize), the commercialization of indigenous crops, the development of new markets and extension services for farmers, the introduction of innovations (such as fertilizers, pesticides, and mechanization), and the development and expansion of transportation networks and related infrastructure. On the other hand, the impacts of colonial plantations were considerably negative, as seen by labor exploitation (including low wages, long hours, no benefits, mistreatment, and even outright slavery), and by soil and environmental degradation from the implementation of intensive farming techniques, such as the use of chemical fertilizers.

After African countries started becoming independent in the 1960s, the plantation-style business model became hard to sustain. The management and technical aspects of the plantations had generally been kept exclusively in the hands of the colonists, so there was a sudden skills deficit after their departure. Almost-free or cheap labor, a key part of this farming model, was no longer politically tenable after independence, although today it continues to be a key feature of the large farms that remain. Fickle prices of global commodities and competition from other countries also contributed to the demise of large plantations in Africa.

So the idea of large-scale farming is not new to Africa, although it never took hold or became the dominant agricultural model. Only in a few countries—such as South Africa, Zimbabwe, Kenya, Egypt, and the Ivory Coast—did it really flourish and become a significant part of the economy. But even in these countries, the model has been under tremendous pressure in recent years and continues to evolve rapidly. It will survive, but in forms very different from how it was first introduced.

Today's large international agribusiness deals on the continent take a dangerously and naïvely ahistorical view toward investment in African farming. Such perspectives reduce the chances of win-win outcomes for these deals, thereby making them even riskier than they already are or need to be. The investor of today, wanting to take advantage of the tremendous and largely untapped agricultural potential of Africa, would be foolish not to study the history of the large-scale commercial farming model in Africa.

Sentiments about Land in Africa

In Africa, so many livelihoods, and entire cultural and economic experiences, are directly tied to the land—more so perhaps than on any other continent. Such strong ties in turn engender a strong sensibility about land that is poorly understood by many non-Africans, particularly Westerners. Yet regardless of how this view is perceived or judged—and to outsiders it can seem almost irrational—it is unwise for prospective farmland investors to ignore these sensibilities.

Large-scale investments of any kind are generally done in a very opaque fashion, with negotiations usually conducted secretly between outside investors and host-country officials. Ordinary citizens rarely obtain information on the intricacies of these arrangements. People may grumble and suspect all kinds of things about how these deals are concluded, but generally the schemes are far enough removed from the public consciousness for involved governments and investors to escape popular scrutiny.

This is the same sort of non-transparent spirit in which many of today's farming investment deals are being discussed. Take, for example, the leasing of 100,000 hectares of land from Mali to a Libyan firm in 2009. Local communities were never consulted, and yet the land involved had long been occupied and used by local agro-pastoralists.[1] No doubt, the principals involved in deals such as these believe that they can conduct their business far from public scrutiny, just like easy-to-conceal mining or infrastructure projects. But on the contrary—due to African sensitivities about land— negotiating deals in such an old-fashioned, back-room manner is foolish and dangerous. There are several reasons for this.

First, a big mine can be kept relatively fenced off, so that local communities know little about its goings-on and possible impacts on them. This is simply not possible with vast stretches of farmland.

Second, land with rich soil—the type of land that attracts investors—is typically already occupied and used by locals, even if done so poorly or sparingly. Given how recent the Western ideas of individual ownership and title to land are to most of Africa, there is almost always some community that claims ownership over the land, even if, legally and technically, it may now belong to the state.

So it is very difficult to appropriate a huge piece of farmland in any African country without sparking some sense of dispossession and displacement. Yet this outrage does not just result because of threats to or direct losses of livelihoods. One often hears in news reports that large percentages of African farmland may not currently be in use. Consequently, the Western approach to such land (or perhaps more fairly and accurately, the market-based utilitarian approach) might be characterized as the following: "What's the problem? They are not using it and are not equipped to use it, or capable of using it, maximally, in any meaningful commercial way. So if we take the land, give them at least some token compensation, and then develop the land and provide them with jobs and downstream opportunities, then surely that is a net gain for the natives that they should warmly welcome. So what is the problem? Why all the fuss?"

Such a reductivist approach captures the whole ethos of today's land deals. One must always keep in mind that for better or worse, African ties to the land transcend economic and utilitarian considerations. For example, occupying land that happens to be a community's ancestral burial ground will arouse passion and resentment. Even if this land has not been used for a long time, it still retains a very powerful traditional and symbolic importance for that community. As stated in the International Land Coalition's 2011 review of large-scale land deals across Africa: "Many African communities have a close connection with long-dead ancestors and are seriously traumatized when they are forced to abandon graveyards of their ancestors and other family members."[2]

Make no mistake: This sentimental/cultural tie to a particular piece of land does not necessarily mean that it is off-limits to economic and commercial development in perpetuity. Rather, when the community can be shown and convinced that using it for commercial purposes would definitely and significantly improve community well-being, cultural procedures can be employed to make it acceptable for this kind of use.

However, an investor who is ignorant or contemptuous of these sensibilities, and who brings in the bulldozers simply on the basis of a lease or title deed obtained in the capital city (which, in the view of some communities, may as well be another universe), will right away incur the enmity of the community, rather than its cooperation and support. What is required, and what I fear is often missing in the context of mega-farmland deals, is simple respect for those attached to the land—respect that communities are not used to getting from government bureaucrats and politicians (except during election time), or from most of the foreigners they have interacted with since the colonial era. Such respect is undoubtedly missing in Uganda, where, according to a 2011 Oxfam report, 20,000 locals have been displaced by a British firm intent on—ironically enough—planting new forests to improve the area's environment.[3]

For farming investments—more so than perhaps any other type of investment—the goodwill of neighboring and surrounding communities is essential for long-term success, particularly in terms of security of land tenure. It is simply good business to try and get these communities on one's side, rather than have them suspicious or resentful from the beginning. Indeed, governments and ordinary citizens in most African countries are eager for investments that produce new jobs and related economic opportunities. And there is a growing realization among even the most traditional people that in today's world, the value of land cannot just be evaluated on cultural, ancestral, religious, or sentimental grounds: the land can and must also be put to intelligent use in order to materially improve living conditions. Therefore, there is no wholesale objection to large-scale farming investment.

Nonetheless, the cultural, ancestral, religious, and sentimental elements cannot be ignored. Africa is currently in a state of transition between two approaches of land use and management. One is traditional and precolonial, while the other is newer and Western-oriented. The Africa of today is a hybrid of these two different paradigms. The extent and nature of the mix varies from country to country. Many of Africa's problems—not just those of agriculture and land use—derive from its considerable difficulties in finding the right balance between the old and the new.

Many failed interventions over the years have taught us that the transition to whatever will end up being the ideal mix of old/indigenous and new/imported cannot necessarily be forced or rushed. Some changes will take place faster and more easily than others. Synthesizing a new consciousness is not an easy, straightforward process that can be done according to some formula, as has sometimes been naïvely thought and attempted by governments or "development agencies." Yet many investors today only view the prospects of farming in Africa in narrow, shallow, and ahistorical ways. Such limited perspectives ignore the complex, messy realities that must be understood if investors' ventures are to succeed.

Researching and Respecting Local Sensibilities about Land

For agribusiness investors, acquainting themselves with African conceptions about land is a business-savvy strategy. Taking the time to do this as part of their due diligence will make them more knowledgeable and smarter. Incorporating this knowledge into a business plan helps protect this necessarily long-term kind of investment from social and political risks that may not be obvious at first glance.

Critically, investors should not let their relationships with African governments detract from efforts to focus on the needs of the people. After all, even in undemocratic countries, governments come and go. So while it is still wise—and in fact unavoidable—to engage governments, this must be done in a way that does not tie investment to the tenure of any particular ruling clique or administration. It is important that investments be secure, even as governments come and go.

When an investment is well researched and intelligently and sensitively structured to respect and benefit the people of a country rather than the politicians or the government, then it has a much better chance of lasting and thriving for the long term. I am not convinced that this is the way most of the highest-profile agribusiness deals we hear and read about are being done. Africans need and want local and foreign agribusiness investment for the potential economic benefits, but they also insist that the investments take into account and respect their sensibilities. They insist as well that such investments avoid the many perceived ills of the past. Whereas in a less informed and less free era these sensibilities could be ignored or suppressed, now it is just foolish—and a poor protection of one's investment—not to take these sensibilities into account. Investors should reflect on what has happened in Sierra Leone. There, in the fall of 2011, dozens of locals protested against the leasing of more than 12,000 hectares to a Belgian firm. These protestors, who blocked access to the land project, unsurprisingly claimed that they had never been consulted about the deal.[4]

Agribusiness Perspectives and How Africans Perceive Them

In agribusiness circles, "bigness" is a much-prized quality.[5] It is commonly accepted that economies of scale are the way to be competitive in a global farming environment of ever-more discerning consumers, greater competition, rising production costs, and tighter profit margins. So according to many subscribing to this worldview, the small- or medium-sized commercial farm is endangered. The African small-scale farmer does not feature on the commercial farming radar at all.

This position is implicit in the way today's proposed agribusiness deals are announced and discussed. The most naïve and uninformed investors talk about not just bringing in capital and expertise from abroad, but sometimes even managers and workers as well. While never stated outright, the presumption seems to be that, apart from the actual land, the African side has nothing to bring to the table.

One thinks here of another case in Sierra Leone. A Swiss company has acquired a 50-year lease to grow biofuels (for Europe) on 40,000 hectares in the country. Local farmers were promised 2,000 jobs—yet three years after the deal was concluded, according to those who have reviewed it, only 50 new jobs had been generated.[6] Similarly, the World Bank's *Rising Global Interest in Farmland* study identified a project in Mozambique that had originally promised 2,650 jobs—yet, by 2011, when the report was published, the deal had created only about 40 full-time positions.[7] The Oakland Institute, which in 2011 produced a report on 50 land deals across Africa, found that "not only are these foreign corporations failing to follow through on promises of jobs, in some cases they are actually taking jobs away from local workers by importing more easily exploitable immigrant laborers."[8]

It sometimes seems that Africans are expected to gratefully stand aside as investors take over the land, and to be satisfied with the small crumbs of a few low-wage jobs they may be allowed to obtain. In late 2011 the *Toronto Star* reported on the case of an Indian firm, Karuturi Global Limited, which has leased 300,000 hectares in Ethiopia. Land once used to grow teff—the country's staple grain—is now being used to grow food for export out of Ethiopia. Karuturi does not let locals use the firm's crop residues to feed livestock, and it has also carved an immense ditch on its farm (for draining purposes) that prevents locals from obtaining water for their livestock.[9] Deals structured in this Africa-dismissive way cannot be sustainable in the long term, no matter what guarantees are offered by the governments involved.

It is this unspoken—yet obvious to Africans—dismissive attitude that sparks worry and resentment about these deals and endangers their longevity and ultimate political and social viability. For many Africans, the underlying attitudes of these deals are reminiscent of all that was demeaning to them about colonialism—hence the charges of "neocolonialism" and "landgrabbing."

Seeking an Elusive Common Ground

It is quite understandable that investors, particularly those operating in as risky an area as farming, would want to control as many aspects of their operations as possible. After all, they want to develop and tweak every variable in their businesses for maximum productivity and profitability.

Consequently, there is a part of me that has no trouble understanding why investors would hope that, once they have successfully negotiated for the land, locals would largely step aside to let the financiers develop and run their investments in a way they believe is required for profitability, and as they have seen or experienced it work somewhere else. The reigning thinking about successful agribusiness models imposes fairly narrow and specific restrictions on what is required for success. Today, the criteria for such success revolve around not just the large-scale, but also the mega-scale, in terms of land size, capital investment, tons-per-hectare output, and so on.

This is all very well, and there are probably some situations where these narrow, tightly controlled parameters offer the route to success. Such discussions are controversial, and they comprise a part of the bitter and ongoing ideological debate about the "best" model of farming in the world today. This debate revolves around the mixed concerns of global food security, food affordability, environmental and social justice, and the natural and understandable profitability worries of agribusiness. These issues lurk at the edges of the debate about large-scale agricultural investment in Africa. Some of the most vociferous opponents of these mega-farming deals object to them primarily on the grounds that the model exploits locals; is based on input-intensive farming that pollutes the environment; and is part of an evil conspiracy by a few dominant global agribusiness players to control the world's food supply and to put their own profits above the world's food-security, food-accessibility, and food-affordability needs.

Agribusiness deals can in fact be beneficial for all parties, and can take approaches that are more practical than ideological. Ultimately, however, overseas farmland investment is such a big and intricate issue of so many different local variables that there is no "one-size-fits-all" solution to how farming can and should be done to try to accommodate all the various parameters of farming's importance to mankind.

Partnering with Small-Scale African Farmers

Nonetheless, in the African context, it is important that prospective agribusinesses broaden their thinking about achieving economies of scale. One alternative to the directly controlled plantation model is for the investor to partner with hundreds or thousands of small-scale farmers, who serve as contract growers. There are some crops for which this may not be well-suited, but there are many others for which this can work very well. For example, the Kenya Tea Development Agency employs more than 560,000 contract growers—making it one of the largest such schemes in the world.[10]

The biggest hurdle to this idea of agribusiness partnering with small-scale farmers is not so much the difficulty of making this model of commercial farming work, but rather the large paradigm shift required on the part of investors. For instance, contract-grower models necessitate more research and community involvement than investors may be accustomed to or are interested in. Additionally, farmers will need training and other kinds of technical (and sometimes material) support. Investors may not have the patience to make this type of commitment to farmers, given that they are used to having large groups of tightly controlled laborers who can be hired and fired at will.

This is far from a perfect model, and its successful implementation requires patience and a different way of thinking. Additionally, there is considerable potential for one or both parties to exploit the arrangement, as has often occurred in Asia[11]—a reality that illuminates how goodwill on both sides is essential for success. A case study from Rwanda, for example, concludes that local farmers involved in a project with the Madhvani Group, a large Uganda-based sugar firm, earned less income than they did before signing on to the project. Out-growers were unhappy with the conditions imposed on them, while laborers cited poor labor conditions.[12]

Nonetheless, if done right, the potential benefits are considerable for the farmers, for the host countries, and particularly for the companies willing to make this investment. For example, if the investor partners with neighboring farmers, his or her need for landmass and labor is drastically reduced, particularly as contract farmers become more experienced at producing according to specified quality standards and as the partner farmers become yield-productive. These farmers are business partners who are not under the agribusinesses' direct control. But in return for giving up this control, the investor has relieved himself or herself of considerable management and other headaches of having a large labor office. Additionally, the productivity of the contract farmers will obviously vary, but the agribusiness only pays for product that meets specified standards and so does not directly carry the financial and business risks of low productivity.

Farmers gain under this model as well. Given that they interact with the agribusiness as independent businesspeople, they tend to be highly motivated about making an income. Additionally, the farmers are welcome to grow crops for themselves or other suppliers during off-seasons or at any other time. According to Nicholas Minot of the International Food Policy Research Institute, there are several documented cases of contract farming schemes in Africa that have proven highly beneficial to small farmers. These include 10,000 contract growers of vegetables in Madagascar, who have enjoyed "higher and more stable income than similar farmers," and 32,000 contract growers of groundnuts in Senegal, whose incomes are "55 percent higher than other similar farmers."[13]

When this arrangement works well, a huge additional benefit for the investor is that the community begins to see its own best interests tied up with the success of the enterprise. Not only does this have positive implications for the investor's bottom line, but it also provides long-term social and political protection for investments that can transcend legal documents.

Conclusion

Investors are likely to get burned if they view Africa as an agricultural blank slate on which they can simply write whatever primarily suits them or is convenient for them. African agriculture does indeed offer great potential and exciting opportunities, but only for the smart investor who is willing to do his or her homework diligently in order to stay well clear of the many potential pitfalls. Investors need lateral, outside-the-box thinking—perspectives which, for example, embrace partnerships with small-scale farmers—in order to maximize their engagement with farming in Africa.

Chapter 9

Regional Perspectives: Asia[1]

RAUL Q. MONTEMAYOR

Foreign investment in agricultural ventures is not exactly a new phenomenon in Asia.[2] Large banana and pineapple plantations carrying well-known foreign brands have been operating in the Philippines since the early 1900s. Malaysian agribusiness firms have long expanded their production of palm oil, rubber, and similar industrial crops to nearby countries like Indonesia and the Philippines. In fact, many of the haciendas and plantations that still exist in the region today trace their roots to the colonial period when spices, tea, rubber, and other tropical products were shipped in large volumes to Europe and other overseas markets.

The last few years, however, have seen a distinct spike in the number, scope, and magnitude of investments involving foreign entities in farmland and agricultural ventures. According to estimates published by the International Land Coalition (ILC) in 2012, publicly reported land deals in Asia cover a total of 43 million hectares (ha).[3]

Make no mistake: Large-scale farmland investments in Asia are not exactly overwhelming Asian agriculture, and it is important to emphasize — as the ILC does — that many of those 43 million hectares have not yet been transferred to foreign investors. Indeed, according to a 2011 study of the phenomenon in the Philippines, "Mostly, the new wave of foreign investors seeking land is still doing just that: seeking. There are only a handful of operational projects, largely in the fruit-export sector."[4]

Nonetheless, while relatively few projects are actually operational, there is a flurry of negotiations under way throughout the region between eager investors and equally enthusiastic host governments.[5] Additionally, the deals that have been finalized have sparked controversy (several of them are highlighted in this chapter), with more likely on the way. This chapter identifies the major motivations for undertaking farmland investments in Asia, explains the different modes for these deals, and assesses the actual or potential effects of these investments on host countries in the region. The last section provides some recommendations for managing this trend so that it can approximate a win-win situation for all parties concerned.

Drivers of Overseas Farmland Investments in Asia

In Asia, as in other regions, large-scale land acquisitions are motivated by a variety of factors, particularly those related to commercial interests and food security.

Commercial Motivations

The most common and logical rationale for undertaking overseas farmland investments is commercial in nature. Asian countries may provide the best agro-climatic conditions for producing certain crops, offer significantly lower labor costs, or proffer other competitive advantages that enable investors to maximize profits and financial returns.

Foreign agribusiness investors could also be in a better position to tap nearby domestic markets and to react promptly to market developments if they locate their production and processing activities closer to the demand areas themselves. Agribusiness opportunities abound in Asia, where many countries simultaneously have burgeoning populations, increasing consumption trends, and limited capacities to produce food and supply it to consumers.

In Asia, the reasons for this limited ability to produce and supply food are varied. There is a lack of rural infrastructure—such as roads, irrigation, and ports—which makes the transport of inputs and products difficult and expensive. Rural credit is also a major problem, and consequently farmers scrimp on inputs and so suffer lower yields. Furthermore, due to poor marketing systems, farmers are vulnerable to price volatility and manipulation.

Globalization and the gradual removal of both trade and investment barriers at the international level have made it easier for companies to relocate their supply bases and to pick production areas where they can enjoy optimal tariff- and other trade-related incentives for both their imported inputs and exportable products. An American investor who locates his or her production in a member country of the Association of Southeast Asian Nations (ASEAN) could theoretically benefit from zero-tariff privileges for almost all agricultural products sold to other countries within the ASEAN free-trade area.

The shift toward freer trade regimes has also intensified competition among agribusiness entities, leading many to look for ways to cut costs, improve quality, and gain other competitive edges over their market rivals. Vertically integrating production with processing and marketing operations has become a popular way not only to ensure timely and consistent access to quality raw materials, but also to secure them at potentially lower costs without having to go through manipulative middlemen and assemblers.

Food-Security Motivations

Food-security concerns have emerged relatively recently as a second significant driver of overseas farmland investments. In fact, before the onset of the 2007–8 global food crisis, it was the interest in biofuels that was prompting countries to look for vast tracts of land where they could plant biofuel feedstock. That 2008 crisis, and warnings that similar crises could occur in the near future, have understandably led many countries, particularly those with limited production assets and food-sufficiency capabilities (these include the Asian nations of China, India, Japan, and South Korea), to find new ways to secure access to food for their own populations. Dire warnings about climate change and the future availability of arable land, water, minerals, and other natural resources, on the one hand, and projections that global food requirements will double by 2050, on the other, have further fueled the sometimes-frantic move to secure productive areas offshore.

The impulsive reaction of some countries to impose export restrictions during the food crisis also led many governments to rethink their food-security strategies and to develop contingency measures in case their traditional trading partners are unable or unwilling to supply them with food during future emergency situations. The specter of not only very high food prices but also an actual unavailability of food in the future has induced many government leaders to resuscitate and revitalize their food self-sufficiency programs, and in some cases, to look to offshore food production as an additional safeguard against food riots and other sociopolitical disturbances that may ensue during future food crises.

Further Motivations: Health and Geopolitics

In the Asia context, profit margins and food security do not constitute the sole motivations for farmland investment. Take, for example, public health. The increasing incidence of food contamination, animal diseases, and food-borne toxins have prompted food-safety-conscious countries like Japan to curtail imports of vegetables and other vulnerable farm products from traditional foreign suppliers. In turn, Japanese agribusiness firms have been encouraged by their government to directly undertake and supervise the production of these commodities in foreign countries, and then to process and ship the commodities back to Japan using strict hygiene- and sanitary-related protocols and processes.

Additionally, some Asian governments have used foreign land investments as a tool to pursue their geopolitical objectives. The Indian government, for example, has reportedly encouraged investments in Burma partly to control border tensions and to mitigate the inflow of illegal immigrants into India. For very similar reasons, back in 2003 Thailand spearheaded the Ayeyawady-Chao Phraya-Mekong Economic Cooperation Strategy as a framework for cooperation with Burma, Vietnam, Cambodia, and Laos. Thailand's intention was to generate regional growth, create employment, and reduce income disparities—in order to help address the causes of conflict and cross-border migration between the countries. Finally, China has used its financial resources to expand its sphere of influence, encouraging Chinese state and private enterprises to undertake agricultural investments in other countries, often coupling these with official development assistance and concessional loans.

Modes of Overseas Farmland Investments in Asia

Most countries in Asia have constitutional and other regulatory limits on foreign ownership of land and similar natural resources. Malaysia, which does allow foreigners to directly acquire agricultural land, is an exception. In addition, the Philippines has a land-reform program that imposes restrictions on the sale, transfer, or leasing of land from program beneficiaries to other parties.

Leasing Land

Because of these constraints, the easiest and most common mode by which a foreign entity can undertake overseas farmland investments is by leasing land. Many Asian governments have facilitated this type of investment by entrusting ownership or control of large tracts of public land to certain state agencies, which in turn lease them to foreign corporations. In Cambodia, for example, foreigners must secure an Economic Land Concession (ELC) from the Ministry of Agriculture, Forestry, and Fisheries. According to a 2009 German study, about a million hectares of state land (more than 5 percent of Cambodian territory) was granted to investors through ELCs between 1998 and 2006.[6] Of the 58 projects authorized by ELCs, 26 were managed by foreign investors, comprising a total area of about 300,000 hectares. Most of this foreign investment is undertaken by China (with about 200,000 hectares in land holdings) and other countries based across continental Asia.[7]

Meanwhile, in Laos, investors can acquire a variety of tools to lease land, including land titles, land-tax declarations, and village-head certificates of land ownership. This variety of instruments, together with a weak land-registration system, has led to widespread confusion and conflicts over boundaries, and has also made occupants vulnerable to manipulations by land speculators and investors. As in Cambodia, most of the land investors are from elsewhere in Asia (in fact, such patterns of intraregional investment prevail throughout Asia) — though due to stricter rules on the size and types of land that can be allocated, hectarages are smaller.

The amount of land that can be leased varies by country and type of agricultural activity. In the Philippines, there are generally no limits on the size of areas to be leased. In Cambodia, ELCs can normally allocate up to 10,000 ha per project. Investors can lease a maximum of 2,023 ha in Burma for plantation crops, while the limit for seasonal crops is 404 ha. Leases of land of up to 20,234 ha or more can be allowed in special cases, but need the concurrence of higher authorities. Provincial governments in Laos can approve the lease of lands not exceeding 100 ha, while national government agencies are authorized to allot up to 10,000 ha to investors. There may be some restrictions on the conversion of Asian lands from their original uses, or in the case of the Philippines, the transfer of rights to third parties by land-reform beneficiaries.

Lease rates and payment terms also vary by country and type of project. In Burma, rental fees for fallow lands devoted to perennial crops range from $3 to $6 per hectare per year, while lands used to plant crops in the dry zone are charged $6–16 per hectare per year.[8] Private landowners in the southern Philippines are typically enticed to lease their lands to banana and pineapple plantations for 25–50 years, with rentals averaging $400 per hectare per year paid in lump sum every five years.

Joint Ventures and Partnerships

Another option is for the foreign entity to enter into a joint venture or similar business partnership with a domestic corporation, which then fronts as the lessee of the farmland in question. Joint ventures may allow easier and more trouble-free access to land, while potentially enabling the partnership to reap tax advantages and other incentives normally enjoyed only by domestic enterprises. A possible drawback of this arrangement is that the foreign investor has to share control and profits from the project with local business partners.

In the Philippines, joint ventures are encouraged thanks to the government's emphasis on agribusiness development. Foreigners can form joint ventures with local investors and register their partnership as a domestic corporation. So long as 60 percent of a project's stocks are owned by Philippine nationals, each investment can own up to 1,000 ha. In practice, however, exceptions may prevail with foreign stock ownership. According to one researcher, the Philippine government admits that investors can enjoy 100 percent "foreign-owned activity" on land characterized as "idle, unproductive, or marginal."[9] This likely means not actual ownership—the Philippine constitution bans foreign land ownership—but rather effective control over land for a long period via a lease contract with the government.

Contract Growing

In some instances, foreign investors enter into contract-growing arrangements. This involves the engagement of local farmers to produce certain commodities and raw materials for an agribusiness firm. For example, according to a researcher's interviews with a Philippine agent of a foreign investor in the Philippines, a Mideast financier and a Philippine broker concluded a lease agreement for a banana plantation with a group of Philippine agrarian reform beneficiaries. The agreement awards an annual income to these beneficiaries to work the land in question.[10]

The terms of contracts in these contexts are flexible. In some cases, the firm merely commits to buy from the farmers at pre-agreed prices and terms.

More frequently, the firm provides a much wider range of support services, such as training and technology dissemination, extension services, and the use of farm equipment and facilities. The firm also usually advances the costs for planting materials, farm development, and inputs; in some cases, it arranges for loans on behalf of the producers, using a purchase order from the firm as a collateral substitute. Producers commit to deliver and sell all their output to the firm at pre-agreed terms and conditions, and get back the balance of their sales after deductions for advances and other fees are made. Normally, contract-growing agreements are shorter than lease arrangements and can range from a single crop cycle to at least five years for longer-gestation crops. One variation is the "2 + 3" scheme in Laos, where the farmer contributes land and labor and gets 70 percent of the income from the venture.

Interestingly, contract growing has also become more popular in some Asian countries, but for a rather perverse reason—as a way for agribusiness firms to insulate themselves from labor problems and obligations. In the Philippines, where labor unions are typically active and aggressive, a number of plantations have terminated their lease contracts and entered into contract-growing arrangements with the employees from whom they originally leased the lands. Area expansion is undertaken by recruiting new contract growers, often pirating them from other plantations, instead of leasing additional tracts of land and having to hire more employees as a result.

Contract growing has been increasingly promoted by governments as a fairer and more equitable mode by which small farmers and landowners can engage in business partnerships with investors. Unlike in land-leasing arrangements, contract growers retain some control over their own lands. There is also an opportunity and incentive for the contract growers to be productive, since they can be paid more if they are able to improve their yields and/or quality. And since they are relatively short term, contract-growing agreements allow landowners to negotiate for better terms on a recurrent basis.

Troubling Implications of Overseas Farmland Investments in Asia

There are many significant benefits that can be gained from foreign investments in agricultural ventures in Asian countries. Investments, particularly in rural areas, can have high economic multiplier effects and may generate much-needed employment, tax revenues, technology transfer, and infrastructure and communication services; in so doing, they also improve the access of local farmers to markets and input supplies. It has often been argued further that farmers are better off leasing or selling their land, or working as paid laborers on their own land, rather than continuing to live marginally through subsistence farming.

However, the rapid encroachment on small farms due to overseas farmland investments is raising many eyebrows and warnings because of potential—and, increasingly, actual—disastrous side effects.

Displacement

One common concern has been the large-scale and long-term displacement of small farmers from their land. This is true even when public lands such as forests are leased to agribusiness ventures, since these areas are invariably populated by settlers, indigenous tribes, or other undocumented occupants who have been forced to move out of lowlands. Even when leased public land is largely unoccupied, farmers and landowners on adjacent private plots are often targeted and lured into leasing their land as the agribusiness firms expand their operations and look for areas that are already cleared and arable. Additionally, once foreign investors signify their intentions, it is inevitable that local speculators and opportunists will take advantage of unsuspecting landowners by surreptitiously acquiring control, if not outright ownership, of the latter's land so that the former can later resell the rights over the properties and make huge capital gains.

Given recent history, there is good reason to fear displacement in the Philippines. In the late 1980s and early 1990s, reports abounded of small landowners there being pressured and intimidated into involuntarily leasing their land when Malaysian investors were setting up palm oil plantations in the country's southern reaches.[11] In some parts of the southern Philippines, local agents of palm oil agribusiness investors have been suspected of hiring goons to harass uncooperative landowners. Elsewhere in the Philippines and in other parts of Asia, rogue elements have reportedly been let loose to sow terror in target areas, forcing frantic settlers to evacuate their homes and farms, and making them easy prey for opportunists—who have readily offered to lease the settlers' land in exchange for advance rental payments.

Landlessness is widespread in the Philippines' rural areas and in many other Asian developing countries that have large rural populations dependent on farming. Oftentimes, available land is limited and concentrated in the hands of a small elite. Many settlers who have been innocently cultivating land for generations still do not have firm titles to support their occupation, and can easily find themselves suddenly eased off their land by investors and prospectors who have managed to secure legal titles.

This scenario vividly plays out in Cambodia today. Here, there are reports of farmers losing their lands to companies supported by local politicians and government officials, sometimes without receiving any compensation. The operations of the Phnom Penh Sugar Company, a Cambodian corporation owned by a local politician in partnership with Thai and Taiwanese investors, have affected more than 1,050 families, according to local informants.[12] The company, boasting 9,500 ha in land concessions, has cleared an expanse of land planted with trees, bamboo, rice, and other food crops. Some of this land had been grassland used for grazing by local farmers' cattle and buffalo. Several women farmers have spoken of losing more than half of their modest plots, receiving no compensation, and being denied employment, despite earlier promises from the firm.[13]

Displacement is often fueled by special accommodations given to overseas farmland investments that contradict domestic policies and program thrusts. Some Cambodian farmer leaders, for example, question why established national regulations that encourage farmers to protect and preserve forests are conveniently set aside to enable foreign firms to convert these protected areas into large-scale plantations. In the Philippines, the government has actively wooed foreign investors to establish agribusiness ventures on large tracts of land owned by land-reform beneficiaries. This has raised concerns that tenants newly emancipated by land reform could once again become laborers on their own land in a veritable "land-return" process, putting to waste the long struggle of acquiring land from recalcitrant absentee landowners.

One-Sided Contracts

The one-sided nature of contracts is another common concern. This was a major issue in the Philippines in the past, when farmers and other landowners signed contracts that ceded control of their land to agribusiness investors. Such transactions occurred during the 1980s and 1990s, a period when banana, pineapple, oil palm, and other types of plantations—some of them partly foreign-owned—started expanding in the Philippines.

For example, some of the long-term lease agreements from this period exempted investors from any meaningful liability in case their agribusiness ventures prematurely folded.[14] Some even included a clause obligating the lessors to pay the investors for any permanent improvements that stay on the land, such as irrigation canals, at the time the lease contract expires. The lease agreements have also effectively ceded full control over the land to the agribusiness firms over extremely long periods of 25–50 years, with very little room for landowners to maneuver and with few means to address their grievances. Landowners who have leased their properties to agribusiness companies, for example, are explicitly banned from introducing any improvements or planting any crops on their own land without the express consent of the lessee firm.

The issue of one-sided contracts also cropped up when agrarian reform beneficiaries in the Philippines (to whom many plantations were transferred) ended up leasing back the lands to, or entered into contract-growing arrangements with, the former owners of the plantations. In their haste to consummate the agreements and get advance payments, the reform beneficiaries signed the contracts without any legal advice or detailed negotiations. The Department of Agrarian Reform eventually had to step in to protect the land-reform beneficiaries.

Though such developments occurred in the past, it is not far-fetched to assume that similar problems could arise with the agribusiness investments being scoped out in the Philippines today. In fact, many of the lands currently being eyed in the country are agrarian reform areas, including large tracts of land in predominantly Muslim areas of the southern Philippines. The government often justifies the need for land investments in these violence-ravaged areas by saying that such projects can help promote peace in the region.[15]

One could intuit that contract growers may have more leverage vis-à-vis the agribusiness firms than do outright lessors, since the former's agreements are relatively shorter and they retain some form of control over their land. However, their contracts are often worded such that contract growers are effectively also just workers on their own land.[16] Inputs are supplied exclusively by the company, and contract growers have to strictly follow the company's prescriptions on what, when, and how to plant and maintain crops. Additionally, they are legally bound to sell all of their products to the agribusiness firm on terms that have been negotiated in advance. Because the contract growers are usually not well organized, they generally end up with an agreement that is stacked in favor of the firm. Indeed, the deal mentioned earlier—in which a Middle Eastern investor and a Philippine broker concluded a deal with reform beneficiaries on a banana plantation—is troubling in that the reform beneficiaries working the land receive none of the land's production; are responsible for production input costs; and must meet "volume and quality obligations."[17]

The only bright spot stems from the rising number of contract growers. As more and more agribusiness companies go the contract-growing route, they will have to find a way to attract and retain the required number of contract growers in order to ensure their supply of products. This in turn gives contract growers some leverage in bargaining for new and better contract terms.

Farmers' Welfare

A final concern is the welfare of the small farmers and landowners who have leased or committed the use of their land to foreign agribusiness enterprises. As noted earlier, many in the Philippines have been enticed with advance rental payments averaging about $400 per hectare per year (paid as a lump sum at the start of each five-year period). Assuming a farmer has leased two hectares, this rental payment would amount to a little over $2 per day. Arguably, even a low-technology farmer could easily generate as much if not more income per day on his or her own two-hectare farm. One can only speculate about how much more wealth and output small farmers could generate if they were provided with just the basic levels of support by their government, and about the opportunities in life they and their children have missed out on by opting to cede their land to investors and consequently being relegated to workers, if not squatters, on their own property.

In addition, the promise of full-time employment with agribusiness ventures is not guaranteed. Farmers may be too old, or their children may not qualify for work on the plantations. (In Cambodia, one farmer claimed that the Phnom Penh Sugar Company, after seizing nearly half of her three-hectare plot, rejected her request for employment because of her age.[18]) Agribusiness firms are usually highly mechanized, have low labor-to-land ratios, and will always be on the lookout for ways to cut costs, including the cost of labor. Many periodically hire workers on a casual or contractual basis, lay them off after a prescribed period, and then rehire them on the same basis in order to avoid having to pay mandated benefits to regular employees. The perceptible trend in the Philippines toward contract growing and labor subcontracting is, in fact, seen to be primarily a strategy of agri-based companies to reduce their employee-related costs and obligations, to subvert the power of unions, and to acquire the flexibility to reduce their workforce without having to worry about retrenchment and retirement costs.

Risks to Community Stability: Ethnic and Environmental Considerations

Large-scale farmland acquisitions in Asia have not sparked Madagascar-like scenarios—where public anger over a Korean corporation's agricultural mega-investments helped overthrow the government—yet they do present serious social threats. For example, the introduction of large-scale projects may necessitate an injection of immigrant labor, which could spark or heighten ethnic and cultural tensions between local residents and outsiders. This is ironic, given that several Asian land-acquiring nations are undertaking farming abroad to avoid bringing immigrant labor into their own countries. Indeed, this dynamic helps explain Malaysia's investments in Indonesia and the Philippines (though reduced land availability and urbanization in Malaysia also play a role).

For an example of land acquisitions and concerns about ethnic tensions, consider the case of the Saudi Binladen Group in the town of Merauke in Indonesia's Papua province, which is home to a separatist insurgency led by ethnic Papuans. The company has been granted 1.2 million ha of land in an area known as the Merauke Integrated Food and Energy Estate, an area set aside by the Indonesian government for food production by foreign and domestic investors.[19] Activists warn that this arrangement could expand Merauke's population almost fivefold, from 175,000 to 800,000 people, and exacerbate ethnic tensions and conflicts in the area due to an influx of non-Papuans expected to be brought in as laborers for the farming projects.[20]

Another threat is environmental. Foreign agribusiness investments invariably exploit local natural resources like water, to the detriment of farmers and residents located near the area of operation. Banana plantations require huge amounts of water for both production and processing. In the Philippines, some plantations have actually taken over irrigated rice areas purposely to secure access to much-needed water, and have in the process reduced the availability of irrigation water to the remaining rice farmers in the area. There have also been reports that the large-scale planting of non-indigenous wood species has started to affect the biodiversity and ecological balance in forest areas in Laos and Cambodia. Additionally, timber species like eucalyptus have allegedly strained local aquifers because of their voracious absorption of underground water and nutrients.

Furthermore, agribusiness projects may employ fertilization and pest- and insect-control methods that pollute adjacent water and air resources and could be toxic to nearby residents. Many large plantations employ aerial spraying of insecticides, which may contaminate non-targeted areas. Poisonous pesticides sprayed on plants may find their way into aquifers or irrigation canals, and end up harming people who eventually use the water for drinking or farming.

Unless properly monitored and regulated, agribusiness investors will fully exploit land and other natural resources in their drive to generate returns over short periods of time. The application of massive doses of inorganic fertilizers and inputs, deep plowing, radical recontouring of soils, and year-round planting could eventually render the land barren, infertile, and essentially unusable by the time the lease contracts expire. Even water catchment areas, mangroves, and forests can be severely damaged by intensive agribusiness activities. Mono-crop agriculture could also seriously affect the biodiversity in and around project areas.

It is worth highlighting the activities of Hong Lai Huat (HLH) Agriculture Cambodia Limited in Cambodia. While not a foreign entity, the environmental questions raised by its investments bear mentioning. In 2009, the Cambodian government granted it about 10,000 hectares to raise corn—to be used for export, not to feed local communities. While 10,000 hectares is of modest size relative to other large-scale farmland investments, a 2010 study by a Cambodian nongovernment organization (NGO) revealed that this land includes part of a wildlife sanctuary, a forest conservation zone, and a community forestry project endorsed and supported by the Environment Ministry since 2007.[21]

Fortunately, following pressure from local NGOs, the Cambodian government informed the corporation that 1,000 hectares of evergreen and semi-evergreen forest must be protected and conserved; that the Ministry of Environment would launch two or three community forestry projects on the grounds of the project; and that in order to generate livelihood support for local communities, the government and the company would jointly manage ponds for raising fish.

Region-Wide Effects on Trade and Food Security

Foreign land projects could catalyze far-reaching changes in Southeast Asia's food trade—changes both negative and positive. In regards to the former, since many of these investments aim to address the food security of investing countries, not of host countries, harvests could well be exported back to the investing nation. This means that one of the region's few rice-importing countries, the Philippines (which is actually the largest rice importer in the world), could end up with a larger net rice-stock deficit. The situation would grow even more perilous should foreign investors opt to convert lands traditionally used for staples and food crops into other higher-value non-consumable commodities like cut flowers, vegetables, fruits, and industrial crops like oil palm.

Indeed, the long-term food security of Southeast Asia on the whole could be adversely affected if such investments are carried out on a significant scale. In 2002, the region was estimated to have produced 150 million tons of paddy (unhusked rice), or about one-fourth of the world's total output, from an area equivalent to 45 percent of the region's cropped hectarage.[22] The region consumed 95 percent of its production during the year. Although per capita rice consumption in the region is projected to decline over time, aggregate demand is still expected to rise as a result of population growth. Given this delicate balance, even a slight reduction in the planted area could transform the entire ASEAN region into a net rice importer if rice yields do not improve and compensate for the change. The region's rice self-sufficiency is further threatened by projections that climate change will significantly reduce water availability and rice output in major rice-production areas along the Mekong River, particularly in Vietnam.

Of course, it is equally possible that rice hectarage, cropping intensity, and yields could increase appreciably as a result of the foreign investments, especially if the production projects are situated and successful in heretofore marginally productive lands. Even rice farmers who are not directly involved in the projects could experience yield gains if they secure access to better planting materials, technology, and even irrigation facilities as a result of the investments. If productivity and output improve significantly and over a wide area, traditional rice importers like the Philippines, and to some extent Indonesia, could end up importing much less or even graduating into rice exporters. In turn, Cambodia, Laos, and Burma, with their vast tracts of underdeveloped lands, could become major rice exporters, rivaling Vietnam and Thailand.

Significantly, in response to the 2007–8 global food crisis, many Southeast Asian countries have embarked on major food-production programs in a bid to raise their self-sufficiency levels. Happily, short-term efforts to boost production have yielded appreciable results for most countries in Southeast Asia. If these trends continue and the foreign land investments simultaneously succeed in raising yields and output in the region, overall food sufficiency, supply, and security could be significantly enhanced at both national and regional levels.

Access to critical food staples in the future will undoubtedly be affected by how marketing systems evolve in reaction to changes in production and consumption patterns in the region and worldwide. At present, governments in Asia still wield heavy influence over their rice sectors. The Philippines' National Food Authority and Indonesia's Badan Urusan Logistik continue to operate sizable programs for providing price and related subsidies to rice producers and/or consumers. The Vietnamese government regulates the outflow and sales of rice products abroad through a network of state enterprises. A similar system, albeit one using private rice traders and exporters, still exists in Thailand. The Malaysian government provides various subsidies to rice producers and tries to keep rice prices within targeted ranges through a price-setting and inventory control system involving traders and other grain-business enterprises.

However, the entry of large-scale foreign investors into the production and marketing of staples like rice could change the dynamics of the rice trade. Most of these investments are undertaken by private enterprises, sometimes with the backing of their governments but outside the direct control of the governments of countries where they operate. Some of these investments could evolve into fully integrated operations undertaking production, processing, and marketing, thus operating virtually outside the influence of commodity markets for the supply of raw materials, but maintaining a distinct capacity to supply target markets as opportunities arise. Hence, there is a high probability that private businesses could eventually become competitors of state enterprises in the supply of rice to local markets and in the export of the staple to markets abroad. In turn, a more competitive and liberalized marketing system that includes a variety of private players could potentially respond more predictably and promptly to market signals, therefore mitigating the possibility of supplies being withheld by governments from overseas markets due to political and other non-economic considerations in the future.

Interestingly, a proposal introduced by Thailand at the height of the 2007–8 food crisis to organize an Organization of Rice Exporting Countries, similar to the Organization of Petroleum Exporting Countries (OPEC), gained little support from regional players. Vietnam reportedly rebuffed the idea. The Philippines publicly criticized the proposal as ill-timed and inimical to its long-term food-security interests. A related proposal to establish an ASEAN Rice Reserve System, and subsequently a wider East Asia Emergency Rice Reserve with the participation of Japan, Korea, and China, has likewise received lukewarm support. However, in October 2011 ASEAN nations did agree to form a "regional rice pool."[23] Under this arrangement, countries would pre-position and dedicate rice stocks for use by needy countries during rice shortages and crises arising from calamities and other market emergencies (the accord also allows for some stocks to be purchased from other countries under special or concessional terms). It remains to be seen, however, if this would be effective when actual emergencies arise.

At the moment, the volumes being committed are miniscule, in part because of the high cost of carrying inventories, and also because exporting countries like Thailand and Vietnam would understandably prefer to sell their excess stocks on the open market rather than wait for emergencies to hit. Additionally, the need for such a reserve system may have diminished in light of the apparent resolve of traditional rice-importing countries like the Philippines and Malaysia, and to some extent Indonesia, to achieve more comfortable levels of rice self-sufficiency in the near future.

This apparent hesitance of governments to act together to better influence rice trading in the region in the name of food security provides a window on more active involvement of private traders and enterprises. While it could be argued that private businesses will behave on a purely commercial basis irrespective of food-security considerations, a more competitive market involving a larger number of players could provide some assurance that supplies will go to wherever they are needed most in reaction to market price movements. Governments will in any case retain most of their proprietary programs and policies to ensure that the domestic situation does not get out of hand during emergencies, and that private traders do not abuse their access to local markets.

Recommendations

Overall, while overseas farmland investments can and do bring substantial economic and other benefits to local communities, there is no assurance that small landowners, contract growers, and other rural residents will get an equitable and commensurate share of the benefits from these investments. Nor are the long-term interests of the host countries—with respect to food security, environmental sustainability, socioeconomic development, and even poverty alleviation—necessarily and automatically promoted as a result of such investments. Clearly, proactive steps need to be taken to ensure that overseas farmland investments are not purely extractive and opportunistic in nature and purpose. International land investments must provide concrete and lasting benefits to local landowners, rural communities, and the recipient country on the whole.

What will this entail?

First, governments need to craft and adopt clear policies that will take into full consideration the overriding interests of the country—including food security, rural development, and poverty alleviation—and also the long-term environmental sustainability of land and natural resources. Clear land-use policies and regulations can then be laid out, together with guidelines for foreign investment in domestic agricultural ventures. A clear farmland investment modality will protect national interests while at the same time help foreign investors reduce their start-up costs and minimize future risks to their business ventures.

Second, foreign investors must strictly adhere to the host country's labor, environmental, and land-use rules and other such regulations, and should be dealt with firmly if they fail to do so. They should follow restrictions on what types of plantation crops can be planted in certain areas; rules on what they need to undertake to protect the land, water, and other environmental resources in the areas they operate in; and regulations with respect to labor employment. If they apply for and are given investment incentives, their operations should also be monitored to ensure that they comply with their commitments and operational plans.

Additionally, it is critical that these laws and regulations apply equally and as forcefully to locals. After all, most of the excesses and abuses surrounding land deals are carried out by host-country military forces and politicians. Sometimes this is done for their own personal enrichment (such as through land speculation), and sometimes it is done in cahoots with investors.

Third, given that much of the land targeted by foreign agribusiness investors is owned and/or occupied by small farmers and settlers, there is clearly a need to provide legal assistance to ensure that local landowners and land users are not lured into one-sided contractual agreements. At the same time, a system to protect their historical, ancestral, and legal rights should be put in place so that they cannot be indiscriminately and unfairly dispossessed of their rights and properties. As much as possible, prospective lessors should be organized so that they can negotiate on a more even footing with investors, and possibly even engage as co-investors instead of just lessors in the agribusiness venture. As a general rule, leases, contract-growing arrangements, and similar contracts could be checked by appropriate government agencies or private assistance or legal advisory firms before they enter into force.

Fourth, civil society has a major role to play in ensuring that host-country interests are not unduly compromised as a result of foreign land investments, and that vulnerable sectors like farmers and small landowners are not exploited and taken advantage of in the process. This can be done effectively by raising public awareness of both the benefits and costs of the foreign investments, and by undertaking research and public information campaigns that give a full picture of what is actually happening. National and regional platforms could be established to monitor developments at various levels, and to facilitate the exchange of information across sectors and countries. In cases where particular investors are found to be violating rules or abusing the privileges extended to them, civil-society organizations can take the initiative to expose misdeeds and pressure government agencies to take necessary disciplinary action. If these efforts are not sufficient, civil-society organizations can lead consumer boycotts and undertake mass action to pressure the investors and their local partners to rectify their mistakes and compensate aggrieved parties.

The involvement of civil society is particularly essential in Southeast Asia, and especially in nations like Indonesia and the Philippines, where nongovernment organizations are active and effective. Several years ago, outcries raised by NGOs in the Philippines helped scupper a deal that would have allowed China (through Chinese state and private enterprises and local investors) to lease up to a million hectares of Philippine land. And, as noted earlier, NGOs in Cambodia helped bring attention to—and compel government responses to—the controversial activities of the Phnom Penh Sugar Company.

Finally, it must be stressed that overseas farmland investments are not the cure to the problems that continue to confront large masses of small farmers and landless rural workers in Asia. While these investments can provide tangible benefits, and steps can be taken to ensure that they do so, the hard work remains for governments to assume and execute their responsibility of building the roads, installing the irrigation, delivering the health and education services, and providing the other basic infrastructure and services that will enable farmers to generate profits from their farms and raise their families out of chronic poverty. These masses of small farmers—not foreign entities—are the real and most strategic investors that governments should encourage and support. And unlike foreign investors, who can easily pack up and leave if things go bad, these small farmers are also the most loyal and resilient investors, if only because they have nowhere else to go.

Chapter 10

Regional Perspectives: Latin America

BASTIAAN P. REYDON AND
VITOR B. FERNANDES

Problems involving land property in Latin America have been the subject of controversy, legislation, and political struggle ever since the occupation of its territory by European colonizers. In recent years, however, the need for food and energy production, the exigencies of environmental preservation, and the speculative use of land have all sparked a new wave of debate over land acquisition.

The aim of this chapter is to analyze the process of land acquisition by foreigners in Latin America in general and Brazil in particular. It undertakes a study of foreign investment in the agriculture and livestock sectors of this region and country, concluding that there has been growing investment in agriculture and that land has been acquired in great quantities. In the discussion on Brazil, the chapter demonstrates the powerful influence of land acquisitions by discussing their considerable impact on land prices.

Additionally, the chapter uses the Brazilian case to show that attempts to regulate the entry of foreigners, by way of prohibitions, do not work satisfactorily. This is because the country, by not having a robust legal/institutional framework for agrarian administration, has no effective control over foreigners' involvement in land. An indication of this lack of regulation is that the funds for the purchase of many acquisitions have not entered the country officially.

Foreign Investment in the Agriculture and Livestock Sectors of Latin America

According to a study on private investment in global agriculture conducted by the private consulting firm HighQuest Partners in 2010, the acquisition of land in Latin America has mainly occurred through private agricultural land management companies, which garner funds and administer land for investors. The latter include wealthy family groups and financial institutions based in the region, or in North America or Europe.[1] Due to the enormous supply of land it offers, Brazil stands out as the biggest regional frontier for new agricultural investments—despite the presence of legislation meant to curb foreigners' access to land.

HighQuest's data found that 24 percent of the companies and investment funds involved in the study have their headquarters in South America.[2] Within the region, Brazil appears to be the main center of attention, followed by Argentina. Uruguay and Paraguay hold a certain level of interest for investors as well. HighQuest estimates that a third of the value of global capital allocated to Latin America's agriculture and livestock sectors is being invested in Brazil.

A 2011 report of the International Land Coalition affirms the popularity of Brazil and Argentina among investors, but argues that investments in these countries are concentrated in the purchase of shares in companies that hold land, rather than in the direct acquisition of land.[3] This is in contrast to the direct land acquisitions that have occurred in Africa and Southeast Asia.[4] In considering these findings, it is essential that one not presuppose the existence in Latin America of a regulatory, political, and economic context identical to the cases in Africa and Southeast Asia. In fact, the context in Latin America is very different from that of these other regions.

A 2011 briefing at the UN Food and Agriculture Organization (FAO) office in Chile provided an overview of "land-grabbing" in Latin America. It compared the phenomenon's manifestations in Latin America with those in other regions:

> . . . The region is different from the processes in Africa where transnational (transregional) deals are more prominent and widespread, but Latin America and the Caribbean [are] closer to the Southeast Asian case. In the latter, intra-regional land investments by (trans)Southeast Asian companies are substantial, probably more important than investors from outside the region, at least for now. But the critical role played by domestic/national elites in Latin America and the Caribbean

is a similar phenomenon in all other regions of the world: Africa, Asia, and post-Soviet Eurasia.[5]

In Latin America, land acquisitions occur in countries (such as Brazil) that do not belong to the usual profile of "frail" or "weak" states, therefore going against the conclusions of the predominant line of thinking that claims that "land grabbing" only occurs in countries with "weak" or "frail" governance structures. Additionally, the same 2011 briefing contends that the effects of land deals are not as profound in Latin America as they are elsewhere in the world:

> In some instances, large-scale lands deals in Latin America and the Caribbean [have] resulted in the [. . .] displacement of the rural poor. But more generally, [they have] not resulted in mass dispossession—at least not [on] the scale that we see in many places in Africa and some parts of Asia (. . . we [do] see some hotspots where [the] expulsion of population[s] from their lands ha[ve] occurred, most especially in Colombia). On many occasions, land deals [have] resulted in the incorporation—adversely or otherwise—of smallholder and farm workers into the emerging commercial farm and plantations enclaves. The mixed outcomes in terms of incorporation (adversely or otherwise) are similar to what we see in the emerging land-oriented ventures in Asia and Africa.[6]

Researchers participating in this briefing also noted that the impacts of foreign acquisitions on food production are very small in Latin America, and nonexistent in Brazil—a striking conclusion, given what is often reported about food-security concerns arising from these deals in Africa and Asia. The reasons for this relative lack of negative impacts on Latin American food security are that large-scale land deals have mostly taken place "outside the staple food sector," and have mostly occurred in sparsely populated areas.

In Latin America, the countries where land acquisitions occur the most are Brazil, Argentina, Chile, Colombia, Ecuador, Paraguay, Peru, and Uruguay, and to a lesser extent the Central American states of Panama and Guatemala. The main purpose of land acquisitions in these cases is to produce sugarcane, soybeans, and oil palm—important crops that can be produced for food, livestock feed, and fuels. Investors also acquire land in Latin America to use for the production of timber.

The key investing sources in Latin America range from international investors and intraregional investors to national or domestic capital and finance companies, along with central governments. Intraregional investment—whereby Latin American nations invest in other Latin American nations—occurs throughout much of the region, including in Brazil, Argentina, Bolivia, Chile, Colombia, Ecuador, Paraguay, Peru, and Uruguay. The investors active in these areas come from Brazil, Argentina, Chile, and Colombia. By contrast, international investment in the region—led by investors hailing from outside Latin America—occurs on a smaller geographic scale. Brazil, Argentina, Colombia, Mexico, Peru, and Uruguay witness such investment. Financiers lead it from the Gulf states, China, Europe, South Korea, Japan, and—in the case of Colombia, Mexico, and Peru—the United States.[7]

Researchers conclude that "the extent of large-scale investments in the region has witnessed a major surge" in recent years, a surge that "is underway in far more countries in Latin America and the Caribbean than previously assumed."[8] This trend risks producing significant and troubling economic and social effects. A 2011 economic analysis of land deals in Ecuador, for example, reveals that "the returns on capital are far higher than the returns to labor." The results of this type of investment, it warns, "are largely irreversible. Peasant societies are destroyed and natural resources depleted."[9]

Such concerns bear particular attention in Brazil, where the volume and intensity of the deals have been the highest in the region. To this point they have not had many social and environmental impacts—due in great part to the large amount of arable land still available. (In terms of the environmental impact, this book's chapter on this subject notes that the considerable large-scale projects involving soybeans and sugarcane in Brazil have not caused, and are not predicted to eventually cause, much deforestation—and water footprints are relatively modest compared to those found in other nations.) However, the situation could change if the extent of these land deals continues to grow, and if they start to encroach on fragile forest land in the Amazon or to displace smallholders in undeveloped areas. There are also long-term emissions concerns; the environmental-impacts chapter in this volume warns that certain large-scale biofuels crop projects in Brazil could incur carbon debts that will take decades to repay.

Foreign Investment in the Agriculture and Livestock Sectors of Brazil

The importance of Brazil as a locus for land investment is not in question. The central issue is to understand the characteristics and logic of this investment in Brazilian land, and to think about the primary mechanisms available for its control. It bears mentioning here that these acquisitions in Brazil are indicative of a far broader dynamic—one dominated by the attractiveness of Brazil as a new global axis for the supply of agricultural commodities. In the words of HighQuest:

> Brazil is recognized as the largest frontier for new farmland development. The availability of new land (estimated [at] 40 to 70 million hectares); a legal system which facilitates foreigner investments in farmland; and a relatively clear legal and environmental regulatory system have attracted foreign investment in Brazilian farmland.[10]

As for the total volume of foreign direct investment in Brazil, it has grown significantly, more than doubling between 2002 and 2008 (see Table 10-1). Brazil's primary sector, excluding minerals, boasts the highest average annual growth rates (AGR) of those sectors listed in Table 10-1. (A country's primary sector is focused directly on the use of natural resources, and includes agriculture and forestry.) In this sector, direct investment was $70.9 million in 2002, yet climbed to $796 million by 2007.[11] While other sectors had more FDI in terms of dollar amounts, their AGRs are considerably behind those of the primary sector.[12]

TABLE 10-1   Foreign Direct Investment (FDI) in Brazil, by Sector (in US$ millions)

Sector	2002	2003	2004	2005	2006	2007	2008	AGR*
Primary, Excepting Mineral Extraction	70.9	181.9	207.0	253.0	213.6	796.0	619.2	0.71
Industry	7,553.3	4,506.0	10,707.8	6,402.8	8,743.8	12,166.1	14,013.0	0.25
Trade and Services	10,585.1	6,909.4	8,484.7	12,924.4	12,124.4	16,556.4	16,877.8	0.12
Total FDI	18,778.3	12,902.4	20,265.3	21,521.6	22,231.3	33,704.6	43,886.3	0.20

* AGR = Average annual growth rate

Source: FAO data.

TABLE 10-2   Foreign Direct Investment (FDI) Flows and Stocks in Agriculture (in US$ millions)

Receiving Country	Flows, 2005–7 Avg	Receiving Country	Stocks, 2007 or Latest Year Available
China	747.0	China	6,156.2
Malaysia	671.2	USA	2,561.0
Brazil	420.9	Vietnam	1,753.1
Russia	187.7	Canada	1,497.8
Indonesia	119.6	Indonesia	1,001.4
Cambodia	87.0	Russia	953.0
United Kingdom	84.7	Chile	949.7
Poland	73.9	Italy	624.3
Papua New Guinea	71.1	Australia	624.2
Romania	67.7	France	616.4
France	61.5	Ukraine	557.6
Ukraine	57.3	Hungary	493.9
Vietnam	51.4	United Kingdom	490.8
Peru	51.0	Poland	446.3
Chile	49.5	Romania	412.8
Tanzania	40.5	South Korea	400.5
Honduras	36.2	Brazil	383.6

Source: UNCTAD, World Investment Report 2009.

In recent years, Brazil has been a significant recipient of FDI flows into agriculture. According to the UN Conference on Trade and Development (UNCTAD), for the period 2005–7, Brazil received $421 million, signifying one of the world's highest volumes of FDI flows in the agriculture sector, surpassed only by China and Malaysia (see Table 10-2).[13] Table 10-2 notes that Brazil also has the seventeenth-highest FDI stock, at $383.6 million. It is useful to compare such robust FDI flows into Brazil's farming with those into African agriculture, which, as underscored elsewhere in this book, are relatively low—and reflect the low level of global investment in the world's agricultural production on the whole. Brazil offers an exception to this prevailing global trend.

However, these UNCTAD figures are contested. While UNCTAD values annual direct investment in Brazil's agriculture and livestock at $420.9 million, others report an average annual volume for agriculture and livestock of around $178.2 million over the same period.[14] On the other hand, High-

Quest has found that in Brazil there are investments valued at $1.35 billion (far larger than the UNCTAD estimates).[15]

What is truly striking, however, is the number of foreign-owned rural properties (and the expanse of the land they occupy) registered with Brazil's National Institute for Colonization and Agrarian Reform (INCRA), the country's official registry. Brazil has 34,371 rural properties in the hands of foreigners, extending over a total area of 4.3 million ha.[16] Between 2008 and 2010 alone, 2.3 million ha were acquired.[17]

Foreign Investors and Their Motives in Brazil

Researchers have created a typology of agricultural investors in Brazil, which fall into eight categories:

1. Agricultural capital investing in the same sector of activity. New investment in acquisitions on the part of both domestic and foreign agribusiness companies interested in expanding their activity in the sector. Main crops are sugarcane (ethanol), wood pulp, soybeans, corn, and cotton.
2. Agricultural capital investing in synergistic and/or convergent sectors. New investment in acquisitions on the part of both domestic and foreign agribusiness companies interested in expanding their activity in the same sectors or in new convergent sectors. Main crop is soybeans.
3. Non-traditional agricultural capital responding to new synergies. New capital entering sectors in which foreign investors did not previously participate. For example, oil companies coming into the alcohol sector. Main crop is soybeans.
4. Rural property companies that have emerged in response to the appreciation of land values and the prospects for Brazilian agriculture. Various types of companies, ranging from international funds to real estate developers specializing in the creation of new properties for subsequent resale, particularly on the agriculture and cattle-raising frontiers. Main crop is wood pulp.
5. Nation-states that are rich in capital but poor in natural resources in search of guaranteed food and energy supplies. Despite this being more common in Africa and Asia, this type of investment has also been present in Brazil, particularly coming from Arab countries, China, and India. Main crops are grain, poultry, and soybeans.
6. Investment funds attracted by the diverse prospects for agricultural commodity appreciation. This type of investment was commonly seen

prior to the 2008–9 financial crisis. These are generally joint ventures of national capital and international enterprises located in Brazil. Main crops are sugarcane (ethanol), wood pulp, soybeans, milk, and grain.

7. Investments related to environmental services incentives. The large number of native forests that still exist in the country, linked to the international need for their preservation, has led to some important investments, mainly in the second half of the 1990s and the first half of the following decade, when land values in Brazil were quite low. Policies of payments for environmental services (of the carbon-credit type) offer powerful incentives for this type of investment. Main crops are wood pulp and sugarcane (ethanol).

8. Mining and oil exploration companies. The quest for new sources of oil and the heavy demand for a wide range of minerals are significantly increasing investment in land in Brazil. In the Amazon region, these investments are perhaps the main factor accounting for conflict with indigenous communities. This type of investment results in new uses for land, and often becomes a source of discord in relation to traditional communities and farmers.[18]

These researchers undertook a study of the number of news reports covering these categories of investments in Brazil (between 2008 and 2010). News about acquisitions mostly occurred with categories one (eleven news reports) and six (nine news reports), despite there being a significant number of acquisitions with companies acting more speculatively (category four, five news reports). Curiously, categories one and six garnered more media attention than the "land-grabbing" category five (five news reports), which attracts so much press coverage in Africa and Asia.

The Brazilian Central Bank's records on FDI in agriculture and livestock between 2002 and 2008 show that the largest investments have occurred in the food sector, which is a fairly industrialized sector. The sector receiving the next highest volume of investment was the alcohol-production sector, followed by paper and wood pulp. This shows how foreign investment in Brazil is heavily shaped by the productive agribusiness sectors.

Also corroborating the productive direction of land acquisitions in Brazil is the fact that these acquisitions occur in highly productive regions. Research shows that 82.4 percent of the foreign investment in Brazil's agribusiness that went through the Brazilian Central Bank (between 2002 and 2008) was concentrated in the southeast.[19] Next came the midwest and the south, with 7 and 5.5 percent of investment, respectively. These findings are substantiated in part by other studies, which conclude that the majority of foreign properties are located in the central and southern areas of Brazil.[20]

The Evolution of Land Values in Brazil, and the Role Played by Foreign Acquisitions

The powerful influence of international land acquisitions in Brazil can be seen from its impact on land-property markets and land values. To understand this better, one must appreciate the historical dynamics of land prices in Brazil. One of the most significant milestones in the evolution of land values in the country was the 40 percent drop in the price of land following the Plano Real in 1995. This plan stabilized the value of the local currency, ending a cycle of many years of inflation and depriving land of some of its speculative uses. After this drop in 1995, the price of land remained flat for a further five years at an average selling price of around $1,000 per hectare.

Only in the first decade of the new millennium did land prices bounce back. They started to rise from the end of 2002, mainly as a result of the recovery in commodity prices. Figure 10-1 exhibits the evolution of the selling price of land for cultivation, based on data collected by the agribusiness consultancy group FNP in 2010.

There was accentuated growth in the price of land between 2007 and 2008; this is the consequence of the increased interest of both Brazilian and

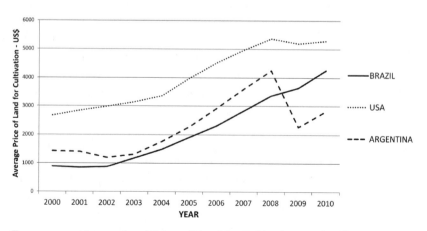

FIGURE 10-1   International Prices of Land for Cultivation (US$ millions). *Source:* FNC consultancy group, 2010.

overseas groups in producing ethanol. The slower growth in the price of land that took shape in 2008 is the product of the economic crisis that ravaged the world that year. Yet the interesting point to note is that, in spite of the extent of the crisis, the average selling price of land in Brazil did not fall; it merely suffered slower growth. In other words, the acquisition of land has had a strong impact on the land market over the last decade, as it has helped prices to rise.[21]

Legal and Institutional Aspects of Foreign-Owned Land in Brazil

Brazil has been burdened from its early days by a lack of land governance. Until the establishment of the Land Law of 1850, effective regulation over urban and rural soil was not determined by the state. The Land Law attempted to eliminate the prevailing chaos with territorial property by demarcating vacant lands. The practical application of the law, however, proved to be ineffective. Its primary objectives—demarcating private vacant lands and prohibiting the appropriation of land—were not achieved. The effect was that vacant lands could still be occupied. Under these circumstances, establishing a land register was not viable. While registries have since been established—laws now state that occupancies and properties must be registered—they are highly inefficient.

The consequences of poor land regulation are numerous and troubling. One is the impediment of effective agrarian governance, and another is the proliferation of opportunities for nonproductive land speculation. Half of Brazil's 850 million ha of land are not registered at INCRA, the official registry office. Some unregistered land has been set aside by the government for the purposes of national parks, indigenous areas, and the like, yet the rest—nearly 175 million ha—remains officially unregistered (some of this land is registered unofficially with highly inefficient notary offices). In the words of a 2011 study conducted by two Brazilian researchers, "there are no formal registers in any of the official instruments of land ownership for approximately 20 percent of Brazilian territory."[22]

Yet another consequence has been widespread irregularities. The most common one in notary offices today is when several parties claim to own the same piece of land. Another is when landed estates "are registered with an area that is larger than the total area of the state itself."[23] Corruption and fraud also mar the registry process at both notary offices and INCRA.

This troubled regulatory context, combined with the reality of large in-flows of capital into the countryside to acquire land, vividly demonstrate the serious situation with land in Brazil. Recent studies show that there has been an appreciation of land by as much as 600 percent in some states in the country—an indication, as noted earlier, of the high level of involvement (foreign and domestic) in Brazil's agricultural land.

Legal-Institutional Measures to Limit Foreign Access to Rural Land

In the last 40 years, the rules, laws, and opinions intended to limit foreign access to land have demonstrated two clear phases. The first one, between 1969 and 1995, was imbued with a clear nationalist spirit and placed strict limitations on the acquisition of land by foreigners. The second one, from 1995 to the present, has been driven by attempts to facilitate the entry of international capital into the state privatization process. Legislation has been modified so that it is both more permissive of, and less clear about, foreign land acquisitions—which has generated diverse opinions and multiple interpretations.

Even during the period of greater restrictions on foreigners acquiring land, there was no way to enforce relevant laws. In spite of the rules being quite clear and well defined, there were no clear mechanisms for control of the process. This is because Brazil has no agency capable of tracking purchase and sale movements on land property markets.

The legal origins of foreigners' acquisition of rural real estate can be traced to the era of military dictatorship (1964–85). Article 3 of Complementary Act No. 45—a law passed, as many were at the time, without parliamentary approval—established that rural property could be acquired by foreigners, but only if they were permanent residents in Brazil. This was a policy justified on the basis of national integrity, state security, and fair property distribution. Law 5709 was passed in 1971, while Brazil was still in the shadows of military dictatorship, and remains in force today. It permits land acquisitions by foreign individuals resident in Brazil, but places rigid restrictions (more than twenty of them) on such investment. The restrictions include the following:

1. Actual acquisitions are limited, in both continuous and discontinuous areas (small levels of acquisitions can be undertaken without the need to secure a license). Limits are also placed on the sum total of rural

areas belonging to foreigners, and on the amount of land area that can be owned by people of the same nationality.

2. For any real estate transaction conveying land to foreigners, title deeds must be established via public deed.

3. Property registry offices must submit deeds listings of foreigners to the Ministry of Agriculture and INCRA on a quarterly basis.

4. Notary publics may draw up title deeds only after the certification of INCRA.

5. Title deeds that do not comply with these restrictions will be legally void, with those who draw up and record the deeds civilly and criminally liable for their acts.[24]

Law 6634, passed in 1979, defined the parameters of foreign vs. non-foreign ownership: In order not to be considered foreign, at least 51 percent of share capital must belong to Brazilian nationals, and at least two-thirds of the workforce must be Brazilian.

The legal environment changed significantly in 1995 with the establishment of Constitutional Amendment no. 6. This clause facilitated the entry of foreign capital into rural real estate through subsidiaries with mixed national/foreign capital, without creating a restriction proviso in the law that had always been imposed on foreigners insofar as rural properties were concerned. However, the foreign ownership restrictions imposed by Law 5709 remained in effect, as they do today.

Over the last few decades, opinion has differed in Brazil as to the actual legal status of foreign land ownership. In 1998, Brazil's attorney general asserted that companies with foreign share participation could acquire land situated on national territory. Some took this to mean that the attorney general had effectively denied protection or benefit to domestic companies and national capital, thereby giving the government's imprimatur to a policy of relinquishing sovereignty across national territory.[25]

In 2007, the government convened a meeting that sought to address the question of refining national legislation in light of the foreign land acquisitions that had begun to occur across the world. Participants pledged to request a review of the attorney general's 1998 decision, with a mind toward placing limits and restrictions on rural real estate acquisitions by Brazilian companies with share capital predominantly in the hands of foreigners not resident in Brazil, or of foreign companies not headquartered in Brazil. More specifically, this review was aimed to remove any doubts about the application of the restrictions and limits provided for in Law 5709 of 1971.

However, this review of the attorney general's 1998 decision did not occur; authorities feared the possible consequences that approval of the request to review might bring upon the country in the middle of a global economic crisis. Instead, it was postponed until 2010. Eventually, the government published an opinion in the Official Gazette of August 23, 2010, affirming the limitations on foreign land ownership. It warned of the following possible effects if limitations were not robustly implemented:

- Expansion of the agricultural frontier with the advance of crop cultivation in areas of environmental protection and in conservation units;
- Irrational appreciation of the price of land and the incidence of real estate speculation producing an increase in the process of expropriation directed towards agrarian reform, as well as a reduction in the inventory of land available for this end;
- Growth in the illegal sale of public land;
- Use of funds arising from money laundering, drug trafficking, and prostitution for the acquisition of land;
- Increase in land grabbing;
- Proliferation of "stooges" in the acquisition of these lands;
- Increase in the volume of bio-piracy in the Amazon region;
- Inadequately regulated expansion of ethanol and biodiesel production;
- Acquisition of land on the frontier putting national security at risk.[26]

Accordingly, the constitutionality of Law 5709 of 1971 was upheld, and with it the provisions for the necessity of registering land purchases in special books in land registry offices. Moreover, the government's 2010 opinion reestablishes that the records of acquisitions made by Brazilian legal entities with a majority of their share capital held by foreigners, by individuals resident overseas, or by legal entities with head offices overseas must be communicated on a quarterly basis to the State Department of Justice, INCRA, and to the Ministry of Agrarian Development. As regards the size of land involved in these acquisitions, restrictions revert to those dictated by Law 5709. And as for frontier areas, the opinion points to Brazilian laws clearly stating that legal business transactions involving obtaining the right of possession, domain, or any other effective right over rural property involving foreigners (both individuals and legal entities) shall depend upon the prior authorization of the National Defense Council. This limitation is valid for companies with foreign share participation of any kind, and not just for companies with majority foreign capital.

Brazil's attorney general, Luís Inácio Adams, has denied that the August 2010 decision was a direct response to the soaring levels of foreign land acquisitions in Brazil—the government has estimated that foreigners own land equal to about 20 percent of São Paulo State, while China was responsible for almost 70 percent of the soy grown in Goiás State in 2010. However, he admits that Brazilian officials were "alarmed" by China's global farmland acquisitions, and particularly the 1.2 million ha it had sought to lease in the Philippines.[27]

To an extent, the government's 2010 decision has had its intended effect; it triggered at least $15 billion in suspensions of farming and forestry projects in Brazil. Yet 2011 featured a flurry of new Chinese investments—including a $2.5 billion deal to produce soybeans in Bahia State, and a $7 billion long-term package to grow six million tons of soybeans per year in the small town of Uruaçu in Goiás. Brazil's agriculture minister has also indicated that the government may allow foreigners to lease land, in order to get around the obstacles to purchase it.[28] The story remains the same: Brazil seeks to limit foreign land deals, yet the acquisitions continue nonetheless.

Conclusion

Land acquisition in Latin America and Brazil is part of a wider, intensifying global process of seeking areas for investment and capital accumulation. What sets Brazil apart is the nature of its agribusiness, which began as a process of modernization in the 1970s, involving the consolidation of investments, particularly those of the larger companies located both up- and downstream of agricultural activity. What this chapter aims to make clear, however, is that there are no national or local controls over the processes of land acquisition. An indication of this lack of control, as noted earlier, is that a significant proportion of the acquisitions in Brazil are taking place with financial resources that do not enter the country officially.

The media tend to associate the "land grab" phenomenon with speculative movements by financial capital, or with food-security strategies in which capital-rich, food-deficient countries target raw agricultural materials abroad. The Brazilian case confirms both of these tendencies as important components of this new wave of land investment. Empirical information shows that land speculation is rife in Brazil, and that the main sectors and regions where land has been acquired are those with potential productive use. Land is, at one and the same time, a speculative and productive asset.

The problem that remains is one of regulation and control. The study of the Brazilian case shows that no control exists over foreign-owned land or over land in general, as there is no land registration and/or land administration along the lines established by the UN.[29] Our analysis identifies the historic roots of the lack of effective land regulation in Brazil, and the limitations of the present registration system.

It is imperative that land policies be far more directed toward the regulation of unbridled speculation in this market, rather than toward attempts to repress or prevent it outright. Speculation with assets, which includes land, will always take place in capitalist systems. It is up to the state to regulate it, and to society to establish governance over it to forestall harm.

Chapter 11

Regional Perspectives: Central and Eastern Europe and the Former Soviet Union

CARL ATKIN

Buy land—they don't make it anymore.
—Mark Twain

There has been much written in the press over the last few years about arrangements by some Middle Eastern and Asian governments and quasi-governmental corporations to lease land in Africa, Asia, and Latin America. While the 2007–8 food crisis might have whipped up considerable interest in the agricultural-investment space from a food-security perspective, it is a trend that has been going on for a long time amongst straightforward commercial investors. Many US institutional investors have been long-term owners of North American farmland, and a similar trend is now beginning to develop in Europe. Indeed, given the illiquidity of farmland and operating companies, most people investing in the sector are taking a minimum ten-year view. Those who want to make a "quick buck" by exploiting short-term volatility in agricultural markets should probably stick to commodities markets or equities with high-sector exposure, such as fertilizer and machinery manufacturers.

Agricultural land is an interesting asset class, containing the generic characteristics of real estate. It is an inflation hedge, it provides a robust income-generating cash flow, and it is not correlated to other investments, especially commercial or residential real estate. Thus, it is easy to see why high-net-worth individuals, family offices, investment houses, and institutions are keen to get exposure, in spite of the recent government-backed surge in Africa surrounding strategic food-security issues.

Agricultural land is also an emotive asset class; the issues of rural land use, food production, and the control of food-supply systems often evoke political sensitivities. The issues surrounding foreign direct investment in land are clearly more complex and charged than in other industries, such as manufacturing. Agricultural land markets are also highly imperfect. Many suffer from a lack of transparency, and there are often restrictions on ownership and occupation. In developed markets, strong noneconomic drivers such as lifestyle, recreation, and tax planning are often considered more important than agricultural income-earning potential or capital growth based on agricultural productivity. In transition and developing economies, markets are poorly developed (if at all), and even the agricultural value drivers may be almost totally irrelevant.

Overview

This chapter focuses on overseas farmland investments in Central and Eastern Europe countries (CEEC) and in the former Soviet Union (FSU).[1] These areas of the world have received relatively little media attention in this context, given that the focus has largely been on the "race for Africa" and the "race for Latin America." However, foreign investment in agriculture in these countries is long-established (since the early 1990s) and is less politically charged, particularly because agrarian reform and holding consolidations are actively encouraged by many governments and industry groups. Some smallholder groups do oppose such consolidations, yet they tend not to be very well organized, visible, or significant. One exception would be Hungary, where investors accord priority to securing the support of small farmers—particularly because this country has had a very nationalistic government.

Investors interested in farmland and farming in the CEEC and the FSU have a range of expectations about their investments, but these essentially break down into two groups. One group considers such investments principally as a relatively low-risk real estate investment. This group tends to target land within the European Union (EU) or within countries (such as those in the Balkans) that are short-term candidates for EU accession. This is because EU membership brings legal and fiscal stability, and on the whole, private-property rights and legal and cadastral systems (i.e., mapped to show property boundaries) in EU member-states are reasonably well developed.

The other group focuses mainly on operational farming investment. This group wishes to seek superior returns on working capital by accessing large areas of land at relatively low costs (probably by leasing). These investments have tended to focus on the FSU, with the most prolific activities occurring in Russia, Ukraine, and Kazakhstan. Real estate purchase, though time-consuming and bureaucratic, is possible in Russia, but not in Ukraine, where agricultural land is subject to a moratorium. In the FSU, large-scale operators can be grouped into a number of types:

1. Successors to former state farms (*sovkhozi*) and collective farms (*kolkhozi*), which have often become joint stock companies—some of which have flourished, while others have been saddled with high debts and low productivity.
2. Backwardly integrating food-processing companies (that is, firms that have moved down the supply chain into primary production, such as Astarta in Ukraine).
3. Poorly developed entrepreneurial Russian and Ukrainian businesses (that is, poorly developed compared with all the forecasts in the early 1990s, though there have been some notable examples, such as Russian Farms).
4. Western-backed investor businesses (e.g., Landkom, Alpcot Agro, Trigon Agri, and Black Earth Farming Ltd.).

The Status of Farmland in the CEEC and the FSU

Efficient agricultural land use collapsed in the FSU and in many parts of the CEEC in the early 1990s, when organized state and collective farms were dismantled or privatized. Large areas of land were left uncultivated. Yields and output fell as the newly fragmented private-farm sector could not access inputs, capital, or technology. Much land remains unfarmed, fragmented, or both. According to the UN Food and Agriculture Organization, of all the world's land not currently in production, at most 12 percent of it could potentially be farmed—and much of this land is in Russia and Ukraine.[2] There remains, of course, a range of conflicting views about balancing global agricultural production with the preservation of biodiversity and carbon-sequestration capacity. Statistics vary and are notoriously unreliable, but some sources suggest that there could still be up to 20 million hectares of land unfarmed in Russia and Ukraine.[3] This land is often owned by peasants who cannot afford to farm it. In some cases, it has reverted back to state ownership.

As a consequence of the land reforms of the early 1990s (which occurred immediately after the Soviet era and the collapse of the centrally planned system), farmland is often very fragmented. Unlike nations such as Poland, which boasts large tracts of commercial farmland in well-sized units, some countries, such as Romania and Ukraine, have redistributed land to the people in hectare blocks, which means that it needs to be "parceled" into workable agricultural units. In Russia, in particular, individuals tend to hold "virtual land shares" within the former *sovkhozi* or *kolkhozi* (rather than plots), because the process of land reform is usually incomplete—tracking down individuals who may have died or moved away is an immensely bureaucratic and time-consuming process. Thus, while Western operators and investors often wish to establish full land titles, many local businesses never complete the land registration process. Land reform has an important impact not only on value, but also on the ability to collateralize land. Only fully aggregated and registered land has any meaningful collateral value.

So why is there all this investment interest in such a challenging environment? The answer lies in the high quality of the land. The region is fortunate in having some of the most productive and resilient soils anywhere in the world: The so-called Black Earth soils stretching from the southern CEEC region across Ukraine and into Russia are deemed by many to feature some of the most arable land in the world. Most accepted forecasts point to a northward shift of the production belt in the Northern Hemisphere. Europe is relatively robust in terms of output, as seen by the vast tracts of the FSU being opened up for productive agriculture as growing seasons lengthen. Europe also looks well positioned with relatively abundant supplies of fresh water, which are "future-proofed" for the medium term.[4] Europe and the FSU are also "future-proofed" against fluctuations in water supply and climate change. For these reasons, these regions have excellent productivity potential.

Cost-to-market analysis is a fundamental element of any agricultural investment decision, not just in terms of considering long-haul freight rates, but also the practicalities of getting large quantities transported in and out of ports or countries with very limited roads and port facilities. Generally, the CEEC and the FSU have a reasonably developed infrastructure with relatively close access to markets in Europe and Asia, allowing significant competitive advantage over many parts of Africa and Latin America.

Land-Price Development and Outlook

While many land markets in the CEEC and FSU are highly imperfect, one can argue that as a broad rule of thumb, good-quality land with title in Russia trades at about €500 per hectare (about US$675). Similar land in Romania trades for about €2,000 to €3,000 per hectare (US$2,700 to US$4,000), and in Poland and Latvia for €4,500 to €5,000 per hectare (US$6,000 to $6,730). In the United Kingdom, the price is €15,000 per hectare (US$20,000). There is a strong argument that agricultural land prices will converge between the old EU-15 and the CEEC countries within the EU (clearly not to 100 percent, as there are inherent productivity differences, but instead probably to 50 to 60 percent of Western European values). Owing to this convergence, land prices in the CEEC and FSU continued to rise between 2008 and 2010, despite the softening of land prices in Western Europe and North America in the immediate aftermath of the 2008 financial crisis.

CEEC and FSU land markets have not witnessed the huge amount of investment capital that other investment "hot spots" have seen over the last two to three years, notably Argentina and Brazil. For example, high-quality land in Argentina increased in value by between two and four times between 2003 and 2010. This may lead to unsustainable asset bubbles, as "fashionable" investment areas are pursued by numerous investors. In contrast, the development of land prices in the CEEC-FSU region has been more steady and stable, and arguably more robust.

Investment Activities and Challenges in the CEEC and FSU

Current Activities

In countries where title to land is robust (such as in the CEEC), investment propositions are often principally about agricultural real estate exposure, perhaps with some exposure to operational farming through a contract-farming or joint-venture arrangement, although some propositions may be fully operational. Many funds were capital-raising during the 2008–10 period, but at the time of writing (autumn 2011), only a small number had deployed capital into the sector. Rabofarm is an institutional investment fund that uses a leasing model to offer low-risk exposure to CEEC farmland, with a focus on Poland and Romania. Other funds, such as those proposed by the firm Agrotrust, emphasize an integrated own-and-operate model.

Spearhead is one of the largest privately owned investment vehicles in the CEEC region, and the focus there is mainly on large-scale operations. Integrated opportunities can yield significant capital appreciation in the land (on the basis that land values will rise as commodity prices rise, that land prices within the EU will converge, and that the holdings will be improved through operational turnarounds). Additionally, a modest but respectable income return can be generated from leasing the land, or by some form of contracting, joint-venture, or operational-farming arrangement. The range of returns across the region is probably 3 to 5 percent from leasing, and 7 to 9 percent from full operational farming.

One of the difficulties with CEEC farmland investment products is in getting a sufficiently attractive running return that will tempt European institutional investors. High-net-worth individuals and family offices who have dominated this sector until recently place less emphasis on running returns, and often remain content with capital growth. European institutional investors, however, are often more concerned about a stable running return.

Challenges to Agricultural Investment

There are a number of challenges to investing, even in countries like Poland and Romania where land titles are robust. Some countries impose foreign ownership restrictions, negotiated as part of their EU accession treaties. Poland has some of the most onerous limitations, theoretically restricting the ownership of land by foreign nationals and entities until 2016.[5] In practice, however, foreign ownership is possible through accepted work-around solutions, and was likely to become easier as the government embarked on a further sale of state-owned farmland assets early in 2012. Of all the CEEC member states now within the EU, Hungary remains the most resistant to promoting foreign ownership of land, with the current nationalist government signaling little willingness to open up the farmland market fully to foreign capital. This is in marked contrast to Romania, where the government has actively promoted and encouraged foreign investment in farmland and operating businesses.

Tenancy legislation is a complex area. In some Western countries, such as the United Kingdom, tenancies are set by reference to the market, allowing the full income-return potential of the land to pass back to the landowner. In other countries, such as Poland, tenancies are often set by reference to an archaic formula that does not always enable the landowner to enjoy such benefits. Payment is often made in-kind. It is not unusual for

Romanian plot owners to turn up at harvest time with empty sacks in their car trunks, seeking grain for payment. In locations where the farm tenancy market is not well developed, more innovative occupational structures are necessary.

The subsidy and support environment is also worthy of consideration. The CEEC countries of the EU received Special Accession Programme for Agriculture and Rural Development (SAPARD) funding as part of the EU accession program (to help with agricultural modernization). Farmers in EU member states now also receive area-based payments under the Single Area Payment Scheme (SAPS), a simplified version of the Common Agricultural Policy (CAP) payments customarily made to farmers in Western Europe, albeit at lower levels for now. The introduction of SAPS has dramatically improved farm profitability in the recipient countries, but it has led to the usual problem that arises with agricultural support. A lot of the support has become capitalized in the land price or rent, or improved profitability has been lost in the upstream value chain—it is typically not retained in the operational farming business.

SAPS is due to be replaced in 2014 with a new CAP Basic Payment Scheme, which will operate across the whole EU-27. This new structure should help to further harmonize area payments in the CEEC region with those in the old EU-15. Perhaps more importantly, fairly generous grant support is available in many of these countries under the EU Rural Development Regulation arrangement, meaning that public funding up to 50 percent for major infrastructure investments such as grain silos and irrigation systems may be possible. The FSU countries generally receive much lower levels of government support than those in the CEEC region, but there may be subsidies available for inputs such as fertilizers and fuel. In Russia, quite generous capital grants are also available at both state and *oblast* (regional) levels for investment into livestock-production facilities and irrigation infrastructure. This helps to lessen the risk of some large-scale investment opportunities for international investors, and may improve financial returns.

Business structure and personnel are equally important considerations. There are myriad offerings in the area of operational farming, some with very robust and well-thought-out business plans, some with appropriate scenario planning and sensitivity analysis, and, unfortunately, others exhibiting significantly more froth in their expectations of yields and profitability. The principal challenge with all these businesses is operational: Is the management capable of growing the area of cultivated land by tens of thousands of hectares year-upon-year while, at the same time, increasing crop yields—as many business plans suggest they will? For many of these businesses, quality and availability of senior management may prove the ultimate limiting factor. The costs and challenges of clearing land and of correcting long-term deficiencies in soil structure and nutrition should not be understated. Those businesses with strong management teams and operational plans are likely to succeed. Others have little more than knowledge of the opportunity with very limited execution capability.

There are significant structural and cultural challenges in moving farming businesses from a "Soviet structure"—characterized by hierarchical management and complicated remuneration systems linked to machinery work rates—to a Western setup characterized by relatively flat management structures and fewer, better workers remunerated on a salary basis with discretionary bonuses. It is not unusual in larger companies for there to be more non-production staff than field operators. Streamlining administration and bureaucracy is a major challenge in some of these large operating entities.

There has been much debate about the economies and diseconomies of scale in the CEEC-FSU region. Calculating optimum operating efficiency for large agricultural businesses is simple, and works on multiples of large harvesting and cultivation equipment—every business is different, but a good rule of thumb is multiples of 4,000–5,000 hectares. Scale brings with it many advantages—notably the ability to have specialized management resources to deal with government relations and security, meaning these tasks do not have to be dealt with as part of a general farm-management role. Scale also brings disadvantages, and many businesses in the region have clearly suffered from diseconomies of scale. A lack of management attention to detail often means that outlying blocks perform poorly, dragging down both the physical and financial performance of the umbrella business.

Impact of the Global Financial Crisis on Agriculture in the CEEC and FSU

The global financial crisis that hit in 2008 made a significant impact on agriculture in the transitional economies of the CEEC and FSU, restricting access to working capital. Fertilizer and input use fell in 2008 and 2009 as farmers simply could not get credit either from clearing banks or from major agricultural suppliers. Credit also restricts investment. Many businesses (especially privatized *kolkhozi* and *sovkhozi* without external capital) have outdated and unreliable machinery. Soviet-era grain elevators are often crumbling, inefficient, and corrupt. The largest farming businesses have found it necessary to internalize their grain storage—in itself a low-return activity—

as an essential mechanism to access the superior returns from operational farming, which in the FSU might be 15 to 20 percent or more. By comparison, according to KinnAgri data, returns from operational farming in Western Europe range from 1 to 4 percent, and from 4 to 9 percent in the CEEC.

There has generally been a retreat away from riskier investment locations, especially Ukraine (where there is concern about the underlying stability of the macroeconomy and the long-term political direction of the country), and a shift toward the CEEC and South America (which are both seen as more stable). The financial crisis, however, does present opportunities. For example, lots of distressed assets are going very cheap in parts of Russia and Ukraine.

The general view remains, however, that agriculture is more recession-proof than the general economy, acknowledging that agricultural prices do not behave consistently during recessionary periods. For example, the years 1973 and 1974 were characterized by relatively high levels of inflation and significant shortfalls in global crop production. In fact, 1973 marked the beginning of a structural shift to a new and higher level of nominal prices for crop and livestock commodities. In contrast, the years 1981 and 1982 were characterized by large growth in US and world crops and relatively strong demand. Crop and livestock prices at that time were characterized as normal.

To some extent, the agricultural economy is also more recession-proof because of the importance of export markets for many major producing regions (especially the United States and the European Union), and also because food expenditures are not as elastic as most other costs. While there will clearly be impacts on the processing and added-value elements of the supply chain, and on higher-end food services and retail, the fundamental production of commodities for those living in the $2-to-$10-per-day bracket is likely to be much less affected.

The long-term fundamentals for agricultural investment remain sound. Population growth remains unabated. There will be a projected nine billion mouths to feed by 2050. Despite the recent downturn in the economy, the International Monetary Fund is still predicting that between 2011 and 2016 economic growth will register at 7–8 percent per annum in India, and 9–10 percent per annum in China.[6] Dietary shifts (characterized by rising rates of meat eating) probably remain one of the most important drivers of demand growth in the medium term, with the $2-per-day level being the important threshold (this figure represents the level at which basic caloric needs are met and diets typically become more diverse, allowing for more meat and dairy consumption).

Meanwhile, biofuels are likely to remain a central part of US energy policy. A University of Illinois report from September 2008 notes that "An ethanol-fueled spike in grain prices will likely hold, yielding the first sustained increase for corn, wheat, and soybean prices in more than three decades."[7] Barack Obama's emphasis on US energy security is important in this respect.

Finally, the supply fundamentals of restricted land availability for agricultural production; potential water shortages in many current key commodity-producing regions; the unknown effects of climate change; and the limitations of technology to solve agricultural supply challenges all remain realities in today's world. True, a period of higher commodity prices is likely to yield to investment in research and development, and may even produce a new "Green Revolution." However, the time lag associated with such technological developments should not be underestimated; it often takes a decade or more for such technologies to have commercial application.

Impact of Agricultural Investment in the CEEC and FSU

Generally, governments are supportive of foreign investment in agriculture, especially at the regional level. For instance, there is a certain amount of prestige for Russian *oblast* governors who can attract flows of capital into their region. Regional business strategy is, however, not without hindrance. There are pressures to farm all the land (as opposed to leaving it fallow) and to keep dairy and beef cattle rather than growing arable crops—yet many Western farming companies would prefer entirely arable operations, as they are less risky and require less working capital.

At the local level, many companies support initiatives such as village schools, ambulances, or hospitals, but these are usually done on a cash basis that can be accounted for. The old state and collective farms have tended to play a wider social role—for instance, by maintaining roads and giving pensioners free food. Such services have declined, though their demise is not associated with the arrival of Western investors, but rather with a collapse of the old centrally planned farms that were not focused on economic efficiency.

Western operators seem to have a better track record than their indigenous counterparts in paying rent, whether in kind or in cash. Generally, the emergence of new companies (both Western and domestic) has driven up rents for rural peasants, who, in the absence of new operators, often have had no choice but to lease their land back for a minimal amount to the former collective farm that had previously allocated it to them. There is clearly political pressure to create and maintain employment for such laborers, but the recent financial crisis and sustained losses for most of the major operators have put pressure on businesses to downsize workforces.

The experience of Western operators is mixed. At the height of the "bubble" in 2007 (before the financial crisis), many companies raised large amounts of cash very quickly and were under pressure to deploy it quickly. Thus, many companies embarked on a "land grab" strategy that probably got too big too quickly, at the expense of operational efficiency. In contrast, businesses that grew more slowly and integrated land acquisition plans and operational farming plans have tended to be more successful. Some of the less successful investors are now actively divesting land, preferring to focus production on a smaller area. Lease values and land prices have fallen considerably since the height of the market in 2007–8, which itself was clearly unsustainable. Many business plans were overly ambitious about the pace of yield growth, and underestimated the costs of land improvement and the working capital needed to farm vast areas of arable land. Those that are well established will survive—albeit at a much-reduced value—while many ventures never left the starting blocks.

Supply-chain experiences are often negative. The major trading businesses (ADM, Bunge, Cargill, and Dreyfus) are now present in most CEEC and FSU markets, but they do not offer the full suite of risk-management tools available in Western Europe or North America because supply chains generally operate in a more adversarial way. Logistics costs can be substantial if farming businesses are some distance from deep-water ports, and very practical issues such as the availability of rail cars can make crop export complicated. Importing inputs, such as fertilizers and machinery, from outside the region is often time-consuming and bureaucratic, and restrictions on the import of new genetic material seriously impedes the opportunity for yield enhancement in some countries, where some local staple-crop varieties may be over 50 years old. Local fertilizer quality is also variable. Quality management remains a problem in large parts of the meat, milk, and horticultural sectors, with many FSU countries not meeting EU import standards on animal health and welfare. In Ukraine, this problem has led to the backward integration of many large food processors into operational farming, and many large Western retail businesses are sourcing high-quality primary products out of country. There are clearly significant opportunities in the value chain for those that can offer produce to recognized international standards.

Conclusion

From an investment viewpoint, there is generally considerable optimism in the agricultural investment sector, including in farmland, the operational farming businesses, and in the value chain. In the medium term, there are immense opportunities across the CEEC region and in Russia and Ukraine, although the financial crisis has dented confidence in some of these economies, especially in Ukraine.

Execution capability is the critical component of all investment options. Some of the funds, companies, and ventures will achieve and exceed their business plans and become very successful; others will be casualties.

Understanding the challenges of operating in a transitional environment is important, as is having robust structures, corporate governance, financial control, and most importantly, first-class operational management. In regards to the latter, this is likely to mean people with first-class technical farming and business skills, but also people who are tough enough to operate in what is quite a challenging environment.

The agricultural investment sector is based on sound fundamentals, and there are exciting opportunities. However, some bubbles will clearly burst along the way.

Chapter 12

Recommendations and Conclusion

Michael Kugelman

This collection's contributors offer a variety of recommendations for how investors, host governments, and the international community should respond to the race for the world's farmland. The major ones are listed below, not necessarily for the sake of endorsement but more as an effort to stimulate debate.

Recommendations for Investors

1. *Understand and respect local conditions.* Be aware of on-the-ground realities in host countries. Uncultivated land is often used by the poor to serve resource needs; untitled land is not necessarily unclaimed; and the impact of large-scale land acquisitions extends to land—and livelihoods—far beyond the areas where land is acquired.

In the developing world, land is a contentious issue and is strongly associated with memories of colonialism and dispossession—so investor decisions could have considerable implications for political stability. Additionally, natural-resource shortages, degraded land, and soaring population rates predominate in many of the nations where land is sought the most—so land deals could also have serious repercussions for environmental sustainability. Investors should honor any host-country regulations on land use, the environment, labor, and other relevant areas.

2. *Invest in the people, not in the government of the day.* Ruling regimes come and go, but the masses always remain. Financiers should tie their ventures to the interests of local communities. Earning the latter's support is essential for the ultimate success of foreign land investments, because having the people on the investor's side will enhance the stability and sustainability of investments and strengthen bottom lines.

3. *Carefully evaluate the qualifications of local partners.* Many investors come from holding companies, are not agrifood specialists, and therefore lack the necessary expertise for large-scale agribusiness management. Firms should seek assistance from host-country professionals with strong farming and business skills, and also those with the toughness to operate in challenging environments. Investors should be vigilant about vetting potential partners, given the reports of local agents hiring thugs to terrorize smallholders or to swindle land from unsuspecting or intimidated farmers.

4. *Consider the merits of contract farming and assure its benefits for farmers.* Historically, general foreign direct investment (FDI) trends have favored looser arrangements over outright acquisitions of assets. Contract farming offers advantages both for investors (security of supply and reduced labor costs) and farmers (income possibilities and flexibility). However, to be sustainable, contract farming must give farmers sufficient rights to plant and manage their crops. Investors must also take the time to provide adequate technical training and support to contract farmers.

Recommendations for Host Governments

1. *Develop a clear and comprehensive farmland investment framework that reflects national and local interests.* Host nations should devise land-use policies and combine them with guidelines for investing in domestic agriculture. This framework should incorporate matters of food security, rural development, poverty alleviation, and environmental sustainability (including local seed development and seed conservation).

The framework should include the views of those most affected—particularly women and community-based organizations. Working with local communities is essential, as it helps foster an understanding of local power relationships, which can in turn inform strategies to protect against abuses. Additionally, monitoring regimes should be instituted to ensure that investors comply with the framework's regulations.

2. *Uphold the right to food as a human right.* International law recognizes the right to food as a universal human right. Governments—and investing nations and firms—should not endanger the right of local communities to food. They should bear in mind the principles of the UN Special Rapporteur on the Right to Food, which include the stipulation that certain percentages of investor crops be sold in local markets.

3. *Protect the most vulnerable from investor excesses or exploitation.* Foreign land contracts are notoriously opaque and often alleged to be one-sided. Host countries should offer legal assistance to smallholders and land users to help them navigate contractual negotiations and reach more favorable terms. A system to protect historical, ancestral, and legal rights should be established to help prevent land dispossession. Additionally, host governments should strengthen the capacities of their land registries so that land is better protected, and ambiguous land ownership arrangements less liable to exploitation. Finally, contracts and leases should be approved by a legitimate public or private authority in the host country before going into effect.

4. *Empower smallholders.* Large-scale production, whether managed by foreign or domestic actors, is not the only way to boost agricultural yields. From Kenyan and Sri Lankan tea farmers to Asian rubber workers, history shows that with political, financial, and technological support, a nation's smallholders can increase their share of production.

5. *Do not outsource ultimate responsibility for rural development policies to foreign investors.* Though foreign capital in agriculture can bring potential benefits to farmers, governments and governments alone should build the infrastructure and provide the basic services that will help lift farmers out of poverty.

Recommendations for the International Community

1. *Respect international guidelines for responsible investment.* Such regulations, which have undergone several years of negotiations, emphasize transparency in contractual discussions; indigenous food-security and rural-development needs; respect for existing land rights; and environmental sustainability.

However, such international initiatives must be complemented by efforts in host countries to monitor and protect local rights, and by media and civil-society campaigns to highlight both promising and troubling deals and to push for more transparency.

2. *Pursue public-private partnerships to help mitigate negative environmental impacts.* International certification programs, sustainability-reporting arrangements, and corporate social-responsibility guidelines can combine with host-country government regulations to positively influence investor behavior. The European Union's experiences with renewable energy policies suggest that establishing certifications as pre-conditions for investment in a country can improve investors' environmental performance.

3. *Gather more information about foreign agricultural investment.* Despite the proliferation of case studies and regional analyses in recent years, data remains patchy and incomplete. More information is needed on patterns, scales, and impacts. Best practices should be developed not just for large land acquisitions, but also for alternatives such as contract farming and other joint ventures.

Consulting the ample data available on general FDI trends can be helpful in gauging the pros and cons of international land deals. Reviewing the historical record—which contains few examples of successful direct corporate investment in large-scale food staple production, but many of foreign-funded, contract-worker-driven smaller-scale farming—can also be instructive.

4. *Keep a proper perspective.* Leasing or buying up farmland overseas constitutes only one type of investment and one way of safeguarding food security—and the proportion of land under foreign control remains relatively minor. Additionally, large-scale land acquisitions may not necessarily harm smallholders. Technology-intensive, labor-reducing farming production may improve the quality of life in local communities. Finally, despite favorable conditions for continued overseas farmland investment, such investment could be slowed by financiers' fears of falling land and commodities prices, and by the controversial nature of land.

The Future of the Farms Race

Today's international land acquisitions are often linked to some broader chain of events. A former director of the International Food Policy Research Institute has described the hunt for land abroad as a new phase of the 2007–8 world food crisis. The *Economist* has depicted the phenomenon as "outsourcing's third wave," following manufacturing in the 1980s and information technology in the 1990s.[1]

Similarly, some discern the trend as part of an evolving quest for resources. Nineteenth-century gold rushes became twentieth-century oil rushes, which have yielded to twenty-first-century land rushes—and perhaps power rushes as well. August 2009 marked the launch of two "hugely ambitious power-generating schemes." One aims to harness sunlight in North Africa and export 15 percent of Europe's power needs to southern Europe as solar energy. The other plans to dam the Congo River and convey 40,000 megawatts of hydroelectric energy to South Africa.[2] Natural resource expert Michael Klare goes even further, describing the world's land hunger as part of a broader, desperate global competition for the world's dwindling supply of natural resources—from coal and copper to land and lithium.[3]

Still, when one narrows the lens and studies the trajectory of land deals on a country-by-country basis, the image that emerges is not of a monolithic juggernaut, inexorably gobbling up the world's land—it is instead an inconsistent and contradictory picture. Argentina and Brazil are cracking down on international investments in agriculture by reaffirming laws against foreign land ownership and passing new ones. Pakistan, which back in 2009 was intensifying its calls for large-scale direct investment in its farmland, has now signed on to contract-farming schemes.[4] On the other hand, almost 10 percent of the landmass in what is now South Sudan, the world's newest nation, was acquired by outsiders between 2007 and 2010.[5] And according to researchers in India, more than 80 corporations from that country have invested $2.4 billion in East African agriculture "to grow cash crops for the Indian market."[6]

Nonetheless, transcending this muddled picture is one crystal-clear point, one that shines through in every chapter: The developing world needs more investment in agriculture. Farm yields are stagnant, and millions are hungry. Investment in the world's farming is necessary to invigorate agriculture and alleviate global food insecurity.

Beyond the Finish Line

Foreign land deals, if planned and executed appropriately, can conceivably help bring about this outcome. Yet as stated in one of the recommendations above, foreign investors cannot be held uniquely responsible for agricultural development in nation-states; such a burden ultimately rests with governments. After all, to use Montemayor's words, foreign investors can always "pack up and leave if things go bad."

Some may argue that momentum for large-scale agricultural investment is already slowing. Much has been made about the estimated 200 million–plus hectares' worth of land deals approved or under negotiation during the new millennium's first decade, but far less has been noted about the slowing pace of acquisitions during the decade's tail end (from nearly 30 million hectares of acquisitions in 2009 to just over 8 million in 2010, according to the ILC).

Additionally, according to the World Bank, "actual farming" has commenced with only about 20 percent of the announced deals.[7] This could signal a realization among many private investors that, as the Meinzen-Dick/Markelova chapter puts it, in an era of rising land prices better profits can be made by holding onto land than by farming it. Yet it may also illustrate growing investor reluctance to follow through on projects.

Furthermore, technological and political developments suggest the eventual emergence of alternatives to large-scale land acquisitions that can strengthen the food security of both investing nations and those countries hosting investments. Private-sector efforts—such as those by the firm Syngenta—are developing genetically engineered, drought-resistant wheat and corn crops.[8] If these truly take off, a prime objective of many land-seeking states—securing water-rich farmland abroad—could become moot. Additionally, national governments are demonstrating an increased willingness to establish regional food reserves to tap into when local supplies are exhausted or threatened. Montemayor reports that despite earlier resistance, Southeast Asian nations have now agreed to form a regional rice pool. If such reserves are in fact established, nations may have less of an incentive to turn to outside investors to enhance food production.

For sure, the drivers of large-scale land acquisitions—high commodity prices, population growth, dietary shifts, biofuels demand, natural-resource constraints, and, above all, the increasingly precious state of arable land—remain in place today, and some will likely intensify in the years ahead. Yet there is no guarantee that host countries will be swelling with deep-pocketed agribusiness investors several decades hence. Therefore, host governments and local communities should treat any benefits resulting from land deals as a mere down payment toward a more long-term investment in government-led national agricultural revitalization programs—programs that assist the poor rural smallholders and landless laborers who will be around for the long haul.

Figures

Data in the following charts are drawn from the Land Matrix, a database project partnership comprising the International Land Coalition (ILC, based in Italy); Agricultural Research Center for International Development (CIRAD, France); Center for Development and Environment (CDE, Switzerland); German Institute of Global and Area Studies (GIGA); and the German Society for International Cooperation (GIZ).

In the charts below, "reported" refers to deals mentioned in published research, media reports, and government registries. "Cross-referenced" refers to deals drawn from multiple sources. For this category, research based on fieldwork, confirmation by in-country partners, or official land records are considered appropriate evidence; media reports are not.

The data provided here appear in Ward Anseeuw et al., "Land Rights and the Rush for Land" (Rome: International Land Coalition, 2012), www.landcoalition .org/sites/default/files/publication/1205/ILC%20GSR%20report_ENG.pdf.

APPENDIX I TABLE 1   The Global Scale of Land Deals, 2000–2010

	Cross-Referenced	*Reported*
Number of Deals	1,155	2,042
Number of Hectares	70.9 million	203.4 million

These figures refer to deals that have been approved or are under negotiation.

APPENDIX I TABLE 2   The Global Pace of Land Acquisitions

Year	Cross-Referenced (in millions of hectares)	Reported (in millions of hectares)
2008	3.5	6.1
2009	6.9	29.9
2010	1.9	8.3

These figures refer to land that has been acquired.

APPENDIX I TABLE 3   Regional Focus of Land Acquisitions, 2000–2010

Continent	Cross-Referenced (in millions of hectares)	Reported (in millions of hectares)
Africa	34.3	134.5
Asia	28.6	43.4
Latin America	6.3	18.9
Europe	1.5	4.7
Oceania	0.1	0.7
World	70.9	203.4

Appendix I Table 4   Investment Areas and Home Regions of Land Acquirers

LATIN AMERICA	*Number of Hectares Cross-Referenced (in millions)*
Africa	0.06
Oceania	0.1
Europe	0.5
Asia	0.6
North America	1.6
Latin America	1.7

AFRICA	*Number of Hectares Cross-Referenced (in millions)*
North America	3.3
Western Asia	3.7
Europe	6.0
Africa	6.4
Asia	12.3

ASIA	*Number of Hectares Cross-Referenced (in millions)*
Oceania	0.3
North America	0.4
Europe	0.8
Western Asia	1.6
Asia	25.3

EUROPE	*Number of Hectares Cross-Referenced (in millions)*
Europe	1.5

AUSTRALIA	*Number of Hectares Cross-Referenced (in millions)*
Asia	0.1

APPENDIX I TABLE 5   Global Land Acquisitions by Sector

Sector	Number of Hectares Cross-Referenced (in millions)			
	Total	Africa	Asia	Latin America
Biofuels	37.2	18.8	15.8	2.0
Food crops	11.3	4.3	4.3	1.6
Forestry	8.2	2.0	5.5	0.6
Industry	1.6	0	1.6	0
Livestock	0.4	0.2	0	0.2
Mineral extraction (including petroleum)	1.7	0.05	0.3	1.4
Non-food agricultural commodities	1.2	0.5	0.6	0.07
Tourism	2.7	2.7	0	0

Due to rounding, numbers may not add up to the total.

Supplementary Data from Environmental Impacts Chapter

The following tables, prepared by the authors of chapter 5, highlight land-use changes driven by maize, rice, and rubber. These crops figure prominently in large-scale land acquisitions, but scientific evidence surrounding their land-use patterns is wanting. Some of the limited, anecdotal information that does exist is presented here. The crops for which land-use data are more established (jatropha, oil palm, soybeans, and sugarcane, along with tree plantations) constitute the prime focus of chapter 5, and relevant figures are provided therein.

APPENDIX II TABLE 1 Anecdotal Evidence of Maize-Related Land-Use Change

Location	Period	Expansion (in thousands of hectares)	Land-Use Change
Africa/Cameroon	2006	4,000	*
Africa/Egypt	2008–2012	42,000	
Africa/Ethiopia[1]	2009–2011	10,000	Forest to maize and rice
Africa/Madagascar[2]	2009	170,914	
Africa/Tanzania[2]	2011–2012	200,000	Forest to maize and other crops
Africa/Sudan	2011	20,492	Desert to maize (brought into production with irrigation)
Africa/Zimbabwe	2008	250,000	
Asia/Cambodia	2008–2012	10,000	Forested

* Blank cells indicate that data is not available.
[1] For Ethiopia case, area cultivated includes maize and rice.
[2] For Madagascar and Tanzania cases, area includes multiple crops.
Sources: Media reports, investor group websites, and International Institute for Environment and Development.

APPENDIX II TABLE 2   Anecdotal Evidence of Rice-Related
Land-Use Change

Location	Period	Expansion (in thousands of hectares)	Land-Use Change
Africa/Angola	2009	25,000	Agricultural land
Africa/Liberia	2007	15,000	*
Africa/Mali	2009	100,000	
Africa/Cameroon	2006	6,120	33 percent mixed savannah/ farming/hunting; 2 percent abandoned rice farm; remainder unknown
Africa/Ethiopia[1]	2009–present	10,000	Forested
Africa/Kenya	2003	3,700	Swampland
Africa/Madagascar[2]	2009	170,914	
Africa/Nigeria	Apr–Jun 2012	6,000	

* Blank cells indicate that data is not available.
[1] For Ethiopia case, area includes maize and rice.
[2] For Madagascar case, area includes multiple crops.
Sources: Media reports, Institute of Environment and Water [Kenya], and International Institute for Environment and Development.

APPENDIX II TABLE 3   Anecdotal Evidence of Rubber-Related
Land-Use Change

Location	Period	Expansion (in thousands of hectares)	Land-Use Change
SE Asia/Cambodia		10,000	*
SE Asia/Burma[1]		30,000	
SE Asia/Laos		10,000	
SE Asia/Burma		240,000	Agricultural land (unspecified)

* Blank cells indicate that data is not available.
[1] Burma case appears to be industrial-scale plantations on farmers' land, with a promise of 60 percent of profits to plantation workers.
Sources: Media reports.

APPENDIX III

Web Resources

What follows is a selective—not exhaustive—list of Internet-available work produced on large-scale foreign land acquisitions since 2009. It aims to capture the range of published output on the topic in both thematic and regional contexts, and to illustrate the rising volume of output after 2009.

General Resources

GlobalAgInvesting — www.globalaginvesting.com/index.php
[website for an annual conference series for investors allocating capital and managers operating farmland in the global agricultural sector]

GRAIN, "Food Crisis and the Global Land Grab" — farmlandgrab.org
[compilation of online research and news reports about foreign land investment globally]

International Institute of Social Studies of Erasmus University, Rotterdam, "The Land Deal Politics Initiative" (LDPI) — www.iss.nl/research/networks_and _projects/land_deal_politics_ldpi
[site featuring research, news, and events relevant to the LDPI, which seeks to examine land deals in an in-depth and systematic fashion]

Land Portal — landportal.info
[web-based clearinghouse and forum on information related to land acquisitions, facilitated by the Rome-based International Land Coalition]

Oxfam, "Select Bibliography of Reports on Biofuels, Land Rights in Africa & Global Land Grabbing" — www.oxfam.org.uk/resources/learning/landrights/downloads /select_bibliog_reports_biofuels_africanlandrights_global_land_grabbing_at_30091 .pdf
[a detailed annotated bibliography, frequently updated]

193

Oxfam International, "Land Rights in Africa" — www.oxfam.org.uk/resources
/learning/landrights/general.html
[compilation of papers relating to global land deals]

2012 (through February)

Ward Anseeuw et al., *Land Rights and the Rush for Land* (Rome: International
Land Coalition), www.landcoalition.org/sites/default/files/publication/1205/ILC
%20GSR%20report_ENG.pdf
[in-depth report assessing the scale and impacts of large-scale international land
investment, with nearly 30 thematic and regional case studies]

Mikkel Busck et al., *Foreign Land Investments for Biofuel Production: An Analysis of
the Debate and the EU Sustainability Policies on Biofuel* (Roskilde, Denmark: Roskilde
University), dspace.ruc.dk/bitstream/1800/7263/4/Samlet%20rapport.pdf
[provides an overview on EU policies on biofuel sustainability, and examines the
debate surrounding foreign investments in land for biofuel]

Klaus Deininger and Derek Byerlee, "The Rise of Large Farms in Land Abundant Countries: Do They Have a Future?" *World Development* 40, No. 4, www
.sciencedirect.com/science/article/pii/S0305750X11001008
[examines large and small farms in the context of growing investor interest in agri-
culture]

Liz Alden Wily, *Turning Point: What Future for Forest Peoples and Resources in the
Emerging World Order?* (Washington, DC: Rights and Resources Group), www
.rightsandresources.org/documents/quarantined/files/turningpoint/Turning%20
Point%20-%20Final%20PDF.pdf
[features discussion on the role of forests in large-scale land acquisitions]

2011

African Union, African Development Bank, and Economic Commission for Africa,
"Framework and Guidelines on Land Policy in Africa," www.oxfam.org.uk
/resources/learning/landrights/downloads/au-framework-guidelines-land-policy
-africa.pdf
[presents a set of rules to govern land investments in Africa]

Julia Behrman, Ruth Meinzen-Dick, and Agnes Quisumbing, "The Gender Implications of Large-Scale Land Deals," International Food Policy Research Institute Discussion Paper, www.ifpri.org/publication/gender-implications-large-scale-land-deals
[discusses the effects of large-scale land acquisition on rural men and women as it
relates to gender]

Saturnino M. Borras Jr. et al., "Land Grabbing in Latin America and the Caribbean: Viewed from Broader International Perspectives," FAO presentation, www.tni.org /sites/www.tni.org/files/download/borras_franco_kay__spoor_land_grabs_in_latam _caribbean_nov_2011.pdf
[based on research in 17 countries in Latin America and the Caribbean]

Saturnino M. Borras Jr. and Jennifer C. Franco, *Political Dynamics of Land-Grabbing in Southeast Asia: Understanding Europe's Role* (Amsterdam: Transnational Institute), www.uneseuleplanete.org/IMG/pdf/PoliticalDynamicsofLand-grabbinging SoutheastAsia.pdf
[examines the direct and indirect roles Europe plays in large-scale land acquisition in Southeast Asia]

Elisa Wiener Bravo, *The Concentration of Land Ownership in Latin America: An Approach to Current Problems* (Rome: International Land Coalition), www.land coalition.org/sites/default/files/publication/913/LA_Regional_ENG_web_11.03.11 .pdf
[examines the problems posed by the concentration of land ownership in Latin America and provides discussion on the background, trends, and effects of land consolidation]

Lorenzo Cotula, *The Outlook on Farmland Acquisitions* (Rome: International Land Coalition), www.ibcperu.org/doc/isis/13570.pdf
[summarizes the findings of research by the International Institute for Environment and Development on the foreign purchase of agricultural land]

Klaus Deininger and Derek Byerlee, *Rising Global Interest in Farmland: Can It Yield Sustainable and Equitable Benefits?* (Washington, DC: The World Bank), siteresources.worldbank.org/INTARD/Resources/ESW_Sept7_final_final.pdf
[contains analysis of agriculture's role in economic development and includes sections on gender, water management, and bioenergy]

Olivier De Schutter, "The Green Rush: The Global Race for Farmland and the Rights of Land User," *Harvard International Law Journal* 52, no. 2, www.harvardilj .org/wp-content/uploads/2011/07/HILJ_52-2_De-Schutter.pdf
[analyzes property rights of farmers in developing nations and concludes that foreign agricultural investment will likely drive poor farmers from their land due to rising costs]

Laura German, George Schoneveld, and Esther Mwangi, "Contemporary Processes of Large-Scale Land Acquisition by Investors: Case Studies from Sub-Saharan Africa," Center for International Forestry Research Occasional Paper, www.wrm .org.uy/subjects/land_grabbing/CIFOR_land_grabbing.pdf
[provides a legal analysis of the framework and practice of foreign land acquisition in Ghana, Mozambique, Tanzania, and Zambia]

Matt Grainger and Kate Geary, "The New Forests Company and Its Uganda Plantations," Oxfam International Case Study, www.oxfam.org/sites/www.oxfam.org /files/cs-new-forest-company-uganda-plantations-220911-en.pdf
[examines allegations of people in Uganda being evicted from their land after large-scale investment in the area by the London-based New Forests Company]

Charlotte Hebebrand, *Leveraging Private Sector Investment in Developing Country Agrifood Systems* (Chicago: Chicago Council on Global Affairs), www.thechicago council.org/UserFiles/File/GlobalAgDevelopment/Report/CCGA%20GADI%20 Private%20Sector%20Policy%20Paper%20FINAL%20VERSION.pdf
[presents the benefit of private investment in sustainable agriculture, examines examples of transnational corporations that have seen profits while benefiting smallholders in developing countries, analyzes how the US government encourages these investments, and provides recommendations for increasing transnational agricultural investment]

Chris Huggins, *A Historical Perspective on the "Global Land Rush"* (Rome: International Land Coalition), www.landcoalition.org/publications/historical-perspective -global-land-rush
[traces agricultural production and trade using historical and conceptual scopes]

International Conference on Global Land-Grabbing, www.future-agricultures.org /index.php?option=com_content&view=category&layout=blog&id=1547& Itemid=978
[conference featured dozens of presentations; conference website contains links to most conference papers]

Journal of Peasant Studies 38, no. 2, www.tandfonline.com/toc/fjps20/38/2
[special edition dedicated to the large-scale land acquisitions theme]

Tom Lavers, "The Role of Foreign Investment in Ethiopia's Smallholder-Focused Agricultural Development Strategy," Land Deal Politics Initiative Working Paper, www.plaas.org.za/pubs/ldpi-working-papers-africa/LDPI02Lavers.pdf
[analyzes the threats, opportunities, and implications of foreign investment in agricultural land in Ethiopia, and discusses the trade-off between the large-scale benefits of foreign investment and the small-scale risks to local communities]

Mary Ann Manahan, "Is Asia for Sale? Trends, Issues, and Strategies against Land Grabbing," Land Research Action Network (LRAN) (part of LRAN Briefing Paper Series on Land Struggles: Defending the Commons, Territories and the Right to Food and Water), www.rinoceros.org/IMG/pdf/Land_struggles.pdf#page=41
[examines international land deals in Asia based on information from discussions at a meeting of social movements in Kuala Lumpur]

Raul Montemayor, *Overseas Farmland Investments in Selected Asian Countries* (Manila: East Asia Rice Working Group), www.eastasiarice.org/Books/OVERSEAS%20 FARMLAND.pdf
[provides an overview of foreign agricultural investment in several Southeast Asian countries, including possible concerns and policy recommendations]

Rachel Nalepa, "The Global Land Rush: Implications for Food, Fuel, and the Future of Development" (Part of Pardee Papers series at Pardee Center for the Study of the Longer-Range Future at Boston University), www.bu.edu/pardee/files/2011/08 /PP13_GlobalLandRush.pdf
[argues that due to tenuous land rights and poor governance, the global land rush has negative short-term effects and could undermine long-term growth]

Michael Ochieng Odhiambo, *Commercial Pressures on Land in Africa: A Regional Overview of Opportunities, Challenges, and Impacts* (Nakuru, Kenya: International Land Coalition), www.landcoalition.org/sites/default/files/publication/1136/Africa %20Overview%20WEB%2014.07.11.pdf
[studies the negative impacts of foreign land investment in Africa on the poor, including land rights and the environment]

Oxfam International, "Land and Power: The Growing Scandal Surrounding the New Wave of Investments in Land," Oxfam Briefing Paper, www.oxfam.org/sites /www.oxfam.org/files/bp151-land-power-rights-acquisitions-220911-en.pdf
[looks at the role of foreign investment and host governments in land acquisitions in Uganda, Indonesia, Guatemala, Honduras, and South Sudan, with a focus on the negative implications for local communities]

Javier Perez, Myriam Gistelinck, and Dima Karbala, "Sleeping Lions: International Investment Treaties, State-Investor Disputes, and Access to Food, Land and Water," Oxfam Discussion Paper, www.oxfam.org/sites/www.oxfam.org/files/dp-sleeping -lions-260511-en.pdf
[outlines the debate about whether foreign investments in land, water, and resources will harm developing nations' ability to reduce poverty and manage resources]

Roel R. Ravanera and Vanessa Gorra, *Commercial Pressures on Land in Asia: An Overview* (Rome: International Land Coalition), www.landcoalition.org/sites /default/files/publication/909/RAVANERA_Asia_web_11.03.11.pdf
[examines the background and implications of land competition due to both agri-cultural and non-agricultural investment in Asia]

Ben Shepherd, "Redefining Food Security in the Face of Foreign Land Inves-tors: The Philippine Case," Nanyang Technological University (Singapore) / S. Raj-ratnam School of International Studies paper series, www.rsis.edu.sg/nts/HTML -Newsletter/Report/pdf/NTS-Asia_Ben_Shepherd.pdf

[argues that foreign land purchases in the Philippines are likely to worsen food insecurity for the rural poor]

Jamie Skinner and Lorenzo Cotula, "Are Land Deals Driving 'Water Grabs'?" International Institute for Environment and Development briefing, pubs.iied.org/pdfs /17102IIED.pdf
    [examines the treatment of water rights in large-scale land deals]

Liz Alden Wily, *The Tragedy of Public Lands: The Fate of the Commons under Global Commercial Pressure* (Rome: International Land Coalition), www.landcoalition.org /sites/default/files/publication/901/WILY_Commons_web_11.03.11.pdf
    [analyzes the pressure on common land from commercial interests and how it contributes to the vulnerability of the poor]

Fleur Wouters et al., "Foreign Direct Investment in Land in West Africa," International Food Policy Research Institute research note, www.ifpri.org/sites/default/files /publications/wcaotn01.pdf
    [examines aspects of international land deals in West Africa]

2010

Saturnino M. Borras Jr. and Jennifer Franco, "Towards a Broader View of the Politics of Global Land Grab: Rethinking Land Issues, Reframing Resistance," Working Paper for Initiatives in Critical Agrarian Studies, Land Deal Politics Initiative, and Transnational Institute, ramshorn.ca/sites/ramshorn.ca/files/Borras%20%26%20 Franco,%20Politics%20of%20Land%20Grab.pdf
    [argues that a "win-win" arrangement for the purchase of foreign land by transnational corporations is unlikely under current political dynamics, and presents an alternative concept]

HighQuest Partners, "Private Financial Sector Investment in Farmland and Agricultural Infrastructure" (conducted for Organization of Economic Cooperation and Development Working Party on Agricultural Policies and Markets, and issued as a working paper), 2010, dx.doi.org/10.1787/5km7nzpjlr8v-en
    [analyzes private sector investment in global agricultural land and infrastructure]

New York University School of Law (Center for Human Rights and Global Justice), *Foreign Land Deals and Human Rights: Case Studies on Biofuel and Agricultural Investment* (New York: NYU School of Law), www.chrgj.org/projects/docs/landreport.pdf
    [studies large-scale land acquisitions from a human-rights perspective]

Tania Salerno, "Land Deals, Joint Investments, and Peasants in Mindanao, Philippines" (MA dissertation), International Institute of Social Studies, oaithesis.eur

.nl/ir/repub/asset/8717/Land_Deals_Joint_Investments_and_The_Peasantry
-_Tania_Salerno.pdf

[examines a land deal in Mindanao, Philippines, involving a Saudi investor, and how it affected people living in the area]

George C. Schoneveld, Laura A. German, and Eric Nutakor, "Towards Sustainable Biofuel Development: Assessing the Local Impacts of Large-Scale Foreign Land Acquisitions in Ghana" (paper presented at World Bank Land Governance Conference), siteresources.worldbank.org/EXTARD/Resources/336681-1236436879081 /5893311-1271205116054/schoneveld.pdf

[evaluates how Ghana's legal structures have balanced local interests with foreign land acquisition in the central regions of Brong Ahafo and Ashanti]

Adil Yassin, "Large-Scale Transnational Land Acquisition in Ethiopia—Is It an Acceleration for Development? The Case of Bako and Gambella Region in Ethiopia" (MA dissertation), International Institute of Social Studies, oaithesis.eur.nl/ir/repub /asset/8690/Adil_Yassin_RP%202009-10.pdf

[argues that the legal environment in Ethiopia encourages transnational land purchase for economic benefit, without bringing accompanying developmental benefits]

2009

Joachim von Braun and Ruth Meinzen-Dick, "'Land Grabbing' by Foreign Investors in Developing Countries: Risks and Opportunities," International Food Policy Research Institute policy brief, www.ifpri.cgiar.org/sites/default/files/publications /bp013all.pdf

[analyzes how foreign land investment can support development if land use is sustainable and the benefits are shared with the host country]

Deborah Brautigam and Tang Xiaoyan, "China's Engagement in African Agriculture: 'Down to the Countryside,'" *The China Quarterly* 199 (September), www.american .edu/sis/faculty/upload/Brautigam-Tang-CQ-final.pdf

[examines China's engagement in agriculture in Africa from a historical perspective]

Lorenzo Cotula et al., "Land Grab or Development Opportunity? Agricultural Investment and International Land Deals in Africa" (London and Rome: International Institute for Environment and Development [IIED], Food and Agriculture Organization [FAO], and International Fund for Agricultural Development [IFAD]), www.ifad.org/pub/land/land_grab.pdf

[surveys trends, impacts, and legal issues surrounding land deals in Ethiopia, Ghana, Madagascar, Mali, Mozambique, Sudan, and Tanzania]

Lorenzo Cotula and Sonja Vermeulen, "Deal or No Deal: The Outlook for Agricultural Land Investment in Africa," *International Affairs* 85, no. 6, www.chatham house.org/sites/default/files/public/International%20Affairs/2009/85_6cotula _vermeulen.pdf
[analyzes trends in international agricultural investment in Africa and outlines ways to avoid political conflict and spur development]

Shepard Daniel with Anuradha Mittal, *The Great Land Grab: Rush for World's Farmland Threatens Food Security for the Poor* (Oakland, CA: Oakland Institute), www .oaklandinstitute.org/sites/oaklandinstitute.org/files/LandGrab_final_web.pdf
[reports on the threat land acquisitions pose for food security and livelihoods]

Mattia Görgen et al., *Foreign Direct Investment (FDI) in Land in Developing Nations* (Eschborn, Germany: German Ministry for Economic Cooperation and Development), www.scribd.com/doc/29459685/Foreign-Direct-Investment-FDI -in-Land-in-Developing-Countries?query=ELC
[Using Cambodia, Laos, Madagascar, and Mali as case studies, focuses on the challenges of using foreign direct investment in land to secure a sustainable food supply, and outlines recommendations to improve the climate for foreign investment]

David Hallam, "International Investments in Agricultural Production" (paper presented at the FAO Expert Meeting on "How to Feed the World in 2050"), www .rrojasdatabank.info/ak976e00.pdf
[examines the trends, policy implications, and motivations of both investors and host countries as related to foreign investment in agricultural land]

IFAD, "The Growing Demand for Land: Risks and Opportunities for Smallholder Farmers" (Discussion Paper and Proceedings Report of IFAD's Governing Council Round Table, United Nations), www.ifad.org/events/gc/32/roundtables/2.pdf
[provides background on the purchase of agricultural land by foreign investors, and discusses the possible implications for rural populations and how they might benefit from good practices]

Carin Smaller and Howard Mann, *A Thirst for Distant Lands: Foreign Investment in Agricultural Land and Water* (Winnipeg, Canada: International Institute for Sustainable Development), www.iisd.org/pdf/2009/thirst_for_distant_lands.pdf
[focuses on causes, trends, and legal issues surrounding foreign investment in securing land and water rights for agriculture]

United Nations Conference on Trade and Development (UNCTAD), *World Investment Report 2009: Transnational Corporations, Agriculture Production and Development* (New York and Geneva: UNCTAD), www.unctad.org/en/docs/wir2009_en.pdf
[looks at the impact of the global financial crisis on foreign direct investment in developing nations, and the role of transnational corporations in agricultural productivity and food security]

NOTES

Chapter 1

1. Joachim von Braun and Ruth Meinzen-Dick, "'Land Grabbing' by Foreign Investors in Developing Countries: Risks and Opportunities," International Food Policy Research Institute Policy Brief 13, April 2009, www.ifpri.cgiar.org/sites /default/files/publications/bp013all.pdf; "When Others Are Grabbing Their Land," *The Economist*, May 5, 2011, www.economist.com/node/18648855; and Klaus Deininger and Derek Byerlee, *Rising Global Interest in Farmland: Can It Yield Sustainable and Equitable Benefits?* (Washington, DC: World Bank, 2011), siteresources .worldbank.org/INTARD/Resources/ESW_Sept7_final_final.pdf.

2. Ward Anseeuw et al., *Land Rights and the Rush for Land* (Rome: International Land Coalition, 2012), www.landcoalition.org/sites/default/files/publication/1205 /ILC%20GSR%20report_ENG.pdf; and Oxfam, "Land and Power: The Growing Scandal Surrounding the New Wave of Investments in Land," Oxfam Briefing Paper 151, September 22, 2011, www.oxfam.org/sites/www.oxfam.org/files/bp151-land -power-rights-acquisitions-220911-en.pdf.

3. Longgena Ginting and Oliver Pye, "Resisting Agribusiness Development: The Merauke Integrated Food and Energy Estate in West Papua, Indonesia" (paper presented at International Conference on Global Land Grabbing, University of Sussex, United Kingdom, April 8, 2011), www.future-agricultures.org/panel-a -session-summaries/7568-panel-26-politics-resistance-and-mobilization-i; and "Mozambique Offers Brazilian Farmers 6 Million Hectares to Develop Agriculture," MercoPress, August 16, 2011, en.mercopress.com/2011/08/16/mozambique-offers -brazilian-farmers-6-million-hectares-to-develop-agriculture.

4. Marie-Béatrice Baudet and Laetitia Clavreul, "The Growing Lust for Agricultural Lands," *Le Monde*, April 14, 2009, www.truthout.org/041509F.

5. See: "Understanding Land Investment Deals in Africa," Oakland Institute, www.oaklandinstitute.org/land-deals-africa.

6. In some cases, agricultural output stays in the host country and is sold in local markets. A notable example is Chinese investment in Zambian farms. According to a researcher at the International Institute for Environment and Development, China operates about two dozen farms in Zambia—and their products go directly to local markets. Fifteen percent of Lusaka's eggs come from these farms, according

201

to the study. See: Stephen Marks, "China and the Great Global Landgrab," *Pambazuka News*, December 11, 2008, www.pambazuka.org/en/category/africa_china/52635.

7. Abbi Buxton, Mark Campanale, and Lorenzo Cotula, "Farms and Funds: Investment Funds in the Global Land Rush," IIED Briefing, London, January 2012, pubs.iied.org/pdfs/17121IIED.pdf.

8. Michael Kugelman, "Going Gaga Over Grain," *Dawn*, September 17, 2009, www.dawn.com/wps/wcm/connect/dawn-content-library/dawn/news/pakistan/04-grain-qs-04.

9. See Appendix III for a list of online resources on the topic of large-scale land acquisitions.

10. This book's main focus is on foreign land acquisitions, though some chapters also address cases where land is secured by investors inside their own countries. As several contributors make clear, the drivers, risks, and outcomes are often similar in both contexts.

11. Michael Kugelman and Susan L. Levenstein, "Sacrificing the Environment for Food Security," *World Politics Review*, January 20, 2010, www.worldpolitics review.com/articles/4969/sacrificing-the-environment-for-food-security.

12. Horand Knaup and Juliane von Mittelstaedt, "The New Colonialism: Foreign Investors Snap Up African Farmland," *Spiegel Online*, July 30, 2009, www.spiegel.de/international/world/0,1518,639224,00.html.

13. Jessica McDiarmid, "Regulating the Rush for Land," Inter Press Service, October 31, 2011, www.commondreams.org/headline/2011/10/31-8.

14. See: Deininger and Byerlee, *Rising Global Interest in Farmland*.

15. "Outsourcing's Third Wave," *The Economist*, May 21, 2009, www.economist.com/node/13692889.

16. Jeffrey Gettleman, "Darfur Withers as Sudan Sells Food," *New York Times*, August 10, 2008, www.nytimes.com/2008/08/10/world/africa/10sudan.html.

17. Katie Hunt, "Africa Investment Sparks Land Grab Fear," BBC News, August 5, 2009, news.bbc.co.uk/2/hi/business/8150241.stm.

18. Lorenzo Cotula, *Land Grabs: What Is in the Contracts?* (London: IIED, January 2011), pubs.iied.org/pdfs/12568IIED.pdf.

19. Burnod Perrine et al., "From International Land Deals to Local Informal Agreements: Regulations of and Local Reactions to Agricultural Investments in Madagascar" (paper presented at the International Conference on Global Land Grabbing, Sussex, United Kingdom, April 6–8, 2011), bit.ly/zsVBCO.

20. Von Braun and Meinzen-Dick, "'Land-Grabbing' by Foreign Investors in Developing Countries."

21. Montemayor's suggestion would also be applicable to Africa, where locals also sometimes play nefarious roles. For example, one observer notes that in Kenya, "it is local elites who pose the greatest threat to land rights." Michael Ochieng Odhiambo, *Commercial Pressures on Land in Africa: A Regional Overview of Opportunities, Challenges, and Impacts* (Nakuru, Kenya: International Land Coalition, April 2011),

www.landcoalition.org/sites/default/files/publication/1136/Africa%20Overview
%20WEB%2014.07.11.pdf.

22. Alexei Barrionuevo, "China's Interest in Farmland Makes Brazil Uneasy,"
New York Times, May 26, 2011, www.nytimes.com/2011/05/27/world/americas/27
brazil.html?pagewanted=all.

23. Deininger and Byerlee, *Rising Global Interest in Farmland*.

24. Tracy McVeigh, "Biofuels Land Grab in Kenya's Tana Delta Fuels Talk of
War," *Guardian*, July 2, 2011, www.guardian.co.uk/world/2011/jul/02/biofuels
-land-grab-kenya-delta.

25. Rick Westhead, "Africa's Farmland in Demand: 'Is There a Better Place Than
This?'" *Toronto Star*, December 3, 2011, www.thestar.com/news/article/1096210.

Chapter 2

1. This is a summary of ongoing work on the history of large-scale investments in land. An expanded paper with full citations is available from the author.

2. Hans P. Binswanger, Klaus Deininger, and Gershon Feder, "Power, Dis-
tortions, Revolt, and Reform in Agricultural Land Relations," in Hollis Chenery and
T. N. Srinivasan, eds., *Handbook of Development Economics* (Amsterdam: North Hol-
land/Elsevier, 1995), 2659–72.

3. A. J. Christopher, "Patterns of British Overseas Investment in Land,
1885–1913," *Transactions of the Institute of British Geographers* 10, no. 4 (1985):
452–66.

4. Hans P. Binswanger and Mark R. Rosenzweig, "Behavioral and Material
Determinants of Production Relations in Agriculture," *Journal of Development Studies*
22, no. 3 (1986): 503–39.

5. Michael Lipton, *Land Reform in Developing Countries: Property Rights and
Property Wrongs* (New York: Routledge, 2009).

6. Roger G. Knight, "Descrying the Bourgeoisie: Sugar, Capital, and State
in the Netherlands Indies, Circa 1840–1884," *Bijdragen tot de Taal-, Land- en Vol-
kenkunde* 163, no. 1 (2007): 34–66.

7. Anne Booth, *Colonial Legacies: Economic and Social Development in East and
Southeast Asia* (Honolulu: University of Hawaii Press, 2007); and Colin Barlow,
"Indonesian and Malayan Agricultural Development, 1870–1940," *Bulletin of Indo-
nesian Economic Studies* 21, no. 1 (1985): 81–112.

8. Chih-ming Ka, *Japanese Colonialism in Taiwan: Land Tenure, Development,
and Dependency, 1895–1945* (Boulder, CO: Westview Press, 1995).

9. Julia Flynn Siler, *Lost Kingdom: Hawaii's Last Queen, the Sugar Kings, and
America's First Imperial Adventure* (New York: Atlantic Monthly Press, 2012).

10. Alan Dye, "Avoiding Holdup: Asset Specificity and Technical Change in
the Cuban Sugar Industry, 1899–1929," *Journal of Economic History* 54, no. 3 (1994):
628–53.

11. César J. Ayala, *American Sugar Kingdom: The Plantation Economy of the Spanish Caribbean, 1898–1934* (Chapel Hill, NC: University of North Carolina Press, 1999).

12. Muhammed Abu B. Siddique, *Evolution of Land Grants and Labor Policy of Government: The Growth of the Tea Industry in Assam, 1834–1940* (New Delhi: South Asian Publishers, 1990).

13. Personal communication with manager at KDHP.

14. The Smallholder Tea Company in Malawi and the Nshili Tea Company in Rwanda also have significant equity shares by smallholders.

15. Deepananda Herath and Alfons Weersink, "From Plantations to Smallholder Production: The Role of Policy in the Reorganization of the Sri Lankan Tea Sector," *World Development* 37, no. 11 (2009): 1759–72.

16. Cosmas Milton Obote Ochieng, "Development through Positive Deviance and its Implications for Economic Policy Making and Public Administration in Africa: The Case of Kenyan Agricultural Development, 1930–2005," *World Development* 35, no. 3 (2007): 454–79.

17. Donald Mitchell, "Kenya Smallholder Coffee and Tea: Divergent Trends Following Liberalization," World Bank draft paper, Washington, DC, 2011.

18. John A. Tully, *The Devil's Milk: A Social History of Rubber* (New York: Monthly Review Press, 2011).

19. Martin J. Murray, *The Development of Capitalism in Colonial Indochina (1870–1940)* (Berkeley, CA: University of California Press, 1980).

20. Robert W. Clower, Georges Dalton, and Mitchell Harwitz, *Growth Without Development: An Economic Survey of Liberia* (Evanston, IL: Northwestern University Press, 1966); and Greg Grandin, *Fordlandia* (New York: Picador, 2010).

21. Tully, *The Devil's Milk*.

22. Yujiro Hayami, "Plantation Agriculture," in Prabhu L. Pingali and Robert E. Evenson, eds., *Handbook of Agricultural Economics* (Amsterdam: North Holland/ Elsevier, 2010), 3305–22.

23. Samuel Crowther, *The Romance and Rise of the American Tropics* (Garden City, NY: Doubleday, Doran & Co., 1929).

24. Steve Striffler and Mark Moberg, *Banana Wars: Power, Production, and History in the Americas* (Durham, NC: Duke University Press, 2003).

25. John Soluri, *Banana Cultures: Agriculture, Consumption, and Environmental Change in Honduras and the United States* (Austin: University of Texas Press, 2005); and Striffler and Moberg, *Banana Wars*.

26. Striffler and Moberg, *Banana Wars*.

27. Ibid.

28. Douglas Sheil et al., "The Impacts and Opportunities of Oil Palm in Southeast Asia: What Do We Know and What Do We Need to Know?" Center for International Forestry Research Occasional Paper No. 51, Bogor, Indonesia, 2009.

29. Much of this section is based on Klaus Deininger and Derek Byerlee, *Rising Global Interest in Farmland: Can It Yield Sustainable and Equitable Benefits?* (Wash-

ington, DC: World Bank, 2011); and Klaus Deininger and Derek Byerlee, "The Rise of Large Farms in Land Abundant Countries: Do They Have a Future?" *World Development* 40 (January 2012): 701–14.

30. Alan Wood, *The Groundnut Affair* (London: Unwin, 1950).

31. Penelope Rogers, "The 'Failure' of the Peak Downs Scheme," *Australian Journal of Politics & History* 10, no. 1 (2008): 70–82.

32. Jan S. Hogendorn and K. M. Scott, "The East African Groundnut Scheme: Lessons of a Large-Scale Agricultural Failure," *African Economic History,* no. 10 (1981): 81–115.

33. Martin McCauley, *Khrushchev and the Development of Soviet Agriculture: The Virgin Land Program 1953–1964* (London: Macmillan, 1976).

34. Deininger and Byerlee, *Rising Global Interest in Farmland.*

35. Hiram M. Drache, *The Day of the Bonanza: A History of Bonanza Farming in the Red River Valley of the North* (Fargo, ND: North Dakota Institute for Regional Studies, 1964).

36. Geoff Tyler, "Investments in Agribusiness: A Retrospective View of a Development Bank's Investments in Agribusiness in Africa and East Asia," study produced by the Commonwealth Development Corporation, London, 2011.

37. Ian Malcolm, David Little, and David G. Tipping, *A Social Cost-Benefit Analysis of the Kulai Oil Palm Estate: West Malaysia* (Paris: Development Center of the Organization for Economic Cooperation and Development, 1972).

38. Anthony G. Hopkins, *An Economic History of West Africa* (New York: Columbia University Press, 1973).

39. Edmund Dene Morel, *Nigeria: Its Peoples and Its Problems* (London: Smith, Elder and Co, 1911).

40. Jeffery Brannon and Eric N. Baklanoff, *Agrarian Reform and Public Enterprise in Mexico: The Political Economy of Yucatán's Henequen Industry* (Tuscaloosa, AL: University of Alabama Press, 1987). Box 2-2 is also based on the author's visits to ex–henequen haciendas; on Sterling Evans, *Bound in Twine: The History and Ecology of the Henequen-Wheat Complex for Mexico and the American and Canadian Plains, 1880–1950* (College Station, TX: Texas A&M University Press, 2007); and on Maureen Ransom Carty, ed., *Henequén: Leyenda, Historia, y Cultura* (Mérida, Mexico: Instituto de Cultura de Yucatán, 2006).

41. Dwayne Woods, "The Tragedy of the Cocoa Pod: Rent-Seeking, Land, and Ethnic Conflict in Ivory Coast," *The Journal of Modern African Studies: A Quarterly Survey of Politics, Economics, and Related Topics in Contemporary Africa* 41, no. 4 (2003): 641–55.

Chapter 3

1. See: "The Principles for Responsible Agricultural Investment," United Nations Conference on Trade and Development (UNCTAD), www.unctad.org /Templates/Page.asp?intItemID=6123&lang=1.

2. The bulleted information is drawn from the UN Food and Agriculture Organization (FAO), UNCTAD, and World Bank sources, all of which are cited in full below.

3. Lorenzo Cotula et al., *Land Grab or Development Opportunity? Agricultural Investment and International Land Deals in Africa* (Rome and London: FAO and International Institute for Environment and Development, 2009), www.ifad.org/pub/land/land_grab.pdf.

4. Josef Schmidhuber, Jelle Bruinsma, and Gerold Boedskar, "Capital Requirements for Agriculture in Developing Countries to 2050" (paper presented at the FAO Expert Meeting on How to Feed the World in 2050, Rome, June 24–26, 2009), ftp.fao.org/docrep/fao/012/ak974e/ak974e00.pdf.

5. Nadia Cuffaro, "The Record of FDI in Developing Country Agriculture" (paper presented at the FAO Expert Meeting on Foreign Investment in Developing Country Agriculture, Rome, July 30–31, 2009).

6. See, for example, Klaus Deininger and Derek Byerlee, *Rising Global Interest in Farmland: Can It Yield Sustainable and Equitable Benefits?* (Washington, DC: World Bank, 2011), siteresources.worldbank.org/INTARD/Resources/ESW_Sept7_final_final.pdf; Ann-Christin Gerlach and Pascal Liu, "Resource-Seeking Foreign Direct Investment in African Agriculture: A Review of Country Case Studies," FAO Commodity and Trade Policy Research Working Paper, No. 31, FAO Trade and Markets Division, Rome, September 2010, www.fao.org/fileadmin/templates/est/PUBLICATIONS/Comm_Working_Papers/EST-WP31.pdf; and Cotula et al., *Land Grab or Development Opportunity.*

7. Gerlach and Liu, "Resource-Seeking Foreign Direct Investment in African Agriculture."

8. Ali Diallo and Godihald Mushinzimana, "Foreign Direct Investment (FDI) in Land in Mali," document prepared for German Federal Ministry for Economic Cooperation and Development, Division 45: Agriculture, Fisheries, and Food, Eschborn, Germany, 2009.

9. FAO, "Assessing the Nature, Extent, and Impacts of FDI on West African Agriculture: The Case of Ghana and Senegal," consultant report, Rome, 2009.

10. Gerlach and Liu, "Resource-Seeking Foreign Direct Investment in African Agriculture."

11. UNCTAD, *World Investment Report 2009: Transnational Corporations, Agricultural Production, and Development* (Geneva: UNCTAD, 2009), www.unctad.org/en/docs/wir2009_en.pdf.

12. Gerlach and Liu, "Resource-Seeking Foreign Direct Investment in African Agriculture."

13. Sonja Vermeulen and Lorenzo Cotula, *Making the Most of Agricultural Investment: A Survey of Business Models That Provide Opportunities for Smallholders* (Rome and London: FAO and International Institute for Environment and Development, 2010), www.ifad.org/pub/land/agri_investment.pdf.

14. Carin Smaller and Howard Mann, *A Thirst for Distant Lands: Foreign Investment in Agricultural Land and Water* (Winnipeg, Canada: International Institute for Sustainable Development, May 2009), www.iisd.org/pdf/2009/thirst_for_distant_lands.pdf.

15. See: Nadia Cuffaro and David Hallam, "'Land Grabbing' in Developing Countries: Foreign Investors, Regulation, and Codes of Conduct" (paper presented at International Conference on Global Land Grabbing, Institute of Development Studies, University of Sussex, United Kingdom, April 6–8, 2011), www.future-agricultures.org/papers-and-presentations/doc_download/1305-land-grabbing-in-developing-countries-foreign-investors-regulation-and-codes-of-conduct.

16. For more details about these seven principles, known as the Principles for Responsible Agricultural Investment, see: James Zhan, "Principles for Responsible Agricultural Investment" (presentation for UNCTAD, High-Level Session of the Commission on Investment, Enterprise, and Development, Geneva, April 26, 2010), www.unctad.org/sections/dite_dir/docs/diae_stat_2010-04-26_Item5_en.pdf. A separate set of principles, which focus more narrowly on land investments, are known as the Voluntary Guidelines on Responsible Governance of Tenure of Land, Fisheries, and Forests. The draft document covering these guidelines can be accessed from this website: www.fao.org/nr/tenure/voluntary-guidelines/en/.

Chapter 4

1. Oxfam, "Land and Power: The Growing Scandal Surrounding the New Wave of Investments in Land," Oxfam Briefing Paper 151, September 22, 2011, www.oxfam.org/sites/www.oxfam.org/files/bp151-land-power-rights-acquisitions-220911-en.pdf.

2. Song Jung-a, Christian Oliver, and Tom Burgis, "Daewoo to Cultivate Madagascar Land for Free," *Financial Times*, November 19, 2008, www.ft.com/intl/cms/s/0/6e894c6a-b65c-11dd-89dd-0000779fd18c.html.

3. Olivier De Schutter, "Large-Scale Land Acquisitions and Leases: A Set of Core Principles and Measures to Address the Human Rights Challenge," UN Special Rapporteur on the Right to Food, June 11, 2009, www.srfood.org/images/stories/pdf/otherdocuments/20090611_large-scale-land-acquisitions_en.pdf.

4. Klaus Deininger and Derek Byerlee, *Rising Global Interest in Farmland: Can It Yield Sustainable and Equitable Benefits?* (Washington, DC: World Bank, 2011), siteresources.worldbank.org/INTARD/Resources/ESW_Sept7_final_final.pdf.

5. For more on the Voluntary Guidelines, see: www.fao.org/nr/tenure/voluntary-guidelines/en/. For a comparison of the VGs and RAIs, see: The Global Campaign for Agrarian Reform/Land Research Action Network, "A Comparison Between FAO Guidelines for the Responsible Governance of Land and Natural Resources Tenure and Principles for Responsible Agricultural Investment That Re-

spects Rights, Livelihoods, and Resources," www.tni.org/sites/www.tni.org/files /FAO-VG%20Principles,%20Rome,%20Oct%202010%20(English)_0.pdf.

6. Carin Smaller and Howard Mann, *A Thirst for Distant Lands: Foreign Investment in Agricultural Land and Water* (Winnipeg, Canada: International Institute for Sustainable Development, 2009), www.iisd.org/pdf/2009/thirst_for_distant _lands.pdf.

7. Farhad Mazhar et al., *Food Sovereignty and Uncultivated Biodiversity in South Asia: Essays on the Poverty of Food Policy and the Wealth of the Social Landscape* (New Delhi and Ottawa: Academic Foundation and International Development Research Council, 2007), www.idrc.ca/openebooks/337-9/.

8. Andries du Toit, "Adverse Incorporation and Agrarian Policy in South Africa: Or, How Not to Connect the Rural Poor to Growth" (paper presented at conference, "Escaping Poverty Traps: Connecting the Chronically Poor to Economic Growth," Washington, DC, February 26–27, 2009), www.basis.wisc.edu/ept /dutoitpaper.pdf.

9. United Nations Development Program (UNDP), "Sustainable Land Management: The Why and How of Mainstreaming Gender in Sustainable Land Management," part of UNDP paper series on "Gender Mainstreaming: A Key Driver of Development in Environment & Energy," New York, 2007, www.undp.org /environment/sustainable-land-management-library.shtml.

10. United Nations Environment Program (UNEP), "Section B: State and Trends of the Environment: 1987–2007," in *Global Environmental Outlook* (Malta: UNEP, 2007), www.unep.org/geo/geo4/report/02_Atmosphere.pdf.

11. Food and Agriculture Organization (FAO), "How to Feed the World in 2050" (expert paper for the High-Level Experts Forum at FAO Headquarters, Rome, October 12–13, 2009), www.fao.org/fileadmin/templates/wsfs/docs/expert _paper/How_to_Feed_the_World_in_2050.pdf.

12. "Organic Agriculture and Food Security in Africa" (paper prepared for United Nations Conference on Trade and Development [UNCTAD] and UNEP, UNEP-UNCTAD Capacity-Building Task Force on Trade, Environment, and Development, New York and Geneva, 2008), www.unctad.org/trade_env/test1 /publications/UNCTAD_DITC_TED_2007_15.pdf.

13. Cathy Rozel Farnworth, "Gender-Aware Value-Chain Development" (paper prepared for UN Women Expert Group Meeting on Enabling Rural Women's Economic Empowerment: Institutions, Opportunities, and Participation, Accra, Ghana, September 20–23, 2011), www.un.org/womenwatch/daw/csw/csw56/egm /Farnworth-EP-1-EGM-RW-Sep-2011.pdf.

14. George C. Schoneveld, Laura A. German, and Eric Nutakor, "Towards Sustainable Biofuel Development: Assessing the Local Impacts of Large-Scale Foreign Land Acquisitions in Ghana" (paper prepared for the World Bank Land Governance Conference, Washington, DC, April 26–27, 2010), siteresources.worldbank.org /EXTARD/Resources/336681-1236436879081/5893311-1271205116054 /schoneveld.pdf.

15. Margareta Pagano, "Land Grab: The Race for the World's Farmland," *The Independent*, May 3, 2009, www.independent.co.uk/news/business/analysis-and -features/land-grab-the-race-for-the-worlds-farmland-1677852.html.

16. Ibid.

17. "Final Report," UN Committee on World Food Security, Thirty-Seventh Session, October 17–22, 2011, www.fao.org/fileadmin/templates/cfs/Docs1011 /CFS37/documents/CFS_37_Final_Report_FINAL.pdf.

18. Michel Merlet and Clara Jamart, "Commercial Pressures on Land World-wide: Issues and Conceptual Framework for Analysis" (document prepared by AGTER [*Améliorer la Gouvernance de la Terre, de l'Eau, et des Ressources naturelles*] for International Land Coalition, April 2009), www.landcoalition.org/sites/default /files/publication/823/ilc-commercial-pressures-on-land-eng-web_layout-1.pdf.

19. International Fund for Agricultural Development (IFAD), "The Growing Demand for Land: Risks and Opportunities for Smallholder Farmers" (discussion paper and proceedings report of the Governing Council round table, 32nd session of IFAD's Governing Council, United Nations, New York, February 2009), www .ifad.org/events/gc/32/roundtables/2.pdf.

Chapter 5

1. The authors would like to acknowledge the contributions of Rachel Emily Perez in the review of media reports for maize, rice, and rubber (highlighted in Appendix II). We would also like to acknowledge the efforts of Michael Kugelman in reviewing earlier drafts and helping to reach an effective balance between scientific rigor and content, and readability to a wider public.

2. See: Klaus Deininger and Derek Byerlee, *Rising Global Interest in Farmland: Can It Yield Sustainable and Equitable Benefits?* (Washington, DC: World Bank, 2011), siteresources.worldbank.org/INTARD/Resources/ESW_Sept7_final_final .pdf; Ward Anseeuw et al., *Land Rights and the Rush for Land* (Rome: International Land Coalition, 2012), www.landcoalition.org/sites/default/files/publication/1205 /ILC%20GSR%20report_ENG.pdf; World Bank, "Environmental, Economic, and Social Impacts of Oil Palm in Indonesia: A Synthesis of Opportunities and Challenges," World Bank discussion paper, Washington, DC, 2010, www.ifc.org/ifcext /agriconsultation.nsf/AttachmentsByTitle/WB + discussion + paper/$FILE/WB_Oil + Palm + SynthesisDiscussionPaperMay2010.pdf; and George C. Schoneveld, "The Anatomy of Large-Scale Farmland Acquisitions in sub-Saharan Africa," working paper, Center for International Forestry Research, Bogor, Indonesia, 2012. Information regarding biofuels in Africa can be found in Rob Bailis, Laura German, and Jan Willem van Gelder, "Biofuels in Tropical Forest-Rich Countries: Part 1—Production and Trade of Feedstocks and Fuels" (under review by *Energy Policy* as of this writing).

3. The World Bank identifies 202 million hectares (ha) of suitable and available land in Africa, and 123 million ha in Latin America and the Caribbean. By suitable

and available, the Bank means uncultivated, non-forested, non-protected land with high agro-ecological potential in areas with a population density of less than 25 persons/km^2. See: Deininger and Derek Byerlee, *Rising Global Interest in Farmland*, 79.

4. Saturnino M. Borras et al., "The Fundamentally Flawed 'Marginal Lands' Narrative: Insights from the Philippines" (paper presented at the International Conference on Global Land Grabbing, University of Sussex, United Kingdom, April 6–8, 2011), www.future-agricultures.org/papers-and-presentations/cat_view /1551-global-land-grab/1552-conference-papers.

5. Joseph Fargione et al., "Land Clearing and the Biofuel Carbon Debt," *Science* 319, no. 5867 (2008): 1235–38; and L. Reijnders and M. A. J. Huijbregts, "Palm Oil and the Emission of Carbon-Based Greenhouse Gases," *Journal of Cleaner Production* 16, no. 4 (2008): 477–82.

6. These reports are Anseeuw et al., *Land Rights and the Rush for Land*; Schoneveld, "The Anatomy of Large-Scale Farmland Acquisitions in Sub-Saharan Africa"; and Deininger and Byerlee, *Rising Global Interest in Farmland*.

7. Deininger and Byerlee, *Rising Global Interest in Farmland*, and Anseeuw et al., *Land Rights and the Rush for Land*.

8. Deininger and Byerlee, *Rising Global Interest in Farmland*. The World Bank uses expansion in area of land under different crops as a proxy for land-use change.

9. Schoneveld, "The Anatomy of Large-Scale Farmland Acquisitions."

10. Wouter M. J. Achten et al., "Jatropha Biodiesel Fueling Sustainability?" *Biofuels, Bioproducts, and Biorefining* 1, no. 4 (2007): 283–91. For the risks of indirect land-use change, see: Wouter M. J. Achten and Louis Verchot, "Implications of Biodiesel-Induced Land-Use Changes for CO_2 Emissions: Case Studies in Tropical America, Africa, and Southeast Asia," *Ecology and Society* 16, no. 4 (2011): 14.

11. For recent cases of its expansion in sub-Saharan Africa, see: George C. Schoneveld, "Potential Land Use Competition from First-Generation Biofuel Expansion in Developing Countries," Occasional Paper No. 58, Center for International Forestry Research, Bogor, Indonesia, 2010.

12. Schoneveld, "The Anatomy of Large-Scale Farmland Acquisitions."

13. Achten and Verchot, "Implications of Biodiesel-Induced Land Use Changes for CO_2 Emissions."

14. Pablo Pacheco, "Soybean and Oil Palm Expansion in South America: Trends Associated to Food, Feed, and Biofuel Markets," working paper, Center for International Forestry Research, Bogor, Indonesia, 2010.

15. Elizabeth Barona et al., "The Role of Pasture and Soybean in Deforestation of the Brazilian Amazon," *Environmental Research Letters* 5 (April 2010): 024002.

16. Schoneveld, "Potential Land Use Competition."

17. Tim Searchinger et al., "Use of U.S. Cropland for Biofuels Increases Greenhouse Gases Through Emissions from Land-Use Change," *Science* 319, no. 5867 (2008): 1238–40, and Achten and Verchot, "Implications of Biodiesel-Induced Land-Use Changes for CO_2 Emissions."

18. David M. Lapola et al., "Indirect Land-Use Changes Can Overcome Carbon Savings from Biofuel in Brazil," *Proceedings of the National Academy of Sciences of the United States of America* 107, no. 8 (2010): 3388–93.

19. Laura German and Sheila Wertz-Kanounnikoff, "Sino-Mozambican Relations and their Implications for Forests: A Preliminary Assessment for the Case of Mozambique," working paper, Center for International Forestry Research, Bogor, Indonesia, 2012; Joseph Hanlon, "5 Large Land Grants," *Mozambique* 193, January 31, 2012; and International Tropical Timber Organization (ITTO), "Encouraging Industrial Forest Plantations in the Tropics: Report of a Global Study," ITTO Technical Series No. 33, ITTO, Yokohama, Japan, 2009.

20. Justin T. Hallet et al., "Teak Plantations: Economic Bonanza or Environmental Disaster?" *Journal of Forestry* 109, no. 5 (2011): 288–92.

21. Fargione et al., "Land Clearing and the Biofuel Carbon Debt," and Achten and Verchot, "Implications of Biodiesel-Induced Land Use Changes for CO_2 Emissions."

22. Rob Bailis and Heather McCarthy, "Carbon Impacts of Direct Land Use Change in Semiarid Woodlands Converted to Biofuel Plantations in India and Brazil," *Global Change Biology Bioenergy* 3, no. 6 (2011): 449–60.

23. Henny A. Romijn, "Land Clearing and Greenhouse Gas Emissions from Jatropha Biofuels on African Miombo Woodlands," *Energy Policy* 39, no. 10 (2010): 5751–62.

24. Bailis and McCarthy, "Carbon Impacts of Direct Land Use Change," and Wouter M. J. Achten et al., "Life Cycle Assessment of Jatropha Biodiesel as Transportation Fuel in Rural India," *Applied Energy* 87, no. 12 (2010): 3652–60.

25. Achten and Verchot, "Implications of Biodiesel-Induced Land Use Changes for CO_2 Emissions."

26. Holly K. Gibbs et al., "Carbon Payback Times for Crop-Based Biofuel Expansion in the Tropics: The Effects of Changing Yield and Technology," *Environmental Research Letters* 3 (July 2008): 034001.

27. Achten and Verchot, "Implications of Biodiesel-Induced Land Use Changes for CO_2 Emissions."

28. Fargione et al., "Land Clearing and the Biofuel Carbon Debt."

29. Lapola et al., "Indirect Land-Use Changes Can Overcome Carbon Savings from Biofuel in Brazil."

30. Lian Pin Koh and David S. Wilcove, "Is Oil Palm Agriculture Really Destroying Tropical Biodiversity?" *Conservation Letters* 1, no. 2 (2008): 60–64.

31. Tom M. Fayle et al., "Oil Palm Expansion into Rain Forest Greatly Reduces Ant Biodiversity in Canopy, Epiphytes, and Leaf-litter," *Basic and Applied Ecology* 11, no. 4 (2010): 337–45; and Carsten A. Bruhl and Thomas Eltz, "Fueling the Biodiversity Crisis: Species Loss of Ground-Dwelling Forest Ants in Oil Palm Plantations in Sabah, Malaysia (Borneo)," *Biodiversity and Conservation* 19, no. 2 (2010): 519–29.

32. Badrul Azhar et al., "The Conservation Value of Oil Palm Plantation Estates, Smallholdings, and Logged Peat Swamp Forest for Birds," *Forest Ecology and Management* 262, no. 12 (2011): 2306–15.

33. Strategies for mitigating negative impacts on biodiversity include placing corridors of native vegetation between monospecific plantation blocks, and planting different blocks of exotic species in a spatially heterogeneous fashion. See: Eckehard G. Brockerhoff et al., "Plantation Forests and Biodiversity: Oxymoron or Opportunity?" *Biodiversity and Conservation* 17, no. 5 (2008): 925–51; and Rudolf S. Groot and Peter van der Meer, "Quantifying and Valuing Goods and Services Provided by Plantation Forests," in Jurgen Bauhus, Peter van der Meer, and Markku Kanninen, eds., *Ecosystem Goods and Services from Plantation Forests* (London: Earthscan, 2010): 16–42.

34. David M. Lapola et al., "Indirect Land-Use Changes Can Overcome Carbon Savings from Biofuel in Brazil"; and Joseph E. Fargione, Richard J. Plevin, and Jason D. Hill, "The Ecological Impact of Biofuels," *The Annual Review of Ecology, Evolution, and Systematics* 41 (December 2010): 351–77.

35. "The blue water footprint refers to the volume of surface and groundwater consumed (evaporated) as a result of the production of a good; the green water footprint refers to the rainwater consumed. The grey water footprint of a product refers to the volume of freshwater that is required to assimilate the load of pollutants based on existing ambient water quality standards." (Mesfin M. Mekonnen and Arjen Y. Hoekstra, "The Green, Blue, and Grey Water Footprint of Crops and Derived Crop Products," Value of Water Research Report Series No. 47, UNESCO, Delft, the Netherlands, 2010, www.waterfootprint.org/Reports/Report47-WaterFootprint Crops-Vol1.pdf.)

36. Note that values for jatropha water footprints are subject to discussion. See: Winnie Gerbens-Leenes, Arjen Y. Hoekstra, and Theo H. van der Meer, "The Water Footprint of Bioenergy," *Proceedings of the National Academy of Sciences of the United States of America* 106, no. 25 (2009): 10219–23; and W. H. Maes, Wouter M. J. Achten, and Bart Muys, "Use of Inadequate Data and Methodological Errors Lead to an Overestimation of the Water Footprint of *Jatropha curcas*," *Proceedings of the National Academy of Sciences of the United States of America* 106, no. 34 (2009): E91.

37. Kathleen A. Farley, Esteban G. Jobbagy, and Robert B. Jackson, "Effects of Afforestation on Water Yield: A Global Synthesis with Implications for Policy," *Global Change Biology* 11 (2005): 1565–76.

38. D. F. Scott, L. A. Bruijnzeel, and J. Mackensen, "The Hydrological and Soil Impacts of Forestation in the Tropics," in M. Bonell and L. A. Bruijnzeel, eds., *Forests, Water, and People in the Humid Tropics* (Cambridge, UK: Cambridge University Press, 2005): 622–51; and W. M. Putahena and Ian Cordery, "Some Hydrological Effects of Changing Forest Cover from *Eucalyptus* to *Pinus radiata*," *Agriculture for Meteorology* 100, no. 1 (2000): 59–72.

39. Albert I. J. M. van Dijk and Rodney Keenan, "Planted Forests and Water in Perspective," *Forest Ecology and Management* 251, nos. 1–2 (2007): 1–9.

40. Philip M. Fearnside, "Deforestation Control in Mato Grosso: A New Model for Slowing the Loss of Brazil's Rain Forest," *AMBIO: A Journal of the Human Environment* 32, no. 5 (2003): 343–45.

41. Greenpeace played an instrumental role in bolstering industry commitment to sustainability by demonstrating the negative environmental effects of soy in the

supply chains of international food companies, and by carrying out a concerted campaign to encourage these companies to change their sourcing practices. See: "Landmark Soya Moratorium Extended," Greenpeace website, June 17, 2008, www.greenpeace.org/international/en/news/features/amazon-soya-moratorium-renewed-170608.

42. Theodor Rudorff et al., "The Soy Moratorium in the Amazon Biome Monitored by Remote Sensing Images," *Remote Sensing* 3, no. 1 (2011): 185–202.

43. Eugenio Y. Arima et al., "Statistical Confirmation of Indirect Land Use Change in the Brazilian Amazon," *Environmental Research Letters* 6 (May 2011): 024010. The new legislation, which cleared the Brazilian House of Representatives and Senate in 2011, reduces the penalties that landowners who illegally cleared protected forest areas would face, and decreases the proportion of landholdings that must be protected. See: Carter Roberts, "Code Red for Brazil's Forests," *Huffington Post*, December 20, 2011, www.huffingtonpost.com/carter-roberts/code-red-for-brazils-fore_b_1161293.html.

44. The schemes approved to regulate compliance with the EU Renewable Energy Directive include: Abengoa RED Bioenergy Sustainability Assurance, Biomass Biofuels Sustainability Voluntary Scheme, Bonsucro, Greenergy, International Sustainability and Carbon Certification, the Roundtable on Sustainable Biofuels, and the Roundtable for Responsible Soy. See the section of the European Commission's website on renewable energy, ec.europa.eu/energy/renewables/biofuels/sustainability_schemes_en.htm.

45. See the International Council on Mining and Metals Sustainable Development Framework, www.icmm.com/our-work/sustainable-development-framework; Newmont Mining's Environmental Policy, www.newmont.com; and Rio Tinto's Environmental Policy, www.riotinto.com.

46. S. Prakash Sethi, "The Effectiveness of Industry-Based Codes in Serving Public Interest: The Case of the International Council on Mining and Metals," *Transnational Corporations* 14, no. 3 (2005): 55–100.

47. Jan Willem van Gelder and Laura German, "Biofuel Finance: Global Trends in Biofuel Finance in Forest-Rich Countries of Asia, Africa, and Latin America and Implications for Governance," *InfoBrief* 36, Center for International Forestry Research, Bogor, Indonesia, 2011, www.cifor.org/nc/online-library/browse/view-publication/publication/3340.html.

48. Laura German and George C. Schoneveld, "Social Sustainability of EU-Approved Voluntary Schemes for Biofuels: Implications for Rural Livelihoods," Working Paper 75, Center for International Forestry Research, Bogor, Indonesia, 2011.

Chapter 6

1. Nils Herger, Christos Kotsogiannis, and Steve McCorriston, "Cross-border Acquisitions in the Global Food Sector," *European Review of Agricultural Economics* 35 (2008): 563–87.

2. Agricultural labor intensity figures from WRI can be accessed at earth-trends.wri.org/text/agriculture-food/variable-845.html. FAO data on nutrition is available from *The State of Food Insecurity in the World 2010: Addressing Food Insecurity in Protracted Crises* (Rome: FAO, 2010), www.fao.org/docrep/013/i1683e/i1683e .pdf.

3. These figures were generated from data providing agricultural population sizes (for 2011), hectares of arable land (for 2009), and corn yields per hectare (for 2011) for all three countries. This data was obtained from the FAOSTAT database, which is accessible at faostat.fao.org/site/291/default.aspx.

4. "Agriculture Should Be Made an Attractive Proposition," *The Hindu Business Line*, July 31, 2011, www.thehindubusinessline.com/todays-paper/tp-agri-biz -and-commodity/article2311555.ece.

5. See: "Know Your Farmer, Know Your Food," US Department of Agriculture, www.usda.gov/wps/portal/usda/usdahome?navid = KNOWYOURFARMER.

6. Susan Schneider, "Senators Challenge Know Your Farmer Program," Agricultural Law blog, April 29, 2010, aglaw.blogspot.com/2010/04/senators-challenge -know-your-farmer.html.

7. Anteneh Roba, "Looming Threats to Africa: Land-Leasing and Intensive Food Production," *Counterpunch*, July 5, 2011, www.counterpunch.org/2011/07/05 /looming-threats-to-africa/.

8. See: Sarita Sapkota, "The Myth about Creating Employment," *The Himalayan Times*, February 13, 2011, www.thehimalayantimes.com/perspectives /fullnews.php?headline = The + myth + about + creating + employment + &newsid = 50. This quote, however, has several variations. For more details, see "If You Want Jobs Then Give These Workers Spoons Instead of Shovels," Quote Investigator blog, October 10, 2011, quoteinvestigator.com/2011/10/10/spoons-shovels/.

9. HighQuest Partners, "Private Financial Sector Investment in Farmland and Agricultural Infrastructure" (OECD Food, Agriculture, and Fisheries Working Papers, No. 33, OECD Publishing, United States, 2010), dx.doi.org/10.1787/5km7 nzpjlr8v-en.

10. Jerry Hagstrom, "Brazilian to Shake Up FAO: Agency's Newly Elected Director Has New Directive," *The Progressive Farmer*, June 28, 2011, bit.ly /zAs5sJ.

11. "Creating a Framework for Agricultural Investment," FAO Policy Note, FAO's Policy Assistance and Support Service (TCSP), www.fao.org/fileadmin/user _upload/tcsp/docs/Promoting_Investment_in_Agriculture-Policy_Brief.pdf (undated).

12. World Water Assessment Program, *The United Nations World Water Development Report 3: Water in a Changing World* (Paris and London: UNESCO and Earthscan, 2009), www.unesco.org/water/wwap/wwdr/wwdr3/pdf/WWDR3 _Water_in_a_Changing_World.pdf.

13. Klaus Deininger and Derek Byerlee, *Rising Global Interest in Farmland: Can It Yield Sustainable and Equitable Benefits?* (Washington, DC: World

Bank, 2011), siteresources.worldbank.org/INTARD/Resources/ESW_Sept7_final _final.pdf.

14. See Bill Ganzel, "Farm Boom of the 1970s," Wessels Living History Farm, 2009, www.livinghistoryfarm.org/farminginthe70s/money_02.html.

15. Simeon Mitropolitski, "Selling Land in Russia Is Like Selling Your Soul," *International Real Estate Digest*, October 4, 2000, www.ired.com/news/mkt/ru -land.htm.

Chapter 7

1. For additional historical examples, see Joachim von Braun and Ruth Meinzen-Dick, "'Land Grabbing' by Foreign Investors in Developing Countries: Risks and Opportunities," International Food Policy Research Institute (IFPRI) Policy Brief 13, Washington, DC, April 2009, www.ifpri.org/pubs/bp/bp013.pdf.

2. Lorenzo Cotula et al., *Land Grab or Development Opportunity? Agricultural Investment and International Land Deals in Africa* (London and Rome: IIED, FAO, and IFAD, 2009), ftp.fao.org/docrep/fao/011/ak241e/ak241e.pdf.

3. Ibid.

4. Lorenzo Cotula, Nat Dyer, and Sonya Vermeulen, *Fuelling Exclusion? The Biofuels Boom and Poor People's Access to Land* (London: IIED and FAO, 2008), www.iied.org/pubs/pdfs/12551IIED.pdf.

5. Cotula et al., *Land Grab or Development Opportunity?*

6. FAO, "Climate Change, Biofuels, and Land" (information sheet for the High-Level Conference on World Food Security: The Challenges of Climate Change and Bioenergy, Rome, June 2008), ftp.fao.org/nr/HLCinfo/Land-Infosheet-En.pdf. See also: Lorenzo Cotula, *Land Deals in Africa: What Is in the Contracts?* (London: IIED, 2011), pubs.iied.org/pdfs/12568IIED.pdf.

7. Klaus Deininger and Derek Byerlee, *Rising Global Interest in Farmland: Can It Yield Sustainable and Equitable Benefits?* (Washington, DC: World Bank, 2011), siteresources.worldbank.org/INTARD/Resources/ESW_Sept7_final_final.pdf.

8. Not surprisingly, as of this writing, the most recent estimates about these land deals found that the most farmland, by far, had been acquired in Africa—more than three times the amount secured in Asia, the second-most popular region. See: Ward Anseeuw et al., *Land Rights and the Rush for Land* (Rome: International Land Coalition, 2012), www.landcoalition.org/sites/default/files/publication/1205/ILC %20GSR%20report_ENG.pdf.

9. Ward Anseeuw et al., *Land Rights and the Rush for Land*; Liz Alden Wily, *The Tragedy of Public Lands: The Fate of the Commons Under Global Commercial Pressure* (Rome: International Land Coalition, 2011), www.landcoalition.org/sites /default/files/publication/901/WILY_Commons_web_11.03.11.pdf; and Cotula, Dyer, and Vermeulen, *Fuelling Exclusion*.

10. Von Braun and Meinzen-Dick, "'Land Grabbing' by Foreign Investors."

11. Cotula, Dyer, and Vermeulen, *Fuelling Exclusion*.

12. Deininger and Byerlee, *Rising Global Interest in Farmland*.

13. Ibid.

14. Ibid. and Anseeuw et al., *Land Rights and the Rush for Land*.

15. Vera Songwe and Klaus Deininger, "Foreign Investment in Agricultural Production: Opportunities and Challenges," *Agriculture & Rural Development Notes*, Issue 45, World Bank, Washington, DC, January 2009, siteresources.worldbank.org /INTARD/Resources/335807-1229025334908/ARDNote45a.pdf.

16. Elisa Wiener Bravo, *The Concentration of Land Ownership in Latin America: An Approach to Current Problems* (Rome: International Land Coalition, January 2011), www.landcoalition.org/sites/default/files/publication/913/LA_Regional _ENG_web_11.03.11.pdf.

17. Anseeuw et al., *Land Rights and the Rush for Land*.

18. Ibid. and Cotula, Dyer, and Vermeulen, *Fuelling Exclusion*.

19. For more about the lack of consultation with local resource users, see: Cotula et al., *Land Grab or Development Opportunity*; and Cotula, Dyer, and Vermeulen, *Fuelling Exclusion*. For more about women in this context, see: Deininger and Byerlee, *Rising Global Interest in Farmland*, and Julia Behrman, Ruth Meinzen-Dick, and Agnes Quisumbing, "The Gender Implications of Large-Scale Land Deals," International Food Policy Research Institute (IFPRI) Discussion Paper 1056, Washington, DC, 2011, www.ifpri.org/publication/gender-implications-large-scale-land -deals.

20. Anseeuw et al., *Land Rights and the Rush for Land*.

21. Von Braun and Meinzen-Dick, "'Land Grabbing' by Foreign Investors."

22. Cotula, Dyer, and Vermeulen, *Fuelling Exclusion*.

23. Anseeuw et al., *Land Rights and the Rush for Land*; and Cotula, *Land Deals in Africa: What Is in the Contracts?*

24. Deininger and Byerlee, *Rising Global Interest in Farmland*.

25. Von Braun and Meinzen-Dick, "'Land Grabbing' by Foreign Investors."

26. Cotula, Dyer, and Vermeulen, *Fuelling Exclusion*.

27. Anseeuw et al., *Land Rights and the Rush for Land*; and Cotula, Dyer, and Vermeulen, *Fuelling Exclusion*.

28. Tom Burgis and Javier Blas, "Madagascar Scraps Daewoo Farm Deal," *Financial Times*, March 18, 2009, www.ft.com/cms/s/0/7e133310-13ba-11de-9e32 -0000779fd2ac.html; and Rivo Andrianirina Ratsialonana et al., *After Daewoo? Current Status and Perspectives of Large-Scale Land Acquisitions in Madagascar* (Rome: International Land Coalition, January 2011), www.landcoalition.org/sites/default /files/publication/905/CIRAD_OF_Mada_ENG_web_16.03.11.pdf.

29. GRAIN, *Seized! The 2008 Land Grab for Food and Financial Security* (Barcelona, Spain: GRAIN, October 2008), www.grain.org/briefings_files/landgrab -2008-en.pdf. See also: "Outsourcing's Third Wave," *The Economist*, May 21, 2009, www.economist.com/world/international/displayStory.cfm?story_id=13692889.

30. Anseeuw et al., *Land Rights and the Rush for Land*.

31. Deininger and Byerlee, *Rising Global Interest in Farmland*.

Chapter 8

1. Ali Diallo and Godihald Mushinzimana, "Foreign Direct Investment (FDI) in Land in Mali," document prepared for German Federal Ministry for Economic Cooperation and Development, Division 45: Agriculture, Fisheries, and Food, Eschborn, Germany, 2009, 7.

2. Michael Ochieng Odhiambo, *Commercial Pressures on Land in Africa: A Regional Overview of Opportunities, Challenges, and Impacts* (Nakuru, Kenya: International Land Coalition, April 2011), www.landcoalition.org/sites/default/files/publication/1136/Africa%20Overview%20WEB%2014.07.11.pdf.

3. Oxfam, "Land and Power: The Growing Scandal Surrounding the New Wave of Investments in Land," Oxfam Briefing Paper 151, September 22, 2011, www.oxfam.org/sites/www.oxfam.org/files/bp151-land-power-rights-acquisitions-220911-en.pdf.

4. Jessica McDiarmid, "Regulating the Rush for Land," Inter Press Service, October 31, 2011, ipsnews.net/news.asp?idnews=105657.

5. See Gary Blumenthal's chapter in this volume.

6. "The Surge in Land Deals: When Others Are Grabbing Their Land," *The Economist*, May 5, 2011, www.economist.com/node/18648855?story_id=18648855.

7. Klaus Deininger and Derek Byerlee, *Rising Global Interest in Farmland: Can It Yield Sustainable and Equitable Benefits?* (Washington, DC: World Bank, 2011), siteresources.worldbank.org/INTARD/Resources/ESW_Sept7_final_final.pdf.

8. See: "'Understanding Land Deals in Africa': FAQs on How Land Grabs Contribute to Hunger and Conflict," Oakland Institute, December 6, 2011, www.oaklandinstitute.org/sites/oaklandinstitute.org/files/Oakland%20Institute%20Land%20Grab%20FAQs%20EMBARGOED.pdf.

9. Rick Westhead, "Africa's Farmland in Demand: 'Is There a Better Place Than This?'" *Toronto Star*, December 3, 2011, www.thestar.com/news/article/1096210.

10. Nicholas Minot, "Contract Farming in Africa: Opportunities and Challenges" (presentation at the African Agricultural Markets Program Policy Seminar, "Successful Smallholder Commercialization," Kigali, Rwanda, April 22, 2011), www.aec.msu.edu/fs2/aamp/Kigali%20Conference/Minot_Contract_farming_in_Africa.pdf.

11. See Raul Q. Montemayor's chapter in this volume.

12. Muriel Veldman and Marco Lankhorst, *Socioeconomic Impact of Commercial Exploitation of Rwandan Marshes: A Case Study of Sugar Cane Production in Rural Kigali* (Rome: International Land Coalition, January 2011), www.landcoalition.org/sites/default/files/publication/908/RCN_Rwanda_web_11.03.11.pdf.

13. Minot, "Contract Farming in Africa: Opportunities and Challenges."

Chapter 9

1. The material in this chapter is drawn from the author's chapter in *Land Grab? The Race for the World's Farmland*, eds. Michael Kugelman and Susan L. Levenstein (Washington, DC: Woodrow Wilson International Center for Scholars, 2009); and from Raul Q. Montemayor, *Overseas Farmland Investments in Selected Asian Countries* (Quezon City, Philippines: East Asia Rice Working Group [EARWR], 2011), www.eastasiarice.org/Books/OVERSEAS%20FARMLAND.pdf. EARWG is a loose network of farmer organizations and nongovernment organizations from developing countries in the region.

2. In this chapter, unless otherwise stated, "Asia" refers to the following countries in Southeast Asia covered in the author's research: Cambodia, Laos, Malaysia, Burma, the Philippines, and Vietnam.

3. Ward Anseeuw et al., *Land Rights and the Rush for Land* (Rome: International Land Coalition, 2012), www.landcoalition.org/sites/default/files/publication /1205/ILC%20GSR%20report_ENG.pdf.

4. Ben Shepherd, "Redefining Food Security in the Face of Foreign Land Investors: The Philippine Case," NTS-Asia Research Paper No. 6, Centre for Non-Traditional Security (NTS) Studies, S. Rajaratnam School of International Studies, Nanyang Technological University, Singapore, 2011, www.rsis.edu.sg/nts/HTML -Newsletter/Report/pdf/NTS-Asia_Ben_Shepherd.pdf.

5. For an overview and status of foreign agricultural investments in Asia, see: Roel R. Ravanera and Vanessa Gorra, *Commercial Pressures on Land in Asia: An Overview* (Rome: International Land Coalition, January 2011), www.land coalition.org/sites/default/files/publication/909/RAVANERA_Asia_web_11.03 .11.pdf.

6. Mattias Görgen et al., *Foreign Direct Investment (FDI) in Land in Developing Nations* (Eschborn, Germany: German Federal Ministry for Economic Cooperation and Development, 2009), www.scribd.com/doc/29459685/Foreign-Direct -Investment-FDI-in-Land-in-Developing-Countries?query=ELC.

7. Ibid.

8. Dollar figures in this chapter are all US dollar amounts.

9. Shepherd, "Redefining Food Security."

10. Ibid.

11. These reports come from first-hand accounts of small landholder victims in the Philippines, and from the author's conversations with farmer leaders from other Asian countries. Unless otherwise stated, in this chapter references to "reports" and to incidents "reportedly" taking place are based on information obtained either from the author's farmer leader contacts, or from NGO contacts connected with the East Asia Rice Working Group. Information from the NGO contacts could not be verified. Some of the NGO-provided material is based on media reports.

12. Montemayor, *Overseas Farmland Investments in Selected Asian Countries*.

13. Other research points to even more egregious cases of displacement. Researchers from Food First Information and Action Network and the International Institute of Social Studies estimate that a Thai sugar company has acquired 20,000 ha of land in Koh Kong province, displacing 450 families. See: Roman Herre and Saturnino M. Borras Jr., "A Human Rights Perspective on Land Grabbing: The Case of Cambodia" (paper presented at International Conference on Global Land Grabbing, University of Sussex, United Kingdom, April 6, 2011), www .future-agricultures.org/panel-a-session-summaries/7549-panel-9-governance -human-rights-.

14. This information is based on the author's reading of farmland contracts in the Philippines.

15. See: Tania Salerno, "Transnational Land Deals in Mindanao: Situating Ambivalent Farmer Responses in Local Politics" (paper presented at International Conference on Global Land Grabbing, University of Sussex, United Kingdom, April 7, 2011), www.future-agricultures.org/panel-a-session-summaries/7562-panel -20-politics—local-politics.

16. This refers to contract-growing arrangements between farmers and banana/ pineapple plantations and companies in the Philippines; the author has seen and read some of the contracts governing these deals.

17. Shepherd, "Redefining Food Security."

18. Montemayor, *Overseas Farmland Investments in Selected Asian Countries*.

19. See: Takeshi Ito, Noer Fauzi Rachman, and Laksmi A. Savitri, "Power to Naturalize Land Dispossession: A Policy Discourse Analysis of the Merauke Integrated Food and Energy Estate (MIFEE), Papua, Indonesia" (paper presented at International Conference on Global Land Grabbing, University of Sussex, United Kingdom, April 7, 2011), not for circulation; and Longgena Ginting and Oliver Pye, "Resisting Agribusiness Development: The Merauke Integrated Food and Energy Estate in West Papua, Indonesia" (paper presented at International Conference on Global Land Grabbing, University of Sussex, United Kingdom, April 8, 2011), www.future-agricultures.org/panel-a-session-summaries/7568-panel-26-politics -resistance-and-mobilization-i.

20. "INDONESIA: Agriculture Expansion Plan Under Fire," IRIN News, March 26, 2010, www.irinnews.org/printreport.aspx?reportid=88571.

21. "Investigation Report: The Negative Impact of H. L. H. Economic Land Concession to the Suoy Communities in Oral District, Kampung Spue Province," Land and Livelihoods Program, The NGO Forum on Cambodia, May 24, 2010.

22. Ernst Mutert and T. H. Fairhurst, "Developments in Rice Production in Southeast Asia," in *Better Crops International*, Volume 15, Special Supplement, May 2002, oil-palm.info/ppiweb/bcropint.nsf/$webindex/A6E539E7C275E3E485 256BDC00731AA9/$file/BCI-RICEp12.pdf.

23. Alexis Romero, "ASEAN to Form Regional Rice Pool," *The Philippine Star*, November 21, 2011, www.philstar.com/Article.aspx?articleId=750354& publicationSubCategoryId=63.

Chapter 10

1. HighQuest Partners, "Private Financial Sector Investment in Farmland and Agricultural Infrastructure" (study conducted for OECD Working Party on Agricultural Policies and Markets, August 10, 2010), www.oecd.org/officialdocuments /publicdisplaydocumentpdf/?cote=TAD/CA/APM/WP(2010)11/FINAL&doc Language=En.

2. In the HighQuest study, 54 companies and funds were contacted, and 25 were interviewed. As for the location of their offices, the headquarters of the 54 contacted were geographically distributed as follows: 32 percent were based in Europe, 28 percent in North America, 24 percent in South America, 12 percent in the Asia/Pacific region, and 4 percent in the Middle East and North Africa.

3. Lorenzo Cotula, *The Outlook on Farmland Acquisitions* (Rome: International Land Coalition, January 2011), www.ibcperu.org/doc/isis/13570.pdf.

4. It is important to point out, however, that direct land acquisition in Asia rarely takes the form of actual ownership. As discussed in Raul Montemayor's chapter in this book, foreign land transactions in that region typically revolve around lease arrangements.

5. Saturnino M. Borras Jr. et al., "Land Grabbing in Latin America and the Caribbean: Viewed from Broader International Perspectives" (paper presented at the seminar "Dinámicas en el Mercado de la Tierra en América Latina y el Caribe," November 14–15, FAO Regional Office, Santiago, Chile), www.tni.org/sites/www .tni.org/files/download/borras_franco_kay__spoor_land_grabs_in_latam__caribbean _nov_2011.pdf.

6. Ibid.

7. Ibid.

8. Ibid. One must keep in perspective, however, that land acquisitions in Latin America are modest in scale relative to those in Africa and Asia. According to the International Land Coalition's early 2012 estimates—as of this writing, the most current ones available—there have been 19 million ha of land acquisitions in the region. Africa has had 134 million ha, and Asia 43 million ha. See: Ward Anseeuw et al., *Land Rights and the Rush for Land* (Rome: International Land Coalition, 2012), www.landcoalition.org/sites/default/files/publication/1205/ILC%20GSR%20 report_ENG.pdf.

9. Hubert Cochet and Michel Merlet, "Land Grabbing and Share of the Value Added in Agricultural Processes: A New Look at the Distribution of Land Revenues" (paper presented at the International Conference on Global Land Grabbing, University of Sussex, United Kingdom, April 6–8, 2011), www.future-agricultures.org /papers-and-presentations/cat_view/1551-global-land-grab/1552-conference -papers?start=50.

10. HighQuest Partners, "Private Financial Sector Investment in Farmland and Agricultural Infrastructure."

11. Unless otherwise stated, all dollar figures provided in this chapter refer to US dollar figures.

12. Data compiled by John Wilkinson et al., "Dinâmica do Mercado de terras na America Latina: o caso do Brasil" (one of 17 FAO-commissioned country case studies on land acquisitions in South America and the Caribbean, FAO, Santiago, Chile, 2010).

13. United Nations Conference on Trade and Development (UNCTAD), *World Investment Report 2009: Transnational Corporations, Agriculture Production and Development* (Geneva: UNCTAD, 2009), www.unctad.org/en/docs/wir2009_en.pdf.

14. Wilkinson et al., "Dinâmica do Mercado de terras na America Latina: o caso do Brasil."

15. HighQuest Partners, "Private Financial Sector Investment in Farmland and Agricultural Infrastructure."

16. Sérgio Sauer and Sergio Pereire Leite, "Agrarian Structure, Foreign Land Ownership, and Land Value in Brazil" (paper presented at the International Conference on Global Land Grabbing, University of Sussex, United Kingdom, April 6–8, 2011), www.future-agricultures.org/papers-and-presentations/doc_download/1281-english-agrarian-structure-foreign-land-ownership-and-land-value-in-brazil-.

17. Wilkinson et al., "Dinâmica do Mercado de terras na America Latina: o caso do Brasil."

18. Ibid.

19. Ibid.

20. This is substantiated by Borras et al., "Land Grabbing in Latin America and the Caribbean: Viewed from Broader International Perspectives"; and Sauer and Leite, "Agrarian Structure, Foreign Land Ownership, and Land Value in Brazil."

21. Indeed, the Sauer and Leite study suggests that rises in land values are tied to foreign acquisitions.

22. Sauer and Leite, "Agrarian Structure, Foreign Land Ownership, and Land Value in Brazil." See also Bastiaan P. Reydon, "The Agrarian Question Issue in Brazil Requires Land Governance," *Land Tenure Journal* 1 (May 2011): 127–47.

23. Sauer and Leite, "Agrarian Structure, Foreign Land Ownership, and Land Value in Brazil."

24. Wilkinson et al., "Dinâmica do Mercado de terras na America Latina: o caso do Brasil."

25. Ibid.

26. Official Gazette (government of Brazil), August 23, 2010. For more information, see: Walter Stuber and Adriana Maria Gödel Stuber, "Brazil: The Acquisition of Brazilian Rural Land by Foreigners," Mondaq, August 25, 2010, www.mondaq.com/article.asp?articleid=108576.

27. Alexei Barrionuevo, "China's Interest in Farmland Makes Brazil Uneasy," *New York Times*, May 26, 2011, www.nytimes.com/2011/05/27/world/americas/27brazil.html?pagewanted=all.

28. Ibid.

29. These guidelines seek to highlight the benefits of having "relevant and reliable" land information systems in place. See: *Land Administration Guidelines*, UN

Committee on Human Settlements, Economic Commission for Europe (Geneva and New York: United Nations, 1996), www.ica.coop/house/part-2-chapt4-ece -landadmin.pdf. For the Brazil context, see: Reydon, "The Agrarian Question Issue in Brazil Requires Land Governance."

Chapter 11

1. The CEEC include those nations that were part of the Warsaw Pact before 1989 and are now in the European Union. These are principally the Baltic states of the former USSR (Latvia, Lithuania, and Estonia), as well as Poland, the Czech Republic, Slovakia, Hungary, Romania, and Bulgaria. The FSU encompasses the remaining 12 of the former 15 USSR states. Presently, most of the investment interest and activities are in Russia, Ukraine, and, to a lesser extent, Kazakhstan.

2. R. L. Thompson, "The Challenge for Global Population and Food Security" (paper presented at UK National Farm Management Conference, Oxford, United Kingdom, November 2006).

3. These sources include the FAO and European Bank for Reconstruction and Development (EBRD). See, for example, the "Russia Country Profile" provided by the EBRD at www.ebrd.com/downloads/legal/irc/countries/russia.pdf, and "Russia Could Become World's Second Largest Grain Exporter After U.S.," Goliath Business Knowledge on Demand, *Food and Agriculture Report*, October 22, 2008, goliath .ecnext.com/coms2/gi_0199-9618865/Interfax-Russia-CIS-Food-and.html.

4. Indeed, water—not land—is likely to be the limiting factor on agricultural output in many emerging economies, such as India and China. Temperate crop yields in the last 30 years have doubled by tripling water use. Global agriculture is not just living on borrowed time; it is living on borrowed water.

5. The reason for this is historical, rooted in Poland's concern about Germans buying up vast tracts of cheap Polish land, especially in the west of the country that was part of pre-1945 Germany.

6. International Monetary Fund, *World Economic Outlook* (Washington, DC: International Monetary Fund, September 2011), www.imf.org/external/pubs/ft /weo/2011/02/pdf/text.pdf.

7. Darrel Good and Scott Irwin, "The New Era of Corn, Soybean, and Wheat Prices," Marketing and Outlook Briefs 08-04, Department of Agricultural and Consumer Economics, University of Illinois at Urbana–Champaign, September 2, 2008, www.farmdoc.uiuc.edu/marketing/mobr/mobr_08-04/mobr_08-04.html.

Chapter 12

1. "Outsourcing's Third Wave," *The Economist*, May 21, 2009, www.economist .com/node/13692889.

2. Daniel Howden, "The Big Question: Should Africa Be Generating Much of Europe's Power?" *The Independent*, August 25, 2009, www.independent.co.uk/news/world/africa/the-big-question-should-africa-be-generating-much-of-europes-power-1776802.html.

3. Michael T. Klare, *The Race for What's Left: The Global Scramble for the World's Last Resources* (New York: Henry Holt and Company, 2012).

4. Farooq Tirmizi, "Cutting Out the Middle Man: Global Food Giant to Buy Pakistani Rice Directly from the Paddy," *Express Tribune*, October 25, 2011, tribune.com.pk/story/281091/cutting-out-the-middleman-global-food-giant-to-buy-pakistani-rice-directly-from-the-paddy/.

5. Oxfam, "Land and Power: The Growing Scandal Surrounding the New Wave of Investments in Land," Oxfam Briefing Paper 151, September 22, 2011, www.oxfam.org/sites/www.oxfam.org/files/bp151-land-power-rights-acquisitions-220911-en.pdf.

6. Rick Westhead, "Africa's Farmland in Demand: 'Is There a Better Place Than This?'" *Toronto Star*, December 3, 2011, www.thestar.com/news/article/1096210.

7. Klaus Deininger and Derek Byerlee, *Rising Global Interest in Farmland: Can It Yield Sustainable and Equitable Benefits?* (Washington, DC: World Bank, 2011), siteresources.worldbank.org/INTARD/Resources/ESW_Sept7_final_final.pdf.

8. "Syngenta Rolling Out Drought-Tolerant Corn, Cuts Losses 15%," Agriculture Corner website, March 17, 2011, www.agricorner.com/syngenta-rolling-out-drought-tolerant-corn-cuts-losses-15/.

ABOUT THE EDITORS

MICHAEL KUGELMAN is the South and Southeast Asia associate at the Woodrow Wilson International Center for Scholars in Washington, DC. His work largely focuses on water, energy, food, land, and national-security issues, particularly in, but not limited to, South Asia. His recent publications include the coedited volumes *Empty Bellies, Broken Dreams: Food Insecurity and the Future of Pakistan* (Vanguard Press, 2011) and *Land Grab? The Race for the World's Farmland* (Wilson Center, 2009).

SUSAN L. LEVENSTEIN is a program specialist with the US Department of State's Bureau of Educational and Cultural Affairs. Previously, she worked with the Woodrow Wilson International Center for Scholars' Asia Program, where she coordinated more than 150 Asia-themed conferences and worked on three publications. The latter include the coedited volumes *China and the Persian Gulf* (Wilson Center, 2010) and *Land Grab? The Race for the World's Farmland* (Wilson Center, 2009).

ABOUT THE CONTRIBUTORS

WOUTER M. J. ACHTEN is a postdoctoral researcher at the University of Leuven (Belgium). He specializes in life-cycle assessment, carbon footprinting, and land-use impact assessment. He has applied life-cycle thinking mainly to woody bioenergy systems, but also to horticultural products, institutions, and science. He is currently evaluating bio-based polymer production.

CARL ATKIN is head of research and consultancy at KinnAgri Limited, an international agribusiness management and consultancy firm that is part of the Investment AB Kinnevik Group. His business consultancy interests extend across the whole agribusiness value chain, including life science companies and food processors as well as numerous private and corporate farming businesses. He currently spends much time working in Central and Eastern Europe on agribusiness investment projects.

GARY R. BLUMENTHAL is president and chief executive officer of the agricultural consultancy World Perspectives, Inc. He joined the company in 1994 and has owned and managed its diverse business operations since 2002. Previously, he was Special Assistant to the President for Agricultural Trade and Food Assistance under President George H. W. Bush, and chief of staff to Secretary of Agriculture Clayton Yeutter. Earlier in his career he covered the Armed Services Committee for a member of Congress and worked at the Pentagon.

DEREK BYERLEE is an independent scholar and adviser. Formerly, he was rural strategy adviser at the World Bank and co-director of the Bank's *World Development Report 2008: Agriculture for Development*. He was also director of economics at the International Maize and Wheat Improvement Center (Mexico) and associate professor at Michigan State University. He has conducted field research on agricultural technological change and food policy in Africa, Latin America, and Asia, and his recent work focuses on agribusiness, land use, and tropical commodities.

VITOR B. FERNANDES is a master's degree candidate in economic development at the Institute of Economics, University of Campinas (UNI-CAMP), an institution based in São Paulo, Brazil. He also holds a research position at the Center of Agriculture and Environment Research at UNI-CAMP.

LAURA A. GERMAN is an assistant professor with the Department of Anthropology at the University of Georgia. Previously, she worked as a senior scientist with the Forests and Governance Program of the Center for International Forestry Research. Her recent work focuses on understanding and managing the impacts of globalized trade and investment on forests and local communities. Her publications include the edited volume *Integrated Natural Resource Management in the Highlands of Eastern Africa: From Concept to Practice* (Earthscan, 2011).

MANUEL GUARIGUATA is principal scientist in the Forests and Environment Program at the Center for International Forestry Research, where his interests include forestry, climate change, and forestry education. He previously coordinated the Program of Work on Forests at the Secretariat of the Convention on Biological Diversity, and served as a professor on conservation biology and forest restoration at the Tropical Agricultural Research and Higher Education Center in Costa Rica.

DAVID HALLAM is director of the Trade and Markets Division at the United Nations Food and Agriculture Organization (FAO) in Rome. He was previously a faculty member at the University of Reading, where he specialized in the analysis of agricultural commodity markets and policy and directed the university's Center for Agricultural Strategy. He has written widely on agricultural commodity markets, trade, and development, and has served as editor of the *Journal of Agricultural Economics*.

CHIDO MAKUNIKE is an agricultural commodities exporter based in Dakar, Senegal. He partners with Agrecol-Afrique, a Senegal-based sustainable-agriculture training center, to supply dry hibiscus to a tea-making company in Germany. Separately, he is a freelance writer and an agricultural consultant. He also manages a blog called African Agriculture. Previously, he coordinated the Africa office of the International Federation of Organic Agriculture Movements. Earlier, he was a farmer in his native Zimbabwe, where he grew herbs and vegetables.

HELEN MARKELOVA is pursuing a PhD in applied economics at the University of Minnesota. Previously, she was a research analyst at the International Food Policy Research Institute, where she conducted research on how institutions of collective action and property rights affect the livelihoods of the poor.

RUTH MEINZEN-DICK is a senior research fellow at the International Food Policy Research Institute. She is also coordinator of the Consultative Group on International Agricultural Research program on Collective Action and Property Rights, a research program and network involving 15 international centers and more than 400 partner organizations. Much of her work as a development sociologist has focused on water policy, local organizations, property rights, gender analysis, and the impact of agricultural research on poverty.

RAUL Q. MONTEMAYOR is the national manager of the Federation of Free Farmers Cooperatives, Inc. (FFFCI) of the Philippines. He also acts as a private-sector adviser to the Philippine government in the areas of international trade negotiations, rural development, cooperatives, and other agriculture-related issues. Additionally, he serves on the board of several organizations focused on international agriculture. Previously, he was a vice president of the International Federation of Agricultural Producers.

SOPHIA MURPHY is a consultant and senior adviser to the Institute for Agriculture and Trade Policy's Trade and Global Governance program. A political economist, she focuses on the interests of developing countries in international food systems and the reforms needed in developed country agriculture to protect and promote the universal human right to food. Her publications include an analysis of the effects of international market volatility on poverty and hunger, as well as a study of the impact of corporate concentration in the global food system.

BASTIAAN P. REYDON is an economist who teaches at the University of Campinas (UNICAMP) in São Paulo, Brazil. He has conducted postdoctoral research in territorial management at the University of Wisconsin; consulted for various UN organizations, the International Food Policy Research Institute, the World Bank, and USAID; and published five books and numerous articles.

ALEXANDRA SPIELDOCH is an independent consultant on gender, food security, and sustainable development issues. From 2010 to 2011, she coordinated the Network of Women Leaders in Agriculture project with the organization Women Organizing for Change in Agriculture and Natural

Resource Management. From 2006 to 2009, she directed the Trade and Global Governance Program at the Institute for Agriculture and Trade Policy. Earlier, she headed the secretariat of the International Gender and Trade Network.

INDEX

Page numbers followed by "b," "f," and "t" indicate boxes, figures, and tables.